Progress Against Poverty
A Review of the 1964–1974 Decade

This is the first volume in a series entitled

Institute for Research on Poverty
Poverty Policy Analysis Series

PROGRESS AGAINST POVERTY

A Review of the 1964–1974 Decade

Robert D. Plotnick
Felicity Skidmore

Institute for Research on Poverty
University of Wisconsin—Madison
Madison, Wisconsin

ACADEMIC PRESS   New York   San Francisco   London

A Subsidiary of Harcourt Brace Jovanovich, Publishers

This book is one of a series sponsored by the Institute for Research on Poverty of the University of Wisconsin pursuant to the provisions of the Economic Opportunity Act of 1964.

Academic Press, Inc.
111 Fifth Avenue, New York, New York 10003

United Kingdom Edition published by
Academic Press, Inc. (London) Ltd.
24/28 Oval Road, London NW1

Library of Congress Catalog Card Number: 75-31947

ISBN 0—12—558550—0 (Cloth)

ISBN 0—12—558556—X (Paper)

Printed in the United States of America

The Institute for Research on Poverty is a national center for research established at the University of Wisconsin in 1966 by a grant from the Office of Economic Opportunity. Its primary objective is to foster basic, multidisciplinary research into the nature and causes of poverty and means to combat it.

In addition to increasing the basic knowledge from which policies aimed at the elimination of poverty can be shaped, the Institute strives to carry analysis beyond the formulation and testing of fundamental generalizations to the development and assessment of relevant policy alternatives.

The Institute endeavors to bring together scholars of the highest caliber whose primary research efforts are focused on the problem of poverty, the distribution of income, and the analysis and evaluation of social policy, offering staff members wide opportunity for interchange of ideas, maximum freedom for research into basic questions about poverty and social policy, and dissemination of their findings.

Contents

Foreword

For ten years now, the elimination of income poverty has stood as an explicit objective of federal public policy. Since this objective was first suggested by President Kennedy and later implemented by President Johnson, nearly all social policy programs and proposals have had to face up to the basic question posed by this objective: "What does it do—or what will it do—for the poor?" Indeed, at the very inception of the "war on poverty," an agency was established within the Executive Office of the President—the Office of Economic Opportunity (OEO)—a part of whose mandate it was to put this question to all social policy proposals considered by the Administration. A new test had been established that no social policy planner could ignore.

In 1964–1965, when this antipoverty goal was established as a national policy objective, only a rudimentary measure existed of how many poor people there were in the nation. Knowledge regarding the characteristics of the poor population was even less reliable. Indeed, in tackling the mandate to eliminate poverty, early policy planners worked with the crude notion that any family unit with less than $3000 of money income was poor.

As time passed, the measurement of poverty became more sophisticated. Poverty lines were established for families of various sizes. Moreover, these lines varied, depending on whether the family lived on a farm or in an urban area. Each of these lines was adjusted annually to reflect changes in the consumer price level.

This more sophisticated measure of poverty became the established federal government definition. With it, policy planners and analysts were able to evaluate with greater reliability the antipoverty impacts of policy proposals. The number of poor people could be tracked over time, and the changes in the composition of the poor determined. However, even though the objective was established, an agency with concern for income poverty created, and an official poverty measure adopted, the federal government did not issue regular or formal reports charting either the nation's progress in reducing poverty or the effectiveness of various policies in attaining this end.

Now, ten years after the nation accepted the goal of poverty reduction, it seems worthwhile to track the progress that has been made in attaining this goal. While such a progress report might have been prepared by the government itself, it has not been. The Institute for Research on Poverty, therefore, has sponsored this book.

The decision to undertake such a report was not made in a vacuum. Preliminary discussions regarding the structure and approach of the report were held in 1973 with people in the Office of Planning, Research, and Evaluation of OEO. And, after the planning and research staff of OEO was transferred to the Office of the Assistant Secretary for Planning and Evaluation of the Department of Health, Education, and Welfare, further discussions took place. Plans for such a report also were scrutinized regularly at meetings of the National Advisory Committee of the Institute.

In addition to this rather informal guidance, two formal groups were set up to provide the authors, Robert D. Plotnick and Felicity Skidmore, with advice on the form and content of the volume and critiques of the chapters when they were drafted. One such group was composed of experts who were not at the Institute: Edward Gramlich, of the Brookings Institution, Robinson Hollister, of Swarthmore College, and Robert Lampman (while he was at Cornell University on leave of absence from the University of Wisconsin). The second group was an advisory committee of Institute scholars from a wide range of disciplines. This committee included D. Lee Bawden (agricultural economics and economics), Irwin Garfinkel (social work), Joel Handler (law), Matthew Holden, Jr. (political science), Robert Lampman (economics), James Sweet (sociology), Karl Taeuber (sociology), and Burton Weisbrod (economics).

In addition, an early draft of the manuscript was read thoroughly and critiqued in detail by members of the staff of the Assistant Secretary for Planning and Evaluation of the Department of Health, Education, and Welfare. This volume has, therefore, benefited greatly from the constructive suggestions and criticisms of experts in several disciplines, with several perspectives, coming from universities, independent research organizations, and government.

Of this report's many contributions to an appraisal of the nation's progress in eliminating poverty, three stand out. (1) The *antipoverty "budgets"* for 1965, 1968, and 1972 chart for the first time the growth in all public expenditures that provide cash, goods, or service benefits directly to identifiable recipients, and show how the proportion of these expenditures going to the pretransfer poor has changed over the period. (2) *The analysis of changes in the level and composition of posttransfer poverty* addresses the issue of how the level of poverty has changed over the decade and what sorts of people remain in poverty after ten years of public antipoverty effort. Because this analysis relies on a variety of poverty definitions (official and unofficial, absolute and relative) and measures of well-being, the question is answered from a variety of points of view. Each of these viewpoints constitutes an important perspective and stresses different facets of the problem. From the most sanguine viewpoint, progress has been made: The number of poor people has been reduced, and the poverty-income gap has been cut substantially. In contrast, a relative definition, which reflects the degree of inequality in the distribution of income, shows no progress at all in reducing the problem of poverty. (3) The *appraisal of the antipoverty effectiveness of the cash transfer system* provides one measure of the extent to which public policy has lifted people out of poverty. Such an analysis is important because expenditures on cash transfers have been a rapidly growing component of social welfare spending—from $37 billion in 1965 to $80 billion in 1972. No matter what viewpoint is adopted, the poverty problem would be more serious today than in 1965 if this rapid increase in the cash transfer system had not taken place.

This book is an important addition to the poverty literature. It presents the first series describing the numbers and composition of the *pretransfer* poor over time. It charts in detail the changes in the incidence and composition of *posttransfer* poverty since the early 1960s, and assesses the contribution made by public income-transfer policy to these changes. In sum, it provides the only detailed analysis of both the efforts and the achievements of ten years of public policy aimed at reducing income poverty. As the first in what will be a series of biannual reports on poverty sponsored by the Institute, it provides the bench mark against which the second decade of anti-poverty efforts can be appraised.

Robert H. Haveman

Preface

At the request of Robert H. Haveman, then director of the Institute for Research on Poverty, I undertook the task of assessing recent changes in income poverty in the United States. Felicity Skidmore joined me to analyze the concomitant changes in American social policy and place the economic investigations within a broader context. This book represents the results of our inquiries.

Advice and criticism from many members of the Institute have helped shape our research. The findings and interpretations herein, however, do not constitute an official Institute statement or the views of the individuals who so kindly assisted us.

Many persons have given their time and thought in helping us complete this study. A special debt of thanks is owed to Robert Haveman. His daily suggestions, general guidance of our investigations, and careful reading of early drafts contributed immeasurably to the development of the final product. His enthusiasm, encouragement, and good humor were equally important in helping us complete this project.

Robert Lampman was instrumental in the decision to undertake the study. His informed counsel was valuable in helping us develop its overall direction. Irwin Garfinkel offered an essential open door for our day-to-day research problems and helped focus the research. Both of these scholars carefully criticized preliminary versions of the text.

Katharine Mochon was an important participant in the early planning sessions for this book and contributed preliminary research for the first chapter.

We also wish to thank a number of other persons from both inside and outside the Institute for their aid on various parts of this book. Karl Taeuber's suggestions on the entire draft improved both its contents and its style. D. Lee Bawden, Joel Handler, Joseph Heffernan, and Burton Weisbrod commented usefully on various chapters. As outside readers, Edward Gramlich and Robinson Hollister offered valuable counsel and criticism on many aspects of the research.

The cooperation of the Office of Income Security of the U.S. Department of Health, Education, and Welfare was greatly appreciated. Staff members reviewed an early version of the manuscript and made many helpful comments. Moreover, Gordon Fisher, from that Office, shared his unpublished data with me, for which I am most grateful. Without his assistance, the work in Chapter 3 would have been much more difficult and the results less accurate. The survey in Chapter 1 benefited greatly from his extensive knowledge. In no way, however, do the opinions or results reported here represent an official position of that Office or of HEW.

Several people contributed to the success of the empirical investigations. We thank Nancy Williamson for her patient help with the computer programing as well as for her cheerful spirits. Nancy Schofield and Luise Cunliffe also provided valued technical assistance. We are pleased to acknowledge the able research assistance of David Brazell and Carolyn Everett. A special note of thanks is due to Harry Travis. His generous and capable advice was essential to the completion of the multivariate analyses of Chapters 4 and 6. The Center for Demography and Ecology at the University of Wisconsin-Madison provided computer support for this aspect of our work.

My thanks to Susan Elbe, Catherine Ersland, Wendy Haebig, Marlene Kundert, Wanda Montgomery, Mary Sheean, and Norma Walter, of the secretarial staff of the Institute, who efficiently prepared the several incarnations of this work. Marjean Jondrow and Jean Mufti edited the manuscript for publication.

Robert D. Plotnick

1
Growth in Social Programs, 1964-1974

In 1964, the "war on poverty" was declared. Ten years later, it is appropriate to reflect on what has been achieved in that endeavor. This book charts the progress made against poverty during the last decade. Changes in the poverty population and the reasons why they occurred are assessed from several perspectives. Broad trends in the size and demographic characteristics of the poverty population are reported. The impact of economic conditions on the extent of poverty is analyzed. The growth of government social expenditures is traced, and the degree to which they benefited the poor is calculated. Finally, the contribution of the cash-transfer system toward reducing poverty is treated in detail and a brief assessment made of how the growth of in-kind transfers over the period changes this picture.

To set the stage for the detailed empirical discussion of the nation's progress in reducing income poverty that constitutes most of the rest of the book, this first chapter provides a short history of social welfare policy since 1964. Section I includes a brief discussion of the thinking that went into the creation of the Office of Economic Opportunity (OEO), established within the White House as the government agency responsible for eliminating poverty.[1] Section II provides equally brief descriptions of policy developments in the

Katherine Mochon contributed preliminary research for this chapter.

various social policy areas since the early 1960s and gives some assessment of the part played by OEO in the domestic social policy history of the last ten years.[2] Section III introduces the remainder of the book.

I. THE ESTABLISHMENT OF THE WAR ON POVERTY AND OEO

Before 1964, poverty, as such, had not been a special focus of the federal government. During the late fifties and early sixties, accumulating signs signaled that the importance of specific action on behalf of the disadvantaged was beginning to be recognized. The Supreme Court declared school desegregation unconstitutional in 1954. In 1957, a conservative President ordered troops into Little Rock to force compliance with the Supreme Court decision, and Congress passed a Civil Rights Act for the first time in eighty years. In 1959, the Kerr–Mills Act increased the public funds to be allocated to health care for the aged. In West Virginia during the 1960 presidential campaign, John F. Kennedy deplored hunger and found in the public reaction a reflection of his own concern. As soon as he became President, he liberalized and expanded the surplus commodity program and announced a pilot food stamp operation.

In 1962, the Manpower Development and Training Act was passed and soon expanded to cover the disadvantaged. Also in 1962, Michael Harrington published *The Other America,* which received great public attention and, reportedly, was read by President Kennedy. In January 1963, *The New Yorker* published Dwight MacDonald's "Our Invisible Poor," which was widely read. The New Frontier Administration began to recognize that public receptiveness to the issues of poverty amid plenty could provide a rallying point for the coming election of 1964.

In May 1963, a memorandum on poverty, written for the President by Walter Heller, Chairman of the Council of Economic Advisers, included an analysis showing that between 1956 and 1960 the decline in the number of poor families (defined as families with income below $3000) had slowed down from an annual average of 1.0 percent over the period 1945–1955 to 0.4 percent between 1956 and 1960. This analysis predicted that even if the economy were to reach full employment, large groups of the poor (predominantly the aged, the disabled, and the families headed by females) would still remain poor.[3]

The President responded to this memorandum during the summer of 1963, by instructing the staff from various executive agencies—the Council of Economic Advisers (CEA), the Bureau of the Budget, and the Departments of Labor and of Health, Education, and Welfare—to make the case for a major policy to attack poverty. In August 1963, in the midst of this interagency effort, 200,000 civil rights marchers, under the leadership of Martin Luther King, Jr., converged on Washington. The issue of black unemployment was one major focus of the march. In November, President Kennedy asked for antipoverty measures to be included in the 1964 legislative program.

After President Kennedy's assassination in late November, Lyndon Johnson maintained the momentum of the war on poverty, reportedly saying to Heller, "That is my kind of program."[4] The 1964 *Economic Report of the President* included, at President Johnson's express wish, a profile of poverty in the United States, spelling out in detail the composition of the poor, characteristics of poor families, and what had been done to date to alleviate poverty.[5] The report concluded with a series of proposals for "combating poverty" and "organizing the attack."

The emphasis of the Council on a coordinated attack was important. It was out of this framework that President Johnson decided to set up an independent agency within the White House, rather than to assign the war on poverty to an existing department. Sargent Shriver was enlisted to head the task force to draft a bill in line with the ideas expressed in the *Economic Report.*

The early task force days involved some 130 people inside and outside government who contributed their ideas for what was anticipated to be an innovative social venture by the federal government. What emerged from the planning stage was predictable, given the interests of the various task force members. There were two major thrusts—job training programs, and community participation and development.

The proponents of job programs—primarily Willard Wirtz and Daniel Moynihan—viewed the main cause of poverty as lack of jobs. They argued that an antipoverty program should center on increasing employment opportunities and developing job-training programs, particularly for disadvantaged youth. Their ideas continued the 1962 bipartisan effort in the Congress that had achieved passage of the Manpower Development and Training Act (MDTA). This act originally emphasized the retraining of technologically unemployed workers who had been long-time members of the labor force. By 1963, it was already apparent that few of the unemployed fell into this category, and President Kennedy proposed that the act be expanded to involve training in literacy and basic work skills. (It is significant that the President's recommendation to provide MDTA with an antipoverty mission was included in a message to Congress on civil rights and job opportunities for blacks, after a series of White House conferences on racial tension.)

The task force's other major emphasis was on community programs. The genesis of this idea seems to have been twofold. First, the "opportunity theory" of poverty—that pathology lay in the community rather than the individual—had gained credence in the 1950s. This diagnosis had provided a theoretical basis for the community approach to social problems and had stimulated the establishment of Mobilization for Youth, an organization set up on Manhattan's Lower East Side as a testing ground for extending employment, education, and counseling services to youth of the community. At the same time, President Kennedy's Committee on Juvenile Delinquency and Crime, headed by Robert Kennedy, was experimenting with community action pilot projects in seventeen cities across the country. The work of this committee was an important influence on the development of the community organization strategy, which became a major part of OEO activity.

Second, concern had been growing through the fifties and early sixties about the seemingly intractable urban slum and the ineffectiveness of urban renewal in improving center-city conditions. This concern had led to the establishment of the Ford Foundation Grey Areas projects, designed to create independent community agencies to assist persons with little education and few skills to cope with the complexities of urban slum living. These privately funded programs offered good examples of experimentation in community action. They involved grants—initially to school systems and then to cities—designed to stimulate a community-wide approach to physical and human problems in low-income urban areas.

The task force included people who had been involved in these projects—Paul Ylvisacker, Richard Boone, and David Hackett—and it urged a strong community action emphasis that would involve not only an organization of services but also a strategy for the political organization of the poor to effect change in existing community institutions such as schools, welfare departments, and political machines. Discussion of this issue first yielded the phrase "maximum feasible participation." Moynihan argues that the phrase was not originally intended to denote the full participation of the poor, as it was later interpreted. Others, including Adam Yarmolinsky, have argued that, even initially, "maximum feasible participation" was intended to go well beyond Moynihan's interpretation to a totally new idea—a community-based political strategy stimulated by a federal program. No one, however, either among the drafters or among the Senators and Congressmen debating the bill envisaged the possibility of any significant conflict between "the organized poor and the politicians in city hall."[6]

Direct redistribution of money or goods did not figure prominently in the task force discussions, and does not appear to have been considered an important or particularly appropriate weapon in the arsenal by the important planners of the war. In 1966, when OEO formulated and transmitted to the Congress a five-year antipoverty plan, it did include an income-maintenance scheme. The peripheral nature of this scheme was, however, stressed in the letter of transmittal:

> To guarantee income at the poverty level . . . is *not* the approach taken by this plan. An income maintenance program . . . is among the instruments proposed . . . [but] the plan as a whole . . . depends more on economic growth, and on opportunity programs that maximize the anti-poverty effect of that growth, than it does on income maintenance.[7]

Part of the reason for this lack of focus on directly redistributive policies seems to have been the confidence on the part of President Kennedy's economic advisers that expansionary fiscal and monetary policy could produce vigorous and sustainable economic growth (at tolerable price levels). The tight labor markets thus produced would, it was argued, create jobs and continual new government revenues (fiscal dividends) to be spent on social programs. This, in turn, led to the view that the poor did not need handouts as much as enrichment programs to render them more employable.

As Michael Harrington pointed out at the time, this was an oversimplified view.[8] Only the part of the poverty population that is oriented toward and able to function in the labor market has achieved steady gains from macroeconomic strategies. Among other demographic subgroups, the antipoverty effects of growth have not been so powerful. Hence, although growth continued during the late 1960s, its poverty-reducing impact diminished. A complete strategy would thus seem to have required both a vigorous economy and a set of redistribution policies. (For the effects on poverty of macroeconomic policy, see Chapter 5.)

Another part of the reason for the lack of focus on directly redistributive policies is the fact that poverty meant many different things to the designers of the poverty war. Although the Heller memorandum and the 1964 *Economic Report* had documented the extent of *income* poverty, culture of poverty theories and issues of societal barriers were also important parts of "poverty" in the minds of the task force and of the public. According to James Sundquist, "That the word itself embodied various definitions, each leading logically to its own line of attack, only became apparent as the War on Poverty developed."[9] Robert A. Levine extends the ambiguity even further, documenting a confusion between the various meanings to be attached to poverty on the one hand and the concept of equality of opportunity on the other.

> A pretty good case can be made that the intentions of the designers [of the war on poverty] were at least as close to the objective of equal opportunity. The sequence went from the *idea* of equal opportunity, which is relatively difficult to summarize in a single word or paragraph, to the *word* "poverty," to programs that were oriented around the anti-poverty objective because the word had been used. . . . [This] ambivalence is illustrated by the fact that they began a War on *Poverty* centered on an Economic *Opportunity* Act.[10]

And Levine further points out that the problems of poverty affect those people at the bottom of the income distribution, whereas problems of opportunity concern the ceilings that exist on the opportunities of people both below and above any poverty line.

The form of the Economic Opportunity bill and the proposed budget were complete within six weeks from the first meeting of the task force. Table 1.1 shows the various titles of the Act. As can be seen, the biggest share of the proposed budget was for human capital programs—the youth opportunity programs and the work experience program amounted to 58 percent of the total. Most of the rest was accounted for by the urban and rural community action program (33 percent).

The bill was initiated in the executive branch, was strongly supported by President Johnson, and faced a large Democratic majority in both the House and Senate committees. It passed both Houses, and was signed into law by President Johnson in August 1964. As expected, the Democrats exerted strong pressure for its passage. However, the vote—226-185 in the House and 61-34 in the Senate—showed significant Republican opposition; the trampling of this dissent may be a partial explanation for the vehemence of later attacks on OEO. The total budget requested was $962.5 million. The amount finally approved was $800 million, although the relative distribution of the total among the various programs was unchanged. Both amounts were very modest percentages of the federal budget.

TABLE 1.1 ECONOMIC OPPORTUNITY BILL SENT TO CONGRESS, MARCH 1964

	Appropriation Requested (in millions of dollars)
Title I	412.5
Job Corps (OEO-managed), a residential training program for young men and women between the ages of 16 and 21	(190.0)
In-School and Out-of-School Neighborhood Youth Corps (delegated to the Department of Labor), an at-home training and work experience program for young men and women between the ages of 16 and 21	(150.0)
College Work-Study Program (delegated to the Office of Education in the Department of Health, Education, and Welfare)	(72.5)
Title II	315.0
Community Action Program (OEO-managed), a set of comprehensive rural and urban local-initiated and planned programs	
Title III	50.0
Rural Loan Program (delegated to the Farmers Home Administration in the Department of Agriculture), a program of small farm and nonfarm operating loans to rural individuals and cooperatives	
Migrant Farm Workers Program (managed by CAP within OEO)	
Title IV	25.0
Small Business Development Centers (delegated to the Small Business Administration), a program of loans and technical aid to small businessmen who were either to be poor themselves or hire the poor	
Title V	150.0
Work Experience Program (delegated to the Welfare Administration in the Department of Health, Education, and Welfare), a program of work and training for welfare recipients and those—particularly unemployed fathers— whom the administration hoped to make eligible for welfare, via state action	
Title VI	10.0
VISTA (OEO-managed), the Volunteers in Service to America, the domestic counterpart of the Peace Corps	
Administration	
Total	962.5

TABLE 1.2.   OEO BUDGETS, BY PROGRAM OBLIGATION, 1965-1974
(in millions of dollars)

Program	1965	1966	1967	1968	1969	1970	1971	1972	1973	1974
Adult education	4.4	34.1	*	*	*	*	*	*	*	*
College work-study	54.9	.8	*	*	*	*	*	*	*	*
CAP (Local Initiative)	137.8	364.1	353.0	411.1	416.1	416.9	452.4	393.0	469.4	209.5
Concentrated Employment Program	—	—	50.7	73.0	83.0	139.0	*	*	*	*
Emergency Food & Medical Services	—	—	—	12.8	23.2	46.1	48.6	3.5	28.6	9.4
Family planning	—	—	—	9.0	13.8	22.1	18.8	23.9	15.4	*
Follow Through	—	—	—	14.6	32.0	70.3	68.4	*	*	*
Foster Grandparents	—	5.1	5.7	9.5	9.1	*	*	*	*	*
Head Start	96.4	198.9	349.2	316.2	333.9	325.3	360.0	*	*	*
Health programs	—	—	50.8	33.2	58.3	89.1	127.4	129.8	121.5	*
Job Corps	165.0	289.9	190.1	260.2	257.3	158.2	*	*	*	*
JOBS	—	—	—	60.1	113.0	47.0	*	*	*	*
Legal Services	—	24.8	25.2	35.9	47.3	54.7	61.2	67.7	77.2	71.5
Migrant program	14.9	25.5	33.0	25.0	28.5	33.3	36.1	36.5	38.6	*

TABLE 1.2 (cont.)

Program	1965	1966	1967	1968	1969	1970	1971	1972	1973	1974
Neighborhood Youth Corps (In-School)	—	68.4	58.9	49.0	59.2	*	*	*	*	*
Neighborhood Youth Corps (Out-of-School)	—	92.8	147.6	96.3	123.7	97.9	*	*	*	*
Neighborhood Youth Corps (Summer)	130.0	104.3	132.9	113.8	140.5	124.1	*	*	*	*
Operation Mainstream	—	10.3	30.3	22.3	41.0	51.0	*	*	*	*
Public Service Careers	—	—	15.6	7.6	18.5	46.9	*	*	*	*
Rural loans	17.2	32.3	31.9	27.7	12.1	4.1	4.0	*	*	*
Special Impact	—	—	—	19.9	22.4	36.2	37.1	26.8	36.6	38.1
Upward Bound	2.5	24.9	28.2	31.6	30.8	*	*	*	*	*
VISTA	1.8	14.8	20.3	22.4	25.4	27.3	29.6	*	*	*
Work Experience	—	112.0	112.5	100.0	44.3	6.4	*	*	*	*
TOTAL	737.0	1403.6	1623.4	1695.5	1896.1	1824.9	1285.5	681.2	465.4	328.5

*Denotes years when there was no OEO budget item. The programs were not necessarily disbanded. Many were transferred to other agencies.

9

TABLE 1.3. SOCIAL WELFARE EXPENDITURES, 1965-1972
(in millions of dollars)

	Federal		State-Local		Total	
1965						
OEO & related programs	359		0		359	
Other low-income programs	5,995 }	(17)*	2,503	(7)	8,498 }	(12)
Other social welfare expenditures	31,420	(83)	34,205	(93)	65,625	(88)
Total	37,774	(100)	36,708	(100)	74,482	(100)
1968						
OEO & related programs	3,311		0		3,311	
Other low-income programs	8,698 }	(21)	4,379	(9)	13,077 }	(15)
Other social welfare expenditures	46,563	(79)	46,273	(91)	92,836	(85)
Total	58,572	(100)	50,652	(100)	109,224	(100)
1972						
OEO & related programs	4,695		0		4,695	
Other low-income programs	19,959 }	(24)	9,149	(11)	29,108 }	(18)
Other social welfare expenditures	80,362	(76)	70,707	(89)	151,069	(82)
Total	104,016	(100)	79,856	(100)	184,872	(100)

Source: Based on tables in Chapter 3.
*Numbers in parentheses indicate percentages.

Neither the administration nor the Congress apparently was willing to launch a program large enough to justify the rhetoric surrounding it.

Table 1.2 shows the annual budget obligations of OEO from 1965 to 1974.[11] Even at the height of OEO's importance—as measured by its budget—its authorized expenditures were a fraction of what would have been needed if the promises surrounding the creation of OEO were to be given a real chance of fulfillment. But the budget may not be an appropriate measure of its influence, actual or intended, since one branch of thought conceived of OEO as a coordinator and instigator of new efforts on behalf of the poor *throughout* the federal government. These OEO expenditures, it is worth stressing, were only a small part of the total that went for programs directed toward low-income groups over the last ten years. They were only part of the war on poverty, and, particularly in later years, the disappearance of categories from the OEO budget often denoted only the transfer of programs to other agencies.

The relative orders of magnitude involved can be seen in Table 1.3 discussed at the end of this chapter. In 1965, expenditure on federal social programs directed toward low-income groups amounted to $6 billion, of which only $350 million went to OEO and related programs. By 1968, federal expenditure on such programs had risen to $12 billion, of which just over $3 billion was accounted for by OEO. By 1972, the comparable figure was 24\frac{1}{2}$ billion, of which 4\frac{1}{2}$ billion went for OEO and related programs.

What were the programs that grew from $6 billion in 1965 to 24\frac{1}{2}$ billion in 1972? To answer that question, the next section gives a brief overview of the main contours of federal social welfare policy over the last ten years.

II. RECENT SOCIAL WELFARE POLICY DEVELOPMENTS

Recent social welfare policy developments can be divided usefully into five categories: cash transfers, in-kind transfers, direct services, human capital programs, and community development programs.[12]

The first category, cash transfers, includes, but is not always restricted to, direct money grants to people below a certain income level. The goal of such programs is to provide income when a family's usual resources are exhausted. The second category, in-kind transfers, aims at increasing the consumption of goods by the poor but restricts the subsidy to specific items, such as food and housing. The third, direct services, does the same thing for services, such as medical care and legal aid. The fourth, human capital programs, consists of programs, such as education and job training, that enhance the ability of individuals to function in society and, particularly, in the labor market. The fifth, community development programs, can be defined as programs designed to enhance the community participation and political efficacy of the less powerful.

The major policy developments over the last ten years in each of these program categories will be described briefly. In each, the OEO initiatives will be mentioned first, to highlight the activities that were specifically designated as part of the war on poverty.

Cash Transfers

No major cash assistance programs were either funded or administered by OEO during this decade, although OEO Legal Services lawyers had significant effects on liberalizing AFDC and although results from the OEO-funded New Jersey experiment in income maintenance were used in the welfare reform debates. As we have seen, OEO economic planners thought of cash assistance as a necessary item in an antipoverty strategy, but most of the original architects of the war on poverty did not consider new forms of cash assistance to be a major part of that war.

The Social Security Act of 1935 and later amendments established several social insurance and income-tested cash programs—Old Age, Survivors, and Disability Insurance, Unemployment Insurance, Aid to the Aged, Aid to the Blind, Aid to the Permanently and Totally Disabled, and Aid to Families with Dependent Children. OASDI has grown to more than $62 billion in 1975. Unemployment Insurance was extended in 1970 to cover 4.8 million additional jobs; in the same year, a permanent program was created for persons who exhaust their regular state benefits during years of high unemployment. Social insurance reflects the assumption that everyone has some normal earnings flow that only needs supplementation when interrupted. The income-tested programs were thus expected to wither away as social insurance expanded. They have, however, also grown.

The 1961 Social Security Amendments, with the addition of the Unemployed Parent (UP) provision to the AFDC program, recognized the concept that even intact families, containing both parents, might need assistance. This provision enabled certain long-term unemployed parents—in reality, this meant fathers—to apply for public assistance. Two factors, however, have kept this program small. The first is that states may choose not to institute such a program. (In 1974, twenty-seven states had no UP program.) Second, the regulations governing the program are so restrictive that few families actually qualify—fewer than 125,000 families have received benefits at any one time, even in the most recent period.

Three sets of Social Security amendments after 1961 brought further change—the main impetus for which was the continual expansion of the AFDC rolls and budget. The 1962 amendments incorporated the view of the 1961 Ad Hoc Committee on Public Welfare that the way to reduce welfare dependency was through counseling and rehabilitation. They authorized states to provide "rehabilitation and other services" to recipients of AFDC and to set up a "social service plan" for each dependent family.

The cost of the program and the number of AFDC recipients rose increasingly sharply, indicating that provision of social services was not sufficient as a means of reducing poverty. "By 1967, welfare spokesmen in and out of the administration were embarrassed by references to the rhetoric of 1962."[13]

The public welfare amendments of 1967 reflected the growing dissatisfaction. Changes in AFDC were designed to reduce welfare costs and get recipients to work. Under a compulsory work program, the Work Incentive Program (WIN), all recipients were to register for employment or work training. Welfare agencies were required to provide day care for working mothers. And in reaction to growing AFDC costs, a "freeze" or ceiling (never implemented) was placed on federal funds to states to limit the number of dependent children the federal government would aid. Daniel Moynihan called the new measure the first "positively punitive" welfare legislation in the history of the American national government. The amendments did, however, recognize the work disincentive feature of welfare, whereby payments were decreased as earnings increased, dollar-for-dollar and sometimes more. The maximum tax rate on AFDC and AFDC-UP benefits as earnings rose was fixed by the 1967 amendments at 66.7 percent.

The 1967 amendments also failed to stem increases in the welfare rolls. The annual rate of growth of the AFDC population in 1967, 7 percent, grew to 28 percent by 1971 (partly because of raised income eligibility levels and break-even points). A series of welfare reform proposals has since been introduced into the Congress, aimed at guaranteeing, universalizing, and standardizing benefits to all families with children, and also at stopping the rise in caseloads and costs and saving money by rationalizing the patchwork of systems. But they failed to win congressional enactment.

In 1972, further amendments to the Social Security Act represented an important step toward a guaranteed annual income for some groups, requiring, as of January 1974, that public assistance for the aged, blind, and disabled be assumed by the federal government. Benefits were increased, renamed the Supplemental Security Income (SSI), and administered by the Social Security Administration. In the past, benefits in these "adult categories" had varied greatly from state to state and category to category. Under SSI, uniform eligibility standards result, although there are still provisions for discretionary state supplementation.

In-Kind Transfers

In addition to the expansion of cash transfer programs, programs that provide goods rather than money have also increased in the last decade. In this section, we discuss housing and food.

Housing Programs

OEO instituted no significant housing program. The policy developments in this area were mainly the province of the Department of Housing and Urban Development. Since 1937, the federal government has provided public housing for some low-income families. This program provides local authorities with funds for construction of low-rent housing. Only low-income families are eligible to live in these units. Rents cannot exceed 25 percent of a family's monthly income, with upper limits on income being locally established.

Problems of low-income housing persisted into the 1960s, and additional approaches were initiated. In 1964, Congress passed a Housing and Urban Development Act, pulling together several programs into a new department. The Act provided subsidies to local authorities to lease privately owned units for families to rent as public housing. By 1972, 92,000 units of housing operated under this plan, but the major purpose of the Act—to move public housing into better neighborhoods—was not achieved. The vast majority of these public housing units still were in low-income neighborhoods.

In 1965, a federal rent supplement program began, in which the government paid the difference between market rents and one-quarter of the tenant's adjusted income. This subsidy for low-income

1. Growth in Social Programs, 1964–1974

tigation on the administration of welfare focused on four areas: the right to welfare for all persons who meet state standards of ibility; (2) the right to "fair hearings" and a reduction in the ninistrative discretion of welfare agencies; (3) elimination of resi- ce requirements; and (4) the right to a minimally adequate grant. ts brought by legal services lawyers have been successful to some gree in each of these areas. Residency requirements have been allenged and ruled unconstitutional, and the man-in-the-house rule s struck down. Prior hearing must be held before funds are cut off om a welfare recipient accused of violation of welfare rules, and forts are being made to require states to provide a "family mini- um" and to reduce inequities among states.

ledical Services[17]

1967, OEO started a small family-planning program, but OEO's najor health program has been the Neighborhood Health Centers. he Health Centers were started in 1965 and grew to a peak in 1972 vith a budget of more than $130 million a year. They attempted to provide comprehensive medical and dental care for the poor by oulling together services provided by the Children's Bureau, the Public Health Service, and other agencies and by filling remaining gaps. These centers were innovative attempts to provide comprehen- sive family health care in areas where the poor lived, using paramedi- cal aides with medical specialists available, when necessary. Trans- ferred to HEW in 1969, they are being phased out by the current Administration both to eliminate their high cost and to make way for expansion of Health Maintenance Organizations and other health care delivery systems that are intended to provide services for all, rather than separate services for the poor.

HEW instituted a significant health-care delivery initiative in the early 1960s, the Maternal and Child Health Programs. There is evidence that these programs significantly decreased the infant mor- tality rates in their catchment areas, and it has even been suggested that their effect was great enough to show up in the national infant mortality rates—which have indeed dropped appreciably since 1965. Expenditures on these programs grew from less than $35 million in fiscal 1964 to almost $250 million (almost twice the level of OEO health programs) in fiscal 1973. Since then, their funding also has been cut back.

The two largest federal health programs in the last ten years have, however, been concerned with the financing rather than with the

families was also intended to disperse housing units for the poor, but most of the units—69,000 in 1973—were in completely rent-supple- mented projects. The subsidy was targeted directly at the lowest- income families, and participants had, on average, lower incomes than tenants in public housing. It was not, however, universally available to eligible families, and, in fact, it covered only a small proportion.

The Housing and Urban Development Act of 1968 added two more housing subsidy programs to the system. The first—section 236— provided subsidies to lenders so that the interest rate on privately owned, low-income rental projects could be reduced to 1 percent, with the intention that lower costs be reflected in lower rents. The resulting rents were, nonetheless, substantially higher than rents in public housing. Tenants in housing implemented by section 236 did not come primarily from the poverty population (at the end of 1971 their median income was $5000). The second program—section 235, a homeownership program—was intended to encourage home buying and property ownership for low-income families. It provided interest- rate subsidies, reduced mortgage costs, and low down-payments. Here again, it was not the very poorest who were reached. In the homeownership program approximately 5 percent of home buyers have had incomes of less than $4000.

In January 1973, the Administration ordered a moratorium on new subsidized housing starts while housing assistance programs were being evaluated. The major criticisms of the existing programs have centered around the inequities and gaps in the system. Today, only about one in seven families in the income class now being served by subsidy programs actually receives some benefit.

Food Programs

OEO also had little to do with food programs. The only such program under its auspices was the Emergency Food and Medical Program, mandated by Congress in 1967 to provide money to literally penniless people so that they could buy food stamps. Al- though this was a small program, its influence was somewhat broader in that it provided outreach services to assist poor people to receive benefits from the Department of Agriculture food stamp and com- modity distribution programs. It also stepped in to assure that these programs actually delivered, and it kept a number of Department of Agriculture supplemental feeding projects from having to close by paying administrative costs that Agriculture did not agree to pay.

The first major food program in the country was a food stamp program that functioned between 1939 and 1943. President Eisenhower subsequently instituted a very limited program of direct distribution of surplus commodities under the Department of Agriculture. With the election of President Kennedy in 1960, federal expenditures on food programs began to increase. He expanded the surplus commodity program by executive order and persuaded Congress to pass a food stamp program, also under the Department of Agriculture. In 1961, the commodity distribution program amounted to $143 million. The food stamp program was a very modest $1 million. By 1969, commodity distribution had grown to $264 million and food stamps to $248 million. By 1973, the food stamp program had become by far the largest and most important in-kind transfer program.[14] The number of beneficiaries had increased from less than 2 million in 1968 to 13 million.

On 1 July 1974, legislation made food stamps available in all counties and to all persons qualifying under the income test. More than 30 million people became eligible, and that number is now close to 40 million. The food stamp program, thus, has become a universal guaranteed annual income for food, although it is estimated that not many more than one-half of those eligible are receiving benefits, so far. Eligible families may purchase coupons and use them like cash for most food items. The price a given family pays for food stamps varies with its income, while the face value of the total amount of the stamps for which a family is eligible varies with family size.[15] For a family of four with no other income, the annual benefit is $1850. As family income rises, the benefit is reduced by between twenty-five and thirty cents for every extra dollar of income.

The food commodities program was substantial throughout the sixties and early seventies. Before June 1974, counties could choose between a food stamp program and a food commodities program. Now that it is mandatory for all counties to offer food stamps, the food commodities program is being phased out. It had been a program available for public assistance recipients and others certified as "low income," although the quantity of commodities received did not (unlike the food stamp program) vary with income. The food, which could include butter, lard, cheese, flour, cereals, dried milk and eggs, vegetables, and rice, was intended as a supplement to a family's food expenditures. The program was designed primarily to remove agricultural surpluses and to aid in farm price supports; thus, the types of goods that were available varied from month to month.

The third major food program, child nutrition, p[...] lunches, and milk to children at school. The scho[...] the largest, has succeeded in supplying and subsi[...] many children—the number now reaches 23 million[...] for free lunches is an intricate procedure and of[...] gating those children who qualify for lunches to [...] tables. The stigma involved for these children may [...] families from applying for free meals. It is estimat[...] one-third of those children eligible for school lunch [...] benefit.

Direct Services

Two categories of service programs have received [...] attention in the last decade—legal services and medical c[...]

Legal Services

The institution of legal services for the poor was one of [...] contributions to the poverty war. It has had conseque[...] yond the delivery of services, touching on one of the ma[...] the early OEO planners—the changing of social institution[...]

At the turn of the century, private legal aid societies [...] established to enable the poor to receive help, but the res[...] the outreach were never large. When OEO was establishe[...] tuted 250 legal services projects, which were directed [...] guidelines to ensure community involvement (for instanc[...] cluding community residents on governing boards) and to [...] law reform as well as legal services as a major goal.

Frustrations with the inadequacy of dealing with the leg[...] lems of the poor on a case-by-case approach led to law reform[...] in test cases and class actions—cases that have an impact o[...] numbers of poor persons who, although not involved in [...] litigation, stand to benefit from the outcome. Legal services l[...] have brought cases in California to prevent the reduction of m[...] aid to the poor, in the District of Columbia to prohibit lan[...] from engaging in retaliatory evictions, and in Michigan to s[...] revisions in state housing laws. In the consumer field, law refor[...] concentrated on usury, unfair use of garnishment, and contracts[...] deny consumer defenses—areas in which the indigent most oft[...] victimized.

delivery of health care. In the first Johnson Administration, both Medicare (for the aged) and Medicaid (for the welfare population and other medical indigents) were passed by Congress as additional titles to the Social Security Act and put into operation in 1966. The intent was to finance care for certain needy population groups without interfering with the private sector. Government expenditures under these programs were large and grew rapidly, amounting by 1970 to $7\frac{1}{2}$ billion for Medicare and almost $3 billion for Medicaid. Amendments to the Social Security Act in 1972 resulted in some cutbacks in coverage (while extending benefits to those with chronic kidney disease and those disabled who are entitled to Social Security or Railroad Retirement benefits). Costs, however, continue to rise. In fiscal 1975, Medicare is expected to spend $13 billion on medical services for 23 million persons, and Medicaid is expected to spend $12 billion for 29 million persons.

Because of these continually soaring costs, and also because of the still inadequate and incomplete coverage of persons in medical need, public attention has been shifting in the early 1970s to comprehensive national health insurance. More than one dozen insurance bills have been introduced, and, currently, there are several bills before the Congress that vary in their reliance on private insurance companies and in the generosity of their benefits. None, however, has passed so far.

Human Capital

The two major types of human capital programs in the last ten years have been manpower development and education.

Manpower Programs

Manpower constituted one of the major program areas for OEO. In the original OEO Act, there were three manpower programs. The first was Job Corps, one of the most criticized and controversial of all the OEO programs. It was initiated because of a strongly felt need for vocational training for teenage, male school-dropouts who were on the streets rather than in regular employment. One part of the program provided functional literacy, and the other trained the somewhat literate in urban vocational skills. The second OEO program was the Neighborhood Youth Corps (NYC), also a diverse set of programs designed for teenagers who might otherwise be on the streets. It provided part-time jobs during the school day for people still in school, and a summer program and a year-round out-of-school program for youths who had either graduated or dropped out of school. It was essentially a work experience program in low-level public employment jobs. The third original OEO manpower program was the Work Experience Program, designed to be a work and job training program, for people on welfare or eligible for welfare. In 1967, the Concentrated Employment Program was instituted in an effort to focus existing Economic Opportunity Act manpower funds plus some pre-vocational training funds on extremely poor inner-city neighborhoods, in order to provide literacy and discipline training in communities with high concentrations of poor persons, who would then be fed into on-the-job training in entry-level private-sector jobs.

Two major manpower developments since 1960 were not OEO-funded.[18] First, the Manpower Development and Training Act of 1962 (MDTA) preceded and influenced OEO. It originally was designed to mitigate the effects of technological unemployment through the use of retraining programs and, subsequently, to deal with youth unemployment by training. The second was the Work Incentive (WIN) program, passed by Congress with the 1967 welfare amendments. WIN was designed to make possible the enforcement of the AFDC work test by ensuring the availability of work programs and day care. The OEO Work Experience program was phased out in response to WIN.

The relative magnitude of these manpower programs can be gauged from their total budget figures for fiscal 1969. The largest component was $257 million to Job Corps, followed by $226 million to the Manpower Development and Training Act, $154 million to Job Opportunities in the Business Sector, $124 million of the Out-of-School Neighborhood Youth Corps, and $59 million to the Concentrated Employment program.

The federal government first had entered the area of manpower policies with financial aid to the states for vocational education under the Smith–Hughes Act of 1917. In the 1930s, the Federal–State Employment Service was instituted to administer an unemployment insurance program and to help place the experienced unemployed in jobs. Occupational training programs did not appear on the scene until the 1960s, with passage of the MDTA.

Manpower programs were regarded as part of an antipoverty complex for the first time in OEO programs, and they broadened the target group for manpower programs to include not only youth but also the most disadvantaged groups in the community. This change in emphasis also influenced the development of MDTA, which in the second half of the decade transferred funds from predominantly institutional funding (used for formal classroom education and skill training) to the subsidized On-the-Job Training (OJT) program. This, in turn, meant relatively more resources going into subsistence allowances and other subsidies to the *trainees* themselves—true of the Job Corps (which also provided housing), OJT, JOBS, WIN, and NYC.

Cost—benefit analyses of these programs produced varying verdicts. The MDTA program—particularly, MDTA on-the-job training—generally has shown up well in evaluation studies. Job Opportunities in the Business Sector scored well, but there may have been little net increase in the number of disadvantaged who gained employment—rather a displacement effect on other low-skilled workers in traditional jobs. The Neighborhood Youth Corps and Job Corps yielded mixed results, and the record of the WIN program has not been good.

Education Programs

OEO's major effort in education was in preschool education—the Head Start program. The major purpose of Head Start was to provide educational activities for four-year-old and five-year-old children from disadvantaged families, in the hope of narrowing the cognitive gap between them and the average child before the start of regular school in the first grade. Other goals were to improve the health of the children through physical examinations, to provide school lunches, and to create a physical environment conducive to learning. Head Start got underway very quickly, enrolling about one-half million children for the summer of 1965. Year-round programs followed. It was transferred to HEW in 1971–1972, and its funding has continued to grow. Evaluations of Head Start as an educational program have not been able to show enduring educational gains. When viewed as a health or community action program, it has been evaluated more favorably.

A new program, Follow Through, was specified in the 1967 amendments to the Economic Opportunity Act to provide special services to Head Start pupils for the first few years of formal education, in the hope of solidifying and retaining any initial gains. Follow Through in 1968–1969 had a budget of $15 million and grew to a peak of $69 million in 1971, when it was transferred to HEW.

OEO instituted two other educational programs. The Work Study Program, written into the original Economic Opportunity Act, authorized grants to institutions of higher education to assist in employment of students from low-income families. In 1964–1965, the expenditure for Work Study was $23 million. It was incorporated then into the Higher Education Act of 1965. The other program was Upward Bound, a much smaller program to provide special preparation for college entrance to disadvantaged minority high school students.

Three major non-OEO developments on the education front have become law since 1960. The Higher Education Facilities Act of 1963 provided federal grants and loans for college construction. In 1966, when the largest expenditures came, the federal government spent $67 million on construction grants and $200 million on loans. The Higher Education Act of 1965 included the Work Study program, as well as the Teacher Fellow program (to furnish additional teaching services to "developing institutions" that catered mainly to low-income and minority students), and Educational Opportunity Grants (which participating institutions had to match) to be awarded to students from low-income families. By 1972, funds for these programs and for the Work Study program amounted to $575 million. The 1972 amendments to this Act authorized Basic Opportunity grants of $1400 to low-income undergraduates but replaced the Educational Opportunity Grants with a non-income–conditioned provision. Available funds are grossly inadequate, however, with the result that fewer low-income students than formerly are actually receiving aid.

The third development, and probably the most important from the viewpoint of educating the disadvantaged, was the Elementary and Secondary Education Act, also passed in 1965, which provided in Title I for "financial assistance to local educational agencies serving areas with concentrations of children from low-income families." The amount appropriated the first year was somewhat under $1 billion, which was increased in subsequent years to about $1.5 billion. In 1972, for example, $1.4 billion went to 14,200 school districts, which enrolled 7.3 million of the 8.1 million qualifying children.

Community Participation and Development

The Community Action Program and Model Cities were the two major efforts at community change that were initiated in the 1960s. Each will be discussed in turn.

Community Action Programs

The Community Action programs were the programs most definitively the province of OEO and the poverty war, providing a major justification for setting up a separate agency. The community action idea had three major objectives: (1) to coordinate the provision of the various services in poverty areas; (2) to deliver new services to the poor or old services in new ways, if necessary by setting up services in competition with those already in existence to force service improvements; and (3) to produce social change, by giving the poor a share in the decision making that affected them. These were not considered separable objectives; every part of every Community Action Program was assumed to be pursuing all three aims. CAP programs were of two kinds—the so-called national-emphasis programs and local-initiative programs.

The national-emphasis programs, with funds earmarked by the Congress, included the major OEO service programs described above—Head Start, Head Start Follow Through, Upward Bound, Legal Services, Comprehensive Health Services, and Family Planning. Any one Community Action Agency rarely operated all such programs. The usual practice was for some programs to be delegated to other public and private agencies.

The local-initiative programs were the nucleus of the community change strategy. In 1964, when the Economic Opportunity Act was first passed, Community Action was entirely a local-initiative program and no funds within the CAP appropriation were earmarked at the national level. To quote Robert Kennedy's testimony before Congress, "A total effort to bring about broad community change cannot be done by the Federal Government. We can only help by stimulating local action. It must be done by local people and local agencies working closely together."[19]

As the 1960s progressed, however, funds were progressively earmarked for certain operating programs at the national level, leaving a residual to be budgeted by communities for local initiative. In addition, as the operating programs increased in size and reputation, they were transferred to other government departments and agencies. In part, this was a deliberate strategy designed to leave OEO the flexibility to be innovative and experimental. But it was also partly due to the increasingly controversial position of OEO. The programs able to attract public support were gradually given more secure homes—the Department of Labor for manpower programs, for example, and the Office of Child Development (HEW) for Head Start.

Were the Community Action Programs successful in attaining their objectives? It would be generally agreed that the first objective—coordination of service delivery in poor areas—failed. In this, OEO's efforts were no more or less successful than other efforts at service coordination, before and after. Service deliverers already set up in the target areas were unwilling to relinquish their positions of influence or their budgets.

The second objective—delivery of many kinds of service—was variously achieved, as the program histories in previous sections demonstrate. Head Start—as measured by political popularity, at least—was extremely successful; Job Corps was not. By another measure of success—longevity—most of the programs can be considered to be successful because they still survive, although under the aegis of other government departments.

The third objective—to produce social change by increasing the participation of the poor—is the most controversial. CAP has been accused of being responsible for the riots of 1966 and 1967, although there is evidence that most CAPs served to diffuse the riots rather than foment them. It has also been criticized for being entirely ineffective.

Aside from these extremes, certain generalizations about CAP seem already widely accepted. First, given the budgets actually allocated, the hopes for Community Action were vastly inflated, as were the hopes for OEO programs in general. Second, the idea that the structure of society could be changed from within the current power structure in favor of the less powerful, without stimulating resentment and obstruction, is, in retrospect, naive. Third, the people who influenced the conception and organization of Community Action had a theory of participation and organization, but they had no clear formulation of what the objectives of such participation and organization should be. Once pressure had been built up, they did not have well-formulated objectives for that pressure.

An indication that CAP was perceived as effective in its political activity is that the established political authorities felt sufficiently threatened to make vigorous efforts to curb Community Action. By the summer of 1966, the OEO bill emerged from the House committee with specific amounts earmarked for the less controversial national-emphasis programs, rather than leaving the budgetary decision to the local CAP agencies. In 1967, Congresswoman Edith Green, responding to the antagonisms of the mayors across the country, sponsored a successful amendment to enable local governments (that is, the existing power structure) to assume the sponsorship of Community Action Programs. Also in 1966, Congress passed a new attempt at community development, designed to provide a less controversial alternative to Community Action. (See the section on Model Cities.) These efforts to limit Community Action's independence were, in fact, reactions to a problem that already had ebbed in importance. By the summer of 1966, accommodation to the local power structure on the part of most CAPs had been already made.

Evaluations of Community Action Programs have found them to score high on their ability to produce increased membership in community organizations and increased demands and petitioning by citizens who were poor. CAP programs and the controversies surrounding them have also helped change the frame of reference of the political debate. The National Welfare Rights Organization and many other citizen-action groups were founded, at least partly, because of the stimulus provided by CAP. School boards across the country also have been compelled to respond to the challenge from "Head Start programs oriented toward innovation, parent participation, and poor kids, none of which many school boards had been particularly interested in before."[20]

The major achievement of Community Action Programs was probably the amount of employment provided by them to community persons at the local level. This effect was not great in the urban CAPs. But 75 percent of CAPs were in rural areas; in these, particularly in the South, the employment effect was quite marked.

The local-initiative CAP programs have been authorized by Congress for each of the next three years, 1975–1977, at an annual rate of $330 million, with an extra $50 million for 50–50 matching local funds. Not only have the national-emphasis programs survived, therefore, so have the local-initiative ones, which may be considered the crux of the "maximum feasible participation" strategy.

Model Cities Program

The Model Cities program was initiated by the Johnson Administration and passed by Congress in 1966 as the Demonstration Cities and Metropolitan Development Act, under the administration of the Department of Housing and Urban Development. It was seen as an alternative to Community Action that was more firmly under control of local governments. The program, which involved block grants to cities, was to be carried out in two stages. First, funds would be provided for planning a program; then, for those plans that were approved, cities would receive supplementary grants for the programs to be carried out by a city demonstration agency. ("Demonstration city" was quickly changed to "model city" in light of the summer events of 1966 and 1967.)

In the first two years of implementation, the Model Cities and CAP programs were funded at approximately the same levels. However, the two programs differed in approach. The CAP program addressed poverty as a whole; the Model Cities program was concerned with the effect on inhabitants of a physically blighted local environment. With city hall rather than the neighborhood in ultimate control, urban renewal and "comprehensive coordination of physical and social plans" were to be the means to right the situation.[21] By 1969, 150 cities were eligible for planning grants under the direction of the Department of Housing and Urban Development. Recently, the Model Cities program has been modified by cutbacks in funds and a shift in focus from programs concentrating on the neighborhood to programs for entire cities. The concept of the program as encompassing a few demonstration cities has changed in favor of uniform per capita revenue sharing.

III. CONCLUSION

The programs briefly described here are the major federal social efforts of the last decade explicitly directed toward low-income and disadvantaged groups. These constituted what are generally known as the war on poverty and great society programs. During the period we have reviewed, federal expenditures on them grew from slightly over $6 billion in 1965 to $24\frac{1}{2}$ billion in 1972—a fourfold increase.

The biggest growth took place in program expenditures for the welfare-eligible population. AFDC payments, food stamps, and Medicaid made up 41 percent of the total in 1972 (up from 21 percent of a much smaller total in 1965) and have continued to grow. This must be considered a paradoxical outcome: In 1964, the major thrust was to be on human capital and community participation programs— designed to increase the earnings capacity and political power of the disadvantaged rather than merely to increase their posttransfer command over goods and services.

The effect of human capital and community participation programs is difficult to measure, and any ultimate outcome can only be expected to appear generations later. But we can certainly already say that the latter had a significant impact on the increasing recognition in Congress and the Executive that the poor's material needs must be met. As Gilbert Steiner has put it:

> Transformation of public assistance ... and massive additions ... [to] recipient totals ... have their explanations in other social and social policy developments: civil rights, civil disorder, legal services, medical services, community action.[22]

The effects on income of cash and in-kind transfer programs are easier to measure. The rest of this book is devoted to their measurement, as well as to the measurement of the effects of other government social welfare expenditures—that is, food, housing, health, and human capital programs such as education—over the period.

Table 1.3 shows total government expenditures on social welfare, and the proportion of these that were devoted to programs specifically directed to low-income groups (See p. 10). As can be seen, total social welfare expenditures in 1965 amounted to $74.4 billion, of which 12 percent went for programs for which persons qualified specifically because of their low-income status—and only one-half of 1 percent was accounted for by OEO and related antipoverty programs. By 1972, total social welfare expenditures had grown to almost $185 billion, of which 18 percent went for programs directed to low-income persons and 2.5 percent (still a small percentage) went for OEO and related antipoverty programs.

Thus, to understand how the position of the poor changed over the last ten years, it is necessary not simply to assess the effects of the great society programs or even those targeted at the low-income groups, but to analyze the effect of all social welfare expenditures.[23] How did the increase from $75 billion to $185 billion affect the relative position of the poor? To help provide an answer to this complex question, Chapter 3 develops and analyzes a set of "budgets" that allocate these expenditures in order to provide estimates of the benefits from government social welfare expenditures that actually went to the poor over the period. Before this is done, however, Chapter 2 will discuss the various meanings of poverty, to prepare the reader for the budget analysis that follows.

Chapter 4 describes the major changes in the poverty population that occurred between 1964 and 1974—particularly between 1965 and 1972. Chapter 5 begins the analysis of why these changes occurred by considering the effects on the poverty population and various groups within it of macroeconomic fluctuations. Chapter 6 continues the analysis of why the characteristics of income poverty changed between 1965 and 1972 by assessing the contribution of transfers in reducing poverty. Chapter 7 summarizes the main themes and results of the analyses reported in the previous five chapters and, projecting to the next decade, discusses likely issues for social policy. Four appendices follow, providing supplementary statistical evidence.

NOTES

[1]The story of OEO has been told, in whole or in part, before. It will not be told again here.

[2]For a most illuminating set of general articles, which has been a major influence on the material in this chapter, see *The Great Society: Lessons for the Future,* a special issue of *The Public Interest,* no. 34 (Winter 1974).

[3]This analysis of the poor was written by Robert J. Lampman, a staff member of the Council on leave from the University of Wisconsin. See Sar A. Levitan, *The Great Society's Poor Law* (Baltimore: Johns Hopkins Press, 1969).

[4]Quoted in John C. Donovan, *The Politics of Poverty* (New York: Pegasus, 1967), p. 7.

[5]U.S., President, *Economic Report of the President Together with The Annual Report of the Council of Economic Advisers,* transmitted to the Congress, January 1964 (Washington, D.C.: U.S. Government Printing Office, 1964), (Sudocs Number Pr36.9:964. The Superintendent of Documents Classification System keys government publications according to the agency producing them. Government materials in most of the more than 1000 depositories of government documents in the United States are organized using Sudocs numbers.)

[6]Adam Yarmolinsky, "The Beginnings of OEO," in *On Fighting Poverty,* ed. James Sundquist (New York: Basic Books, 1969), p. 51.

[7]U.S., Senate, Committee on Governmental Operations, Subcommittee on Intergovernmental Relations, Letter of Transmittal to Charles L. Schultze from Sargent Shriver, 30 June 1966, in *A New Federalism,* Hearings on the Impact of the President's Proposals for a New Federalism on the Relationships between the Federal Government and State and Local Governments, Part II, 93d Cong., 1st sess., 1973, (Y4.G74/6: F31/14/Vol. 2).

[8]Michael Harrington, *The Other America: Poverty in the United States* (New York: Macmillan, 1962).

[9]Sundquist, *On Fighting Poverty,* p. 8.

[10]Robert A. Levine, *The Poor Ye Need Not Have With You* (Cambridge, Mass.: The MIT Press, 1970), pp. 30 and 32. © 1974 MIT Press, reprinted by permission.

[11]Gordon Fisher, "Federal Outlays Benefitting the Poor—Detailed List of Programs," mimeographed (Washington, D.C.: Department of Health, Education, and Welfare; Office of the Assistant Secretary for Programs and Evaluation, June 1974).

[12]There was also a sixth category: legal and administrative changes—including the Civil Rights Acts, voting rights legislation, Affirmative Action concepts (including the establishment of the Equal Employment Opportunities Commission), school desegregation efforts on the part of HEW following the Supreme Court ruling, the 1964 tax cut, and revenue sharing of the early 1970s. These changes did certainly influence the program developments

described later. However, they will not be discussed explicitly in this chapter, with the exception of the activities of OEO's Legal Services Program. They are surveyed in Phyllis A. Wallace, "The Development of Equal Opportunities in Employment and Housing Since the Early 1960s," and Frank N. Jones, "The Development of the Law and Legal Services Affecting Low-Income Families," in *A Decade of Federal Antipoverty Policy: Achievements, Failures, and Lessons,* ed. Robert H. Haveman (New York: Academic Press, forthcoming). Direct services are included with in-kind transfers in subsequent chapters.

[13]Gilbert Steiner, *Social Insecurity: The Politics of Welfare* (Chicago: Rand McNally, 1966), p. 39.

[14]Medicaid is actually larger, but we have classified it for our purposes as providing a service rather than a commodity. See the next section.

[15]There are both an assets test and a work test, but neither is rigorously enforced.

[16]For a more detailed discussion of legal services, see Jones, "The Development of the Law and Legal Services."

[17]For a detailed review of federal health care since 1964, see Karen Davis, "A Decade of Policy Developments in Insuring Adequate Health Care for Low-Income Families," in Haveman, *A Decade of Federal Antipoverty Policy.*

[18]A third major development, oriented more toward the unemployed than toward the poor and disadvantaged specifically, was the Emergency Employment Act of 1971 and its more recent successors. (In fiscal 1973, only 18 percent of public employment program participants were found to be "disadvantaged" by the Labor Department's poverty-related definition.)

[19]Quoted in Charles Brecher, *The Impact of Federal Antipoverty Policies* (New York: Praeger, 1973).

[20]Levine, *The Poor Ye Need Not Have With You,* p. 144.

[21]Peter Marris and Martin Rein, *Dilemmas of Social Reform: Poverty and Community Action in the United States* (London: Routledge and Kegan Paul, 1967).

[22]Gilbert Y. Steiner, "Reform Follows Reality: The Growth of Welfare," *The Public Interest,* no. 34 (Winter 1974), p. 64. © 1964 by National Affairs, Inc. Reprinted by permission.

[23]All government expenditures, of course, have redistributive effects, if only through the tax system that has to finance them. Assessing the redistributive effect of total government spending is, however, obviously beyond the scope of this volume.

The Measurement of Poverty

Any discussion of the poverty problem and progress in its elimination is crucially affected by the choice of a definition of "poverty." Different definitions have given and will continue to give quite dissimilar views on the nature of the poverty problem, the appropriate policies to remedy it, and the effects of past economic and social conditions and of government policies on the poor.

In subsequent chapters of this book, two economic definitions of poverty are used in the analysis. Changes in the poverty population revealed when the official Social Security Administration (SSA) poverty lines are applied will be compared to changes shown when a "relative" measure is adopted. The SSA definition—the "absolute" definition—indicates progress toward raising the incomes of all citizens above a minimum level, while the alternative relative approach gauges the degree to which inequality in the income distribution has changed.

Because it is important to understand the strengths and weaknesses of our poverty measures, the first two sections of this chapter present issues that arise in the measurement of poverty. Section I focuses on definitions that are concerned only with economic aspects of well-being and includes a description of the SSA poverty lines. Section II briefly reviews more wide-ranging concepts of poverty, which include economic, political, social, and psychological variables. Section III discusses the two definitions used in this book.

I. ECONOMIC DEFINITIONS

An economic perspective on poverty typically begins with the assumption (which may be seriously challenged) that the well-being of families is primarily and positively related to their ability to consume goods and services. According to this view, more consumption leads to greater welfare (assuming other aspects of a family's situation are unchanged). This reasoning suggests that a family is "poor" if its consumption possibilities are "low" according to some established standard. Because it is widely accepted that "income," measured in dollar terms, is the best indicator of ability to consume, economic definitions of poverty view a poor family as one whose *income* falls below the *poverty threshold*. Many variations on this theme have arisen from the range of answers given to two operational questions—first, How should income be counted, and second, What is the proper poverty threshold?

The Official Poverty Definitions

The most widely recognized responses to these two questions, used exclusively by government and extensively by researchers, have been those given by the Social Security Administration in 1965,[1] as modified in recent years.[2] The resulting definition—adopted by the federal government as "official" poverty lines in 1969—answered the first question by letting total family income be its pretax, post-transfer *cash* income for the year, excluding capital gains or losses.[3] This concept of income, while recognized by the SSA as having important shortcomings, was chosen because, in 1965, the only available data for measuring poverty defined income in this manner.

In answering the second question—what is the proper poverty threshold?—the SSA attempted to establish a set of money-income lines that would represent equivalently low levels of economic welfare—that is, poverty thresholds—for families in different circumstances. To do this, it first estimated the annual food costs for families of varying size and composition, assuming they ate the "economy" diet developed by the Department of Agriculture. A nonfarm family of three or more was judged to be "poor" if its purchase of the "economy" food budget would absorb more than 33 percent of its cash income, a figure suggested as reasonable by studies of household budgets.[4] Hence, the poverty thresholds were established by multiplying the food budget by a factor of three. For couples, food costs were multiplied by 3.88 to obtain their poverty-

TABLE 2.1.   OFFICIAL POVERTY THRESHOLDS IN 1972, BY SIZE OF
FAMILY, SEX OF HEAD, AND FARM-NONFARM RESIDENCE

Size of Family	Nonfarm		Farm	
	Male Head	Female Head	Male Head	Female Head
All unrelated individuals				
Under 65 years	$2254	$2085	$1916	$1772
65 years and over	2025	2000	1722	1698
All families				
2 persons, head under 65 years	2823	2729	2399	2258
2 persons, head more than 65 years	2532	2516	2154	2141
3 persons	3356	3234	2838	2702
4 persons	4277	4254	3644	3598
5 persons	5048	4994	4301	4355
6 persons	5679	5617	4849	4900
7 or more persons	7000	6841	5963	5771

Source: U.S. Department of Commerce, Social and Economic Statistics Administration,
Bureau of the Census, "Characteristics of the Low-Income Population, 1972,"
Current Population Reports, Series P-60, No. 91 (Washington, D.C.: U.S.
Government Printing Office, 1973.) (C56. 218: p-60/91).

line income; for individuals the factor was 5.92.[5] For the farm
population, poverty lines were set at 85 percent of the nonfarm ones
to account roughly for the in-kind income—mainly home-grown
food—that farmers earn.[6] Lastly, the poverty lines were allowed to
rise in step with the Consumer Price Index so that they would
represent the same purchasing power each year.[7] Table 2.1 displays
the official poverty lines for 1972. (For 1975, the lines would be
about 28 percent higher after adjusting for inflation.)

The official definition of poverty has a number of problems associated with it, most of which are shared by our relative measure. To
understand better the faults and merits of our definitions, the remainder of this section examines the economic issues involved in
defining poverty. We first consider conceptual issues of defining
income, then look at practical problems that limit the choice of an
income measure. Methods of setting a poverty line also are treated.
Discussion of these issues provides, at the same time, a wide-ranging
economic critique of the official view.

Conceptual Issues of Defining Income

Treatment of Taxes

Disposable cash income (income net of income and payroll taxes) is a more exact measure of a family's purchasing power than is pretax income. Measuring disposable income accounts for tax changes, such as the recent jumps in Social Security taxes, that can decrease a family's "take-home" pay without altering its pretax income. Further, two families with equal pretax incomes may have different amounts of disposable income if one receives mostly tax-free income—Social Security payments, for example—while the other earns taxable income. The SSA's definition of income, therefore, is biased upward since it does not assess the impact of direct taxes upon spendable family income.[8]

In-Kind Transfers

A second problem of the official definition of income is the omission of government and private in-kind transfers—such as food stamps, Medicaid, and fringe benefits. Large shares of many in-kind transfer programs go to the low-income population. These benefits increase the real purchasing power of the recipients in almost the same way that cash transfers do.[9] However, with the SSA's definition of income limited to cash income, the impacts on measured poverty of large increases in in-kind transfers cannot be determined.

Benefits of Government Services

The SSA's income definition does not account for the value of public services received by families. Nonetheless, these services—education and police and fire protection, for example—are forms of in-kind income that contribute to family welfare. An income measure can properly ignore government expenditures only if they are evenly distributed among households, a situation that does not exist in the United States for many of the most important public activities. Differentials in the quality and quantity of government services are especially noticeable in comparisons between urban and rural localities, and between slums and suburbs. Those receiving the inferior public services not only gain relatively smaller benefits from government activities but, in many cases, are also forced to make out-of-pocket expenditures to compensate for the deficiency of public services. For example, lack of a public sewer system requires installation of private systems; inadequate roads cause higher auto maintenance costs or more miles to be driven.[10]

Net Worth

The SSA approach could be modified by accounting for net worth holdings as well as current income. This addition may reveal that some people with poverty incomes are, or could be, enjoying rather high consumption levels by liquidating their assets. Some retired couples or rich students might be examples. Indeed, a study that added the annuitized value of net worth to current cash income found significant shifts in the number and composition of the poor compared to what resulted from the standard definition.[11]

The above four points suggest that the SSA's notion of family income is too narrow an indicator of the ability to consume. A broader measure of economic welfare can be obtained—given suitable data—by adding to cash income the dollar value of government services, in-kind transfers, and the annuitized value of wealth, and by subtracting direct taxes paid.[12]

Permanent Income

The preceding criticisms of the SSA measure might be met by altering the estimate of *current* income used to assess poverty status. A more fundamental criticism has also been advanced. According to this position, *current* income, however carefully charted, can be a misleading sign of poverty status. A family's yearly income may be unusually high or low relative to its normal level, depending upon factors such as spells of unemployment, labor force participation choices of family members, windfall gains or losses, and illness. Income variations due to such causes are particularly important among low-income groups.[13] Estimates of the size and composition of the chronically poor population may be biased when based solely on current income. Instead, the expected long-run or "permanent" income of families should be examined to determine their true levels of well-being—with income defined broadly to include labor earnings, income from property (including its annuitized value), in-kind income, and all transfers.[14,15]

Practical Problems of Income Measurement

Given this range of possible income measures and adjustments, which is preferred for studies of poverty? On theoretical grounds, the comprehensive permanent- and current-income concepts, which include all the forms of cash and in-kind income mentioned above, seem to have the most merit. If our concern is to study long-term poverty and to devise ways to eliminate it, permanent income is the concept on which policy should focus.[16] If, however, interest centers on income-maintenance activities designed to cushion the effects of temporarily low current incomes, the current-income measure is appropriate.

Unfortunately, the lack of data has made it nearly impossible to apply either of these comprehensive measures to many poverty problems. Information useful for the estimation of permanent family income has recently become available but is incomplete and limited to the years 1967–1972.[17] Even if attention is restricted to current income, the necessary nationwide data on family consumption of in-kind income have not been gathered in the years since the SSA first presented its poverty definition. There are substantial problems associated with properly measuring the benefits from government output. And there have been no adequate programs to collect data on family assets. Hence, from a pragmatic view, the SSA's income definition has taken into consideration the information that is available and is faulty only in its failure to consider direct taxes.[18]

Establishing the Poverty Thresholds

Let us turn from the problem of defining income to consider our second question: What is the "proper" poverty threshold?

Criticisms of the SSA Approach

The official poverty lines purport to represent equivalent levels of deprivation for families in different circumstances by accounting for family size and composition and farm–nonfarm residence. But they may neglect important price-level differences among the nation's regions as well as variations among other factors, such as climate— which affects clothing and shelter needs—transportation needs, and the quality of publicly provided goods. These variables also may create differences in equivalent deprivation incomes. However, the quantitative importance of such factors has not yet satisfactorily been determined.[19]

Criticisms of the SSA approach that are more basic revolve around the decision to multiply the "economy" food budget by some factor (3 for families, 3.70 for couples, and 5.92 for unrelated individuals) to determine the poverty-threshold income. Using this particular budget assumes that the poor can obtain the included food items at the prices assigned by the Department of Agriculture. More importantly, the choice of these particular numbers—3, 3.70, and 5.92—while wrapped in the apparent objectivity of budget studies, contains a generous dose of subjective judgment. The official thresholds, despite the particular derivation used to find them, simply reflect one rather stringent view of how much income is needed by different families to reach a minimum "level of decency" relative to average American standards. Their wide acceptance testifies only to their political acceptability and not to the intrinsic validity of the definition.

Absolute Poverty Thresholds

Because the preceding discussion has been conducted with the official poverty definition as its benchmark, it has implicitly been concerned with "absolute" or "minimum decency" measures. That is, the SSA concept is a measure that places a family among the poverty population if it lacks the real income needed to enjoy some *fixed minimum standard of living.* Under the official version, the income that buys the minimum for a family is judged to be a cash income that is triple the economy food budget. Any number of variations could be made by using different adjustments (or none at all) for family size and place of residence, establishing a minimum income by another method, or measuring income in other ways.

A common element of all absolute definitions is that no adjustments to the minimum standard are made in response to rising standards of living in the country as a whole. Absolute standards—at whatever level—define the poverty problem as one that will be "solved" when all family incomes exceed the established poverty thresholds, regardless of what is happening to the real incomes of the rest of the population. This definition directs attention away from politically sensitive questions concerning the proper income distribution. It also ignores evidence suggesting that the socially accepted minimum rises as national per capita income increases.[20]

Relative Poverty Thresholds

Some observers have argued that, in a country like the United States, where average income greatly exceeds bare subsistence levels, poverty is more appropriately viewed as a problem of inequality in the distribution of income rather than as one of low absolute levels of income. They emphasize that in a materialistic society, households with incomes substantially below the average are effectively excluded from participating in the mainstream social and political life of their country. As a result, such households are viewed by society and by themselves as poor.[21] If this logic is accepted, a "relative" definition of poverty—one that defines poverty-level incomes in comparison with the level of income generally prevailing—provides a better measure of the character of the problem and the success of the economy in reducing it than does an "absolute" definition.

The common feature of many relative definitions is that, instead of calling "poor" all those households whose incomes fall below some fixed level, those households are called poor whose incomes fall below a poverty threshold expressed as a stated fraction of average or median income. As the median level of income rises, so does the relative poverty line. Such an approach views the poverty problem as one that will disappear only when the distribution of income becomes sufficiently equal.

No objective procedure exists for selecting a particular fraction. The choice reflects a judgment of what is a "reasonable" and useful criterion for identifying those families with relatively low incomes.

After selecting an operational income measure, one can rank family incomes and determine which are below one-half the chosen fraction of the median income. This straightforward procedure implicitly assumes that a given amount of income enables all families to enjoy the same level of well-being. For example, a family of six with income equal to one-fourth of the median would be judged as poor as a couple with the same income. If, however, it is felt that certain characteristics, such as family size or residential location, significantly affect the level of welfare attainable from a given money income, an index that accounts for interfamily differences is needed to convert all family incomes into common, equal-welfare terms. Determining such an index is analogous to selecting a set of absolute poverty lines that vary according to family characteristics. Once such an index is constructed, each family's income can be rated using the index and assigned an "equal-welfare income." All households with the same equal-welfare income are considered to be equally well-off. Those with equal-welfare incomes below the chosen fraction of the median are considered to be in the poverty population.

Absolute versus Relative Definitions

The virtues of absolute definitions of poverty over relative ones, and vice versa, have been debated for years.[22] We suggest that both forms convey useful information and both should be applied when studying poverty issues.[23] Absolute measures recognize that those with low incomes gain real benefits from rising income and consumption, regardless of their position in the income distribution. Viewing the poor from an absolute perspective highlights an important social dimension of the poverty problem, as well: Many people cannot command some given fixed level of goods and services that is deemed minimally decent by contemporary standards. While social standards may rise in the long run, over short periods the constancy of an absolute standard, adjusted upward only for price changes, provides a meaningful indicator of whether or not and how quickly people are moving beyond the agreed-upon minimum. For analyzing the effects on the poor of general economic conditions and specific government programs over a decade, such a measure may be quite appropriate.

Purely relative indicators acknowledge that people's senses of well-being depend not only on their absolute levels of consumption, but also on their position compared to others. Such measures also emphasize another major social dimension of poverty: the fact that the consumption opportunities of many citizens are far below society's typical standard of living. A relative viewpoint contributes to our understanding of poverty problems by drawing attention to the degree of inequality of the income distribution and by focusing upon the characteristics of those who occupy its bottom strata.

The Income Gap

With any economic definition of poverty, one can, in principle, determine the total number of poor families and identify their characteristics. But there is a related, highly important aspect of the poverty problem that is not revealed by simply counting how many families are poor: Using poverty thresholds fails to distinguish among degrees of poverty. For instance, a situation in which the average income of poor families is half the poverty line is quite unlike one in which the average is 80 percent of the line. Merely counting the number of families below the threshold does not uncover such a difference.

To account for such differences in the extent of poverty, a measure—the "income gap"—has been devised. Applied from the perspective of the absolute definition, the income gap indicates the total amount of money required to bring the income of every low-income family up to the minimum decency level (up to the SSA lines, for example). In the context of the relative definition, the gap measures how much additional money must flow to the poverty population to bring up to the relative threshold the incomes of all its members. When assessing progress against poverty, measuring changes in the income gap provides a valuable supplement to counting the number of poor persons and families.[24,25]

II. WIDE-RANGING DEFINITIONS OF POVERTY

Our review of economic definitions of poverty has centered on two key concepts—the measurement of income and the determination of poverty thresholds. The search for a broader definition of poverty has generated interest in many concepts, all harder than these two to analyze from both theoretical and empirical viewpoints. A rich and intricate debate has developed over how to incorporate concepts such as well-being, class, alienation, culture and subculture, values, and prestige into a more-than-economic view of poverty. We shall be content to sketch only the very broad outlines and flavor of this controversy.[26]

Advocates of wide-ranging poverty indicators all agree that economic definitions are fundamental, yet seriously inadequate. Certainly, a meager level of private consumption is considered to be a major burden of the poor's lot. But also, it is argued, the poor, both as individuals and as a group, possess social and psychological characteristics that may or may not be tied to a lack of economic resources and that might remain to disadvantage them seriously even if their economic problems were alleviated.

The notion of a full-fledged "culture of poverty" has become the best-known alternative to an economic perspective on poverty. This theory argues that the chronically poor have developed, as a reaction to their marginal position in society, certain traits and values that differ from those of the majority. As Oscar Lewis points out, this culture of poverty tends to perpetuate itself, once it has emerged, because its effects are carried from generation to generation. He explains that slum children, by the time they reach the age of six or seven, so thoroughly have absorbed the essential values of their subculture that they are unable psychologically to take full advantage of opportunities or improved conditions as these may arise in their lives.[27] The culture of poverty is alleged to generate a social system with little political activity, little participation in major social institutions, weak and unstable family structures, weak personal identities, short time-horizons, male chauvinism and "machismo," and a sense of submission to "fate." Without denying the correlation between permanently low incomes and these traits, culture-of-poverty theorists argue that it is poverty in this wide sense that must be measured and then attacked, because it is harder to eliminate this type of deprivation than to eliminate poverty due only to a lack of income.

Attempts to include culture-of-poverty notions or other noneconomic conditions in a poverty definition encounter difficulty because measuring many of the most important of these concepts—alienation or instability, for example—casts up severe empirical problems. On technical grounds alone, obtaining wide agreement among scholars that a proposed measure of just one noneconomic characteristic was sufficiently reliable and valid would be difficult. Thus, an attempt to combine various measures of this type into a scale for unambiguously determining who are the members of the poverty population would be premature, at least at this stage of social science.[28]

III. DEFINITIONS OF POVERTY USED IN THIS STUDY

Two distinct measures of poverty will be used in this report to analyze changes in the poor population and the influence of public policy upon those shifts. As is true of any poverty definition, both can be attacked and defended from many angles, depending on the critic's perspective and the uses he requires from the definition. Thus, in no way should one regard these as the ideal definitions; rather, we conceive of them as necessary compromises among the demands of social and economic theory, the limitations of the available statistics, and the needs and objectives of this report.

General Factors Influencing Our Choice

While the importance of noneconomic aspects of poverty has been seriously argued by many thoughtful students of the problem, this report will confine itself to economic definitions of poverty. Though we do not deny the importance of studying and correcting the social, political, and psychological deprivations faced by poor people (and others) in our society, the problems resulting from low income are themselves so severe that the focus on income variables is a valuable compromise between the poles of conceptual comprehensiveness and practical applicability. More pragmatically, the available nationwide population statistics are suitable for determining poverty status only if economic definitions are used.

Our choice of income definition is limited by the available data. The nationwide data collected annually in the Current Population Survey (CPS) contain information only on current pretax cash income. Other survey sources include more comprehensive income data, but they do not suit the needs of this study for other reasons. Hence, we are constrained to use CPS data and cannot apply the notion of permanent income. Nor will we be able to account for taxes, wealth, or in-kind income.

These omissions are regrettable. Any study of poverty that cannot include them is marred to some extent because, as our earlier analysis emphasized, current pretax cash income is not always an accurate indicator of a family's consumption opportunities and its economic welfare. Examining only cash income introduces biases that distort the measurement and analysis of the number and demographic composition of the poor and of the effect of government programs, especially the impact of in-kind transfers, on low-income households.

The Operational Measures

One of the measures we have chosen is the official SSA version. For various reasons, some may argue that these poverty lines should be raised, while others may reject the particular adjustments for family size and location. But among the many possible absolute poverty thresholds that can be constructed, the government's is as plausible as most. The political and historical importance of this definition argues strongly for its use. Further, using it to analyze changes in income poverty makes it possible to compare the effects of the antipoverty policies of the past decade to their stated goal: to bring the incomes of as many families as possible above these lines. Naturally, this is not the sole basis on which to judge the success of government programs, but it is an important one.

Our second measure defines the poverty population in a relative manner and in doing so complements the absolute approach. We divide each family's current cash income by its SSA poverty line. This yields a "welfare ratio" that indicates the fraction by which the family's income exceeds or falls below the SSA minimum decency level. (One can think of this ratio as an index of income relative to needs, where "needs" are defined in relation to the official poverty lines.) Families with the same welfare ratio would be assumed to be equally well-off. We have defined the relative poor as those families with welfare ratios below .44 of the median ratio.

This definition is analogous to the more commonly proposed relative poverty measure that defines the poor as all households with incomes less than one-half of the median income. We use welfare ratios instead of unadjusted dollar incomes to rank households and choose the fraction .44 instead of .50.

The fraction .44 does not reflect a completely arbitrary choice. Rather, it was selected with the following procedure. In 1965, the base year for our demographic analysis of changes in the poverty population, the median welfare ratio was 2.25. All families with incomes below the SSA poverty lines had, of course, welfare ratios less than one. Thus, any household that in 1965 was poor under the SSA definition necessarily had a welfare ratio less than 1/2.25 of the median. Defining the relative poor as those with welfare ratios below 1/2.25 = .44 of the median yielded, in 1965, the *same group* of households as were poor from the SSA absolute perspective.

This unique property of our particular relative measure serves a useful analytical purpose. Changes over time in the low-income population traced out by either definition are measured against exactly the same base. This conveniently allows us to observe how our conclusions about changes in income poverty are affected by the choice of an absolute or relative definition of poverty.

These two measures of poverty do not adjust family incomes for the effect of taxes and in-kind transfers. A recent study has attempted to adjust incomes for these items. The author used this expanded income definition and the SSA poverty threshold to assess changes in poverty and the effects of transfers on those changes. [29] Because these findings supplement in an important way the trends revealed by the two approaches to measuring poverty, a summary of them is included in Chapters 4 and 6.

NOTES

[1] Mollie Orshansky, "Counting the Poor: Another Look at the Poverty Profile," *Social Security Bulletin* **28** (1965): 3-29.

[2] See U.S., Department of Commerce, Bureau of the Census, "Revision in Poverty Statistics, 1959 to 1968," *Current Population Reports: Special Studies,* Series P-23, No. 28 (August 12, 1969) (Washington, D.C.: U.S. Government Printing Office, 1969), (C56.218: P-23/28).

[3]U.S., Department of Commerce, Social and Economic Statistics Administration, Bureau of the Census, "Characteristics of the Low-Income Population, 1971," *Current Population Reports: Consumer Income,* Series P-60, No. 86 (December 1972) (Washington, D.C.: U.S. Government Printing Office, 1972), pp. 14–15 (C56.218: P-60/86).

[4]The proportion of income spent on necessities, especially food, is often regarded as an indicator of well-being. Studies of the actual spending habits of American families indicated that food absorbed about one-third of posttax cash income over a wide range of income classes. Therefore, the SSA decided that the economy food budget of the "truly" poor families (a very stringent budget, which, in fact, the Agriculture Department had suggested for use only temporarily when funds were low) should also absorb one-third of their income. However, the SSA measured this income on a *pretax* basis. In 1972, one-third of the poverty line for a nonfarm family of four was $1426, or 98 cents for food per person per day.

[5]These higher values, 3.88 and 5.92, reflect a belief that, while food costs for a person or couple may be, respectively, one-third or two-thirds the size of food costs for a three-person family, their other expenses do not fall proportionately. That is, one- or two-person units face higher fixed costs, especially housing, relative to their food requirements. For example, commuting expenses of the family head are the same whether he (she) lives singly, with a spouse, or with several family members. Hence, for these smaller units, to provide for these higher costs relative to food needs, the food budgets were multiplied by larger factors.

[6]This ratio was changed by a federal committee from 60 percent in 1965 to 85 percent in 1969 as opinions on the in-kind savings enjoyed by farm people changed. A study that was instrumental in raising the ratio to 85 percent was that of J. Patrick Madden, Jean L. Pennock, and Carol M. Jaeger, in U.S., President's National Advisory Commission on Rural Poverty, "Equivalent Levels of Living: A New Approach to Scaling the Poverty Line to Different Family Characteristics and Place of Residence," in *Rural Poverty in the United States* (Washington, D.C.: President's National Advisory Commission on Rural Poverty, 1968), pp. 545–552, (Pr36.8: R88/R88/2).

[7]This adjustment corrects for general inflation and any tax change that is reflected in higher consumer prices, such as a rise in sales taxes. But it does not adjust the thresholds for other tax changes.

[8]For example, suppose in 1972 one couple received $1823 from Social Security and $1000 of interest payments. The couple would pay no direct taxes and would be exactly on the poverty line. Suppose another couple had $2823 in wage earnings and no other income. Such a household would have paid $147 in Social Security taxes and $2 in federal income taxes, leaving $2674 to spend. The SSA income measure would fail to capture the difference of 5 percent in spendable income. Similarly, low-income earners had 5.85 percent of their wages withheld for Social Security taxes in 1975 but only 3.625 percent in 1965. This change is not taken into account by the SSA income measure.

[9]One dollar spent on in-kind transfers may not be a perfect substitute for a $1 cash transfer because the recipient is constrained to consume the particular commodity (for example, food, in the case of food stamps) but he may have preferred to spend the cash on something else. See Maria Schmundt, Eugene Smolensky, and Leanna Stiefel, "When Do Recipients Value Transfers at Their Costs to Taxpayers?" in *Integrating Income Maintenance Programs,* ed. Irene Lurie (New York: Academic Press, 1975), for a careful discussion of this issue. A paper by these same authors and Robert Plotnick, "Adding In-Kind Transfers to the Personal Income and Outlay Account: Implications for the Size Distribution of Income," Institute for Research on Poverty Discussion Paper 199-74 (University of Wisconsin-Madison, 1974) offers further discussion and an empirical application.

[10]The authors thank D. Lee Bawden for his discussion of these points.

[11]Burton Weisbrod and W. Lee Hansen, "An Income-Net Worth Approach to Measuring Economic Welfare," *American Economic Review* 58 (December 1968): 1315–1329. See also Michael K. Taussig, *Alternative Measures of the Distribution of Economic Welfare,* Industrial Relations Section, Princeton University, 1973; and Marilyn Moon, "The Economic Welfare of the Aged: A Measure of Economic Status and an Analysis of Federal Programs," (Ph D. diss., University of Wisconsin-Madison, 1974).

[12]An effort to extend the SSA's income measure to encompass government in-kind transfers and direct taxes paid is contained in Timothy Smeeding, "Measuring the Economic Welfare of Low Income Households, and the Anti-Poverty Effectiveness of Cash and Non-Cash Transfer Programs" (Ph.D. diss., University of Wisconsin-Madison, 1975).

[13]U.S., President's Commission on Income Maintenance Programs, "Factors Affecting Poverty: A Gross Flow Analysis," by Terence Kelly in *Technical Studies,* prepared for the President's Commission on Income Maintenance Programs (Washington, D.C.: U.S. Government Printing Office, 1970), pp. 1–82, (Pr 36.8: In2/T22); and Thad W. Mirer, "Aspects of the Variability of Family Income," in *Five Thousand American Families: Patterns of Economic Progress,* ed. James N. Morgan et al. (Ann Arbor, Mich.: Institute for Social Research, 1974), vol. 2.

[14]Harold W. Watts, "An Economic Definition of Poverty," in *On Understanding Poverty,* ed. Daniel P. Moynihan (New York: Basic Books, 1969), pp. 322–325.

[15]The notion of "earnings capacity" has been advanced as another alternative to current income measures of economic welfare. (See Irwin Garfinkel and Robert H. Haveman, "Earnings Capacity and the Target Efficiency of Alternative Transfer Programs," *American Economic Review* 64 (May 1974): 196–204). A family's earnings capacity reflects its ability—given the physical assets and marketable skills of its members—to earn income if it uses these assets and skills to their fullest extent. If, for example, the wife in one of two demographically identical families chooses to work, that family will rank higher under a measure of current income, but the difference reflects a stronger taste for income and work, not a difference in the level of economic resources (in this case, the labor market skills of the wife) potentially available to the families. Earnings capacity, therefore, attempts to purge tastes for work from the measurement of economic status, ignores temporary fluctuations in income, and does not include government transfer income. Because of this last property, earnings capacity is probably not an adequate indicator of a family's real consumption opportunities. This approach is perhaps best used as a way of identifying those households with the lowest capabilities for generating income.

[16]The earnings capacity measure may also be useful for such issues (see Note 15).

[17]We are referring to the Michigan Panel Study on Income Dynamics.

[18]For in-the-field administrative decisions, the practical considerations that limit the choice of income definitions are of another sort. A useful definition must allow officials to recognize easily the poor on an individual level, a need that does not concern policymakers or researchers. In this situation, a simple measure that is reasonably equitable and based on information readily available from the poor themselves is essential. (This discussion is taken partly from Joseph J. Kershaw, *Government Against Poverty* (Chicago: Markham, 1970), pp. 11–14.

[19]Harold W. Watts, "The Iso-Prop Index: An Approach to the Determination of Differential Poverty Income Thresholds," *Journal of Human Resources* 2 (Winter 1967): 3–18, and Timothy Smeeding, "Cost of Living Differentials at Low-Income Levels," Institute for Research on Poverty Discussion Paper 190-74 (University of Wisconsin-Madison, 1974).

[20]Eugene Smolensky, "The Past and Present Poor," in *The Concept of Poverty* (Washington, D.C.: Chamber of Commerce of the U.S., 1965), and Robert W. Kilpatrick, "The

Income Elasticity of the Poverty Line," *Review of Economics and Statistics* **55** (August 1973): 327–332.

[21] An excellent discussion of this issue is in Lee Rainwater, *What Money Buys: Inequality and the Social Meanings of Income* (New York: Basic Books, 1974).

[22] For some discussion of this debate, see Eugene Smolensky, "The Past and Present Poor," and Victor Fuchs, "Toward a Theory of Poverty," in *The Concept of Poverty.* See also Robert Lampman, *Ends and Means of Reducing Income Poverty* (Chicago: Markham, 1971).

[23] The following two paragraphs are partly drawn from an unpublished manuscript by Robinson Hollister.

[24] A modified version of the income gap has also been proposed. Observing that a low-income family must forgo the consumption of more and more basic commodities as its income falls lower and lower, this version argues that increasing a family's income from, for example, $1500 to $2000 reduces the burden of poverty to it and to society more than would raising its income from $2500 to $3000. Conceived of in slightly different terms, this version suggests that a family whose income is, say, $1000 below its poverty threshold is more than twice as needy as another whose income gap is only $500. (Many social programs implicitly accept this judgment since the amount of cash or in-kind transfers they provide is greatest for those recipients with the lowest incomes and diminishes as recipient incomes rise.) Following this logic, the measure weights an income gap of $1000 more heavily than two $500 gaps and sums the weighted values to obtain an estimate of the overall extent of poverty. The particular weights are based on the opinions of those constructing the index. Hence, this "disutility index" counts income gaps in such a manner that the greatest reduction in poverty is measured when the incomes of the very poorest rise. See Harold Watts, "The Measurement of Poverty—An Exploratory Exercise," *American Statistical Association Proceedings of the Social Statistics Section, 1967.* Applications of this measure appear in Moon, "Economic Welfare of the Aged," and Smeeding, "Measuring the Economic Welfare."

[25] Another aspect of poverty that is evident from counting the number of poor families concerns the near-poor. The statistical nature of a poverty threshold establishes a sharp, but admittedly artificial, dividing line between poor and nonpoor. Households with incomes slightly below the threshold are included in the poverty population, but those slightly above—the near-poor—are not.

The near-poor deserve attention in many studies of poverty for several reasons. Members of this group in one year are likely to be among the ranks of the poor in the next or to have come from last year's poor. Thus, the near-poor have been and will be strongly affected by policies aimed at low-income families. Many government programs that are income conditioned bring large benefits to the near-poor as well as to the SSA-defined poor.

To help investigate these issues, the notion of near-poor has been given quantitative form. Near-poor families are those with incomes between the chosen poverty threshold and a somewhat higher cut-off point, for example, between 100 and 125 percent of the SSA poverty lines.

[26] For an excellent discussion of this debate, see Charles Valentine, *Culture and Poverty* (Chicago: University of Chicago Press, 1968).

[27] Oscar Lewis, "The Culture of Poverty," in Moynihan, *On Understanding Poverty,* p. 188.

[28] The authors thank Karl F. Taeuber for his discussion of these points.

[29] Smeeding, "Measuring the Economic Welfare." The author also uses in his analysis a relative poverty line that differs from ours, but we will not summarize this part of his work.

Government Assistance for the Poor, 1965-1972

The antipoverty policies of the 1960s and early 1970s, primarily those of the federal government, signaled a fresh public initiative against poverty and stood at or near the center of national attention for several years. However, they formed but a small part, as we have seen, of total governmental expenditures on community and personal welfare. In this chapter, we look at the whole range of federal and state–local government social welfare expenditures from an anti-poverty perspective.

How much benefit (in dollar terms) from social welfare expenditures was received by those families and individuals whose incomes before *public transfers* were below the official poverty lines?[1] That is, to what extent have those who are the pretransfer poor, according to the "absolute" definition, benefited from public programs? Which programs have brought the largest benefits, and which have devoted the largest fraction of their outlays to this group? How have the volume of benefits and their distribution among programs changed between 1965 and 1972?

To answer these questions, we have measured the economic benefits received by the *pretransfer* poor from government expenditures for social welfare in 1965, 1968, and 1972.[2,3] The findings are presented in three tables that have been labeled "antipoverty budgets."

In this analysis, only the absolute pretransfer poor will be treated. Section I of this chapter explains the concept of "social welfare expenditures" (SWE) and describes the nature, scope, and limitations of these budgets. Section II presents the broad changes in total SWE between 1965 and 1972 and includes a discussion of the general trends in benefits to the pretransfer poor. Aid to the poor is analyzed in greater detail in the third section. We examine the changing composition of these benefits and the importance of aid received from special antipoverty programs and, more generally, low-income–conditioned programs. The division between federal and state–local governments of expenditures on the poor is studied also. Concluding comments and a summary are contained in a final section.

I. DESCRIPTION OF THE ANTIPOVERTY BUDGETS

The social welfare expenditures upon which the antipoverty budgets focus include all cash transfer programs as well as those public expenditures that provide food, housing, manpower training, health, and education benefits directly to identifiable recipients. In addition, a few programs outside of these categories but with benefits that can be directly attributed to individuals or families are included. In this approach, no attention is given to government activities that promote individual well-being indirectly or are essentially public goods.[4] These include expenditures on the transportation system; police and fire protection and judicial services; national defense; regulation and the setting of standards; research; and the promotion of economic growth. These activities have major consequences for the social welfare of poor and nonpoor alike, but the conceptual and empirical difficulties of satisfactorily distributing their benefits among various income groups have forced us to omit them.[5]

The distinction between direct social welfare expenditures and those that are public goods or affect welfare only indirectly is not always a clear one. To some extent, the list of programs in our antipoverty budgets reflects some arbitrary choices. However, while various amendments to that list could reasonably be made, the budgets are quite comprehensive and undoubtedly capture the major trends in government social welfare expenditures.

The concept of benefits to the pretransfer poor used in the budgets is much broader than the conventional notion of "income" and should not be confused with it. Estimated benefits do include cash receipts from government programs. Also included in the budgets are in-kind transfers, such as food stamps, public housing, or Medicare, which are not counted in money income. Moreover, our budgets go beyond these two components to encompass aid received by the poor from many social programs that generally are not regarded as providing either cash or in-kind assistance to the recipient. Among these are Community Action, education, employment, and man-power programs.

At the same time, because we are focusing on *transfer* benefits, we do not include any income earned by working for agencies that administer public programs or for private firms under government contract to provide goods needed for a program. (That is, the analysis ignores gains from the *input* or labor market side of all government activity.) Only benefits to the poor that flow from receiving the program *output* are discussed. For example, suppose a family occupying public housing received a rent subsidy of $900 per year and, furthermore, its head earned $2000 as a part-time em-ployee of the housing authority. Assuming the family had no other nontransfer income, it would, of course, be pretransfer poor. The antipoverty budget would credit the family—and hence the poor population—with only this $900 from the subsidy.[6] The only excep-tions to this approach are for work-support manpower programs, where the federal agency provides both a job and supportive services (the Neighborhood Youth Corps, for example).

Because our estimates ignore gains to the poor from the labor market and omit government activities that have indirect, though perhaps large, effects on individual welfare, the antipoverty budgets do *not* portray the full impact of the public sector on the distribu-tion of economic welfare between pretransfer poor and nonpoor. We start with the division of the population into pretransfer poor and nonpoor, then allocate the benefits of social welfare expenditures between the two groups. This procedure overlooks the likely possibil-ity that the volume and composition of government spending itself has affected the number of the pretransfer poor. However, measuring this complex relationship requires a quite different approach that recognizes the general interdependence between government activity and the entire distribution of earnings and property income. Such an analysis is beyond the scope of this report.[7]

These budget estimates present a few technical problems. First, because of insufficient data for several programs, estimating benefits to the poor requires some strong assumptions (see Appendix A for a full description of our methods). Second, benefits to the poor are measured in terms of the cost to the taxpayers (net of administrative expenses) of providing the aid. If poor recipients consider their benefits to be worth less than the taxpayer cost, estimated aid to the poor is overstated. For example, the state may directly subsidize low-income housing when the occupants would prefer a lesser sum in cash and the opportunity to rent from the private housing market. Also, it has been alleged that some public programs have provided employment for professionals, but few worthwhile outputs for the poor or other client groups. Overestimates of benefits are particularly likely for education, employment, and health programs. The costs of providing these benefits are largely the wages paid to the professionals involved (such as the teacher, counselor, doctor, and social worker), and the poor may prefer cash to these forms of transfers.[8] Third, some government benefits obtained by the poor may have partly replaced services formerly provided without charge by the private economy. For example, former charity patients now receive Medicaid. We were unable to estimate the extent of this substitution.

All figures in the three antipoverty budgets are on a fiscal-year basis and in current dollars. They exclude administrative expenses and any cost to recipients of participating in a program. (For example, only the food stamp bonus is measured, not the total value of stamps purchased.) The value of interest subsidies from government loans is not considered.[9] In addition, the distribution of taxes needed to pay for the social programs is not treated.[10]

II. SOCIAL WELFARE EXPENDITURES AND THE PRETRANSFER POOR, 1965–1972

In 1965, 15.6 million households—more than 25 percent of all households—were poor if public transfers were not counted in their incomes. (See Table 3.1, which presents statistics on pretransfer poverty.) The total dollar amount by which their incomes fell below the poverty lines—the pretransfer poverty gap—was $22.1 billion. This was an average gap of $1418 per household, which far exceeded the average pretransfer income of $906. By 1968, pretransfer poverty affected 700,000 fewer households, but the poverty gap had risen to $23.8 billion, or $1593 per household. Four years later, 17.6 million households were poor before transfers, and the poverty gap had jumped to more than $34 billion. As in other years, the average gap—$1944—was well above average pretransfer income—$928.[11]

TABLE 3.1.   BASIC STATISTICS OF PRETRANSFER POVERTY

	Pretransfer Poor Households		Total Pretransfer Poverty Gap[c]	Average Per Household Poverty Gap[d]	Total Pretransfer Income of the Poor[c]	Average Pretransfer Income[d]
	Number[a]	Incidence[b]				
1965	15,609	25.7	22.13	1,418	14.14	906
1968	14,933	23.2	23.79	1,593	12.95	867
1972	17,640	24.8	34.29	1,944	16.37	928

Source: Tabulations of the Survey of Economic Opportunity and Current Population Survey data tapes.
[a] In thousands.
[b] In percentages
[c] In billions of dollars.
[d] In dollars.

The three antipoverty budgets appear in Tables 3.2, 3.3, and 3.4.[12] We divide the discussion of trends in these budgets into three major parts. Before focusing on benefits to the pretransfer poor, we review changes in the magnitude and composition of all social welfare expenditures. Then, the poor's share of these expenditures is examined. Shifts in the amount and composition of benefits going to the poor are analyzed from various approaches.

Aggregate Social Welfare Expenditures

In fiscal year 1965, a time in which major social programs of the Johnson Administration were just being enacted and few OEO funds were being spent, SWE reached $74.5 billion, 39 percent of all public-sector spending.[13] Of that sum, OEO and related antipoverty programs of the early 1960s accounted for merely $359 million, or .5 percent. Cash transfers comprised 49 percent of total SWE; while education absorbed 36 percent; health, 8 percent; and the other smaller categories about 7 percent (see Table 3.5).

Three years later, SWE had jumped to $109.2 billion, an increase of 47 percent. As a fraction of all public expenditures, SWE remained at 39 percent, but its composition markedly changed. The introduction and expansion of Medicare and Medicaid during 1966–1968 more than doubled health outlays; they rose from 8 to 13 percent of total SWE. Cash transfers grew more slowly than other

TABLE 3.2.   ANTIPOVERTY BUDGET, INCLUDING FEDERAL AND
STATE-LOCAL EXPENDITURES, FISCAL YEAR 1965

	Total Expenditures[a]	Benefits to the Pretransfer Poor[a]	Percentage Spent on Pretransfer Poor
Total	74,481	31,052	41.7
Cash transfers	36,643	21,005	57
Social Security and railroad benefits	17,649	10,877	62
Public employee retirement	5,077	2,615	52
Unemployment Insurance	2,506	601	24
Workmen's Compensation	1,763	474	27
Public assistance	4,761	4,232	89
Veterans' benefits	4,128	2,143	52
Temporary disability	253	63	25
Payments to farmers	2,245	202	9
Nutrition	906	339	37
Food stamps	36	32	95
Other	870	307	35
Housing	307	158	51
Public housing	219	112	51
Rent supplement	—		
Model Cities	—		
Other	88	48	52
Health	5,655	3,105	55
Medicare	—		
Medical Assistance for the aged	523	506	97
Veterans' medical care	1,221	244	20
State—local hospitals and public health	2,826	1,735	61
Other	1,086	620	57
Welfare and OEO services	1,412	908	64
Public assistance social services	266	250	94
Community Action	4	4	95
OEO health and nutrition	—		
OEO Legal services	—		
Other	1,142	654	57

TABLE 3.2. — (continued)

	Total Expenditures[a]	Benefits to the Pretransfer Poor[a]	Percentage Spent on Pretransfer Poor
Employment and manpower	693	437	63
Employment services	200	87	44
OEO manpower programs	65	65	100
Other manpower and voca- tional rehabilitation	428	285	67
Public Employment Program	—		
Education	27,125	4,898	18
Student support	488	33	7
Local schools	21,581	4,267	20
Federal elementary and secondary education	624	207	33
State–local higher education	3,609	253	7
Federal aid to higher education	127	12	9
Veterans' education	26	13	50
Vocational–adult education	668	113	17

Note: Entries may not sum to totals because of rounding. Also, in some instances the percentage appearing in column 3 diverges considerably from the ratio of column 2 to column 1. The percentage is correct; the divergence results from rounding of the dollar entries. See Appendix A for more detailed estimates and documentation.

[a] In millions of dollars.

program categories, and consequently fell to 42 percent of the total. Antipoverty programs sponsored by OEO and other agencies, including the massive outlays for Title I of the Elementary and Secondary Education Act, increased tenfold to $3.3 billion, but still only accounted for 3 percent of all SWE.

By 1972, governments were spending $184.9 billion on social programs, a 69 percent rise over the 1968 figure. Because other types of public expenditures grew more slowly during those four years, the portion of the public dollar devoted to SWE moved sharply up from 39 to 46 percent. Shifts in the composition of SWE were less striking than before, but still noticeable. Cash transfers and outlays for health absorbed marginally higher shares than in 1968. Payments to farmers dwindled to less than 2 percent of SWE. The rapid growth of food

TABLE 3.3.   ANTIPOVERTY BUDGET, INCLUDING FEDERAL AND
STATE-LOCAL EXPENDITURES, FISCAL YEAR 1968

	Total Expenditures[a]	Benefits to the Pretransfer Poor[a]	Percentage Spent on Pretransfer Poor
Total	109,224	43,914	40.2
Cash transfers	45,563	24,575	54
Social Security and			
Railroad Benefits	24,112	13,937	58
Public employee retirement	6,494	2,747	42
Unemployment Insurance	2,204	384	17
Workmen's Compensation	2,287	754	33
Public assistance	5,537	4,524	81
Veterans' benefits	4,632	2,181	47
Temporary disability	297	48	16
Payments to farmers	3,020	211	7
Nutrition	1,038	408	39
Food stamps	187	172	92
Other	851	236	28
Housing	412	291	70
Public housing	294	209	71
Rent supplements	2	2	69
Model Cities	2	1	39
Other	114	78	68
Health	14,064	7,704	55
Medicare	4,411	2,073	47
Medicaid	3,329	2,545	77
Veterans' medical care	1,420	284	20
State–local hospitals and			
public health	3,315	1,817	55
Other	1,589	985	62
Welfare and OEO services	2,555	1,869	73
Public assistance social			
services	547	482	88
Community Action	426	405	95
OEO health and nutrition	50	48	95
OEO Legal Services	36	34	95
Other	1,496	900	60

TABLE 3.3—(continued)

	Total Expenditures[a]	Benefits to the Pretransfer Poor[a]	Percentage Spent on Pretransfer Poor
Employment and manpower	2,012	1,592	79
Employment services	322	145	45
OEO manpower programs	884	878	99
Other manpower and vocational rehabilitation	806	569	71
Public Employment Program	—		
Education	40,561	7,264	18
Student support	937	132	14
Local schools	29,036	5,052	17
Elementary and secondary education act	1,344	553	41
Other federal elementary and secondary education	1,230	593	48
State—local higher education	5,623	449	8
Federal aid to higher education	632	93	15
Veterans' education	444	120	27
Vocational—adult education	1,315	271	21

Note: Entries may not sum to totals because of rounding. Also, in some instances the percentage appearing in column 3 diverges considerably from the ratio of column 2 to column 1. The percentage is correct; the divergence results from rounding of the dollar entries. See Appendix A for more detailed estimates and documentation.

[a]In millions of dollars.

stamps, manpower programs, and Model Cities led a broad surge of outlays for nutrition, welfare services, manpower, and housing activities. The combined share of SWE for these program areas rose from 5 to 8 percent. Public spending for education lagged behind, reflecting a slower growth in school enrollments after the booming 1960s. Spending on policies created by or closely related to OEO efforts against poverty rose to $4.7 billion despite hostility from the Nixon Administration during this period. These expenditures remained a small 2.5 percent of all SWE.

Benefits to the Pretransfer Poor

Throughout the period under study, the pretransfer poor received substantial benefits from SWE. In 1965, $31.1 billion, or 41.7 percent of SWE, directly benefited the approximately 15.6 million

TABLE 3.4.   ANTIPOVERTY BUDGET, INCLUDING FEDERAL AND
STATE-LOCAL EXPENDITURES, FISCAL YEAR 1972

	Total Expenditures[a]	Benefits to the Pretransfer Poor[a]	Percentage Spent on Pretransfer Poor
Total	184,871	78,653	42.5
Cash transfers	80,110	42,719	53
Social Security and railroad benefits	40,426	23,367	58
Public employee retirement	11,692	4,443	38
Unemployment Insurance	6,751	1,424	21
Workmen's Compensation	3,794	1,248	33
Public assistance	10,828	9,511	87
Veterans' benefits	6,215	2,641	43
Temporary disability	404	85	21
Payments to farmers	3,234	162	5
Nutrition	3,688	2,582	70
Food stamps	1,866	1,586	85
Other	1,822	996	55
Housing	1,834	1,016	55
Public housing	744	551	74
Rent supplement	75	56	75
Model Cities	500	210	42
Other	514	200	39
Health	24,574	13,826	56
Medicare	7,023	3,371	48
Medicaid	7,548	5,690	75
Veterans' medical care	2,377	523	22
State–local hospitals and public health	5,039	2,671	53
Other	2,587	1,571	61
Welfare and OEO services	5,290	3,822	72
Public assistance social services	2,161	1,750	81
Community Action	458	440	96
OEO health and nutrition	180	173	96
OEO Legal Services	60	58	96
Other	2,431	1,401	58

TABLE 3.4.–(continued)

	Total Expenditures[a]	Benefits to the Pretransfer Poor[a]	Percentage Spent on Pretransfer Poor
Employment and manpower	3,904	2,796	72
Employment services	450	228	51
OEO manpower programs	1,337	1,319	99
Other manpower and			
vocational rehabilitation	1,559	1,093	70
Public Employment Program	559	156	28
Education	62,238	11,730	19
Student support	1,688	347	21
Local schools	42,148	7,376	18
Elementary and secondary			
education act	1,836	879	48
Other federal elementary and			
secondary education	1,632	695	43
State–local higher education	9,700	970	10
Federal aid to higher			
education	518	96	19
Veterans' education	1,889	623	33
Vocational-adult education	2,828	744	26

Note: Entries may not sum to totals because of rounding. Also, in some instances the percentage appearing in column 3 diverges considerably from the ratio of column 2 to column 1. The percentage is correct; the divergence results from rounding of the dollar entries. See Appendix A for more detailed estimates and documentation.

[a] *In millions of dollars.*

households that were below the poverty line on a pretransfer basis (see Table 3.2). Between 1965 and 1968, expenditures benefiting the poor increased 41 percent to $43.9 billion, representing 40.2 percent of total SWE. The decline to 40.2 percent was partly due to the decrease in the fraction of households that were pretransfer poor (see Table 3.1). Four years later, aid to the poor had leaped to $78.7 billion, a 79 percent jump over the 1968 total. The share of SWE spent on this group reached 42.5 percent. Estimates of SWE to the pretransfer poor for more recent years would, we suspect, also fall between 40 and 45 percent.[14] The trend in total benefits to both poor and nonpoor is shown graphically in Figure 3.1.[15]

The number of pretransfer poor households fluctuated during the years 1965 to 1972, which suggests that we also look at the trend in average benefits per poor and nonpoor household. Figure 3.2 visually displays the trend. The $31.1 billion of total aid to the poor in 1965

TABLE 3.5. COMPOSITION OF TOTAL SOCIAL WELFARE EXPENDITURES TO PRETRANSFER POOR FOR 1965, 1968, AND 1972, BY FUNCTIONAL CATEGORIES

	Total SWE		
	1965	1968	1972
Total dollars (in billions)	74.5	109.2	184.9
Composition (in percentages)			
Cash transfers	48.5	41.7	43.3
Payments to farmers	3.0	2.8	1.7
Nutrition	1.2	.9	2.0
Housing	.4	.4	1.0
Health	7.6	12.9	13.3
Welfare and OEO services	1.9	2.3	2.9
Employment–manpower	.9	1.8	2.1
Education	36.4	37.1	33.7
Total	100.0	100.0	100.0

Source: Computed from Tables 3.2, 3.3, and 3.4.

represented an average benefit of $1989. This was more than twice as large as the mean SWE of $964 for the nonpoor. Between 1965 and 1972, average SWE per household rose slightly more quickly for the poor than for the nonpoor. Average per-household SWE of the pretransfer poor were $2941 in 1968, a rise of 48 percent. For other households, the corresponding value of $1324 marked a gain of only 39 percent over 1965. By 1972, the average benefit to a poor household stood at $4459, 52 percent above the 1968 figure. This percentage increase slightly exceeded the 50 percent hike in mean benefits to the nonpoor, which reached $1987 in 1972. Over the whole time period, then, mean SWE directed at the pretransfer poor rose a hefty 124 percent, while the average benefits to the nonpoor increased 106 percent. In constant dollars adjusted for inflation, this rise was 69 percent for the poor and 55 percent for nonpoor.

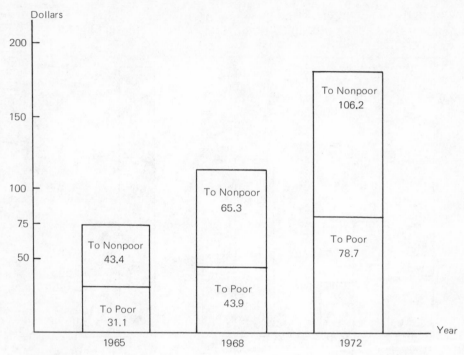

Figure 3.1. Social Welfare Expenditures
Note: In billions of dollars.

Why Haven't Social Welfare Expenditures Eliminated Poverty?

The data suggest that government aid to the poor has been quite substantial in recent years and, during the period examined, increased faster in per-household terms than did SWE for the nonpoor. Moreover, for poor households the ratio of mean SWE benefits to the mean pretransfer poverty gap steadily rose from 1.4 in 1965 to 1.8 in 1968 and 2.3 in 1972 (see Figure 3.3). Given these significant public efforts to provide benefits to the pretransfer poor, one might reasonably ask, Why hasn't *posttransfer* poverty been erased by now?

An answer to this question contains many parts. It should be remembered first that this analysis uses a poverty definition that considers only *cash* income when determining a household's poverty status. Hence, only SWE going to the pretransfer poor in the form of cash transfers contribute to a recorded decline in poverty. Any reduction in need due to government in-kind transfers—such as food

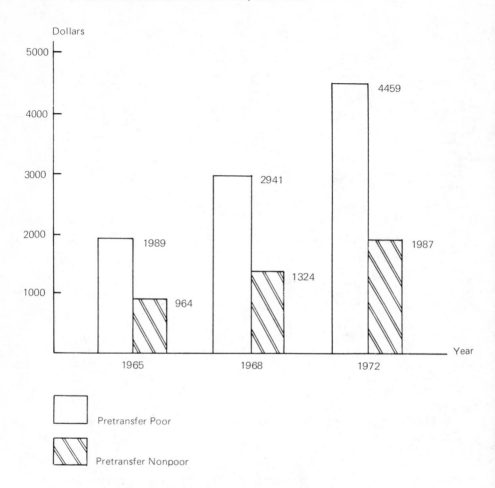

Figure 3.2. Average Social Welfare Expenditures Received by Poor and
Nonpoor Households

stamps or public housing—which are close though not perfect substitutes for cash, is not captured with this approach. Yet these forms
of aid have increased enormously since 1965. Estimates of changes in
the posttransfer poverty population that included the benefits of
in-kind transfers would, therefore, indicate greater progress, but still
not a complete elimination of poverty.[16]

Nonetheless, total cash transfers received by the pretransfer poor
(neglecting completely those transfers going to the nonpoor) were
sufficient by themselves to eliminate the poverty gap in 1968 and

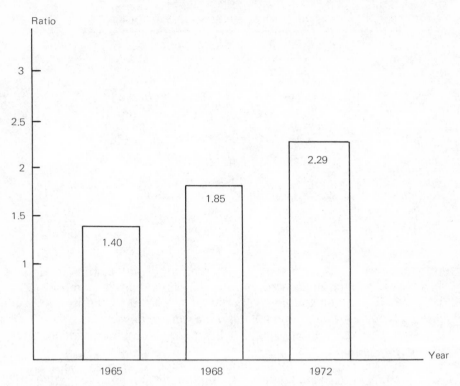

Figure 3.3. Ratio of Average Social Welfare Benefits to Average Poverty
Gap of the Pretransfer Poor

1972. They could almost have done so in 1965. This is shown in the
first two columns of Table 3.6. In fact, the poverty gap declined only
53, 57, and 64 percent for 1965, 1968, and 1972, respectively
(column 4).[17] This difference between the potential and actual
performance of the cash-transfer system in reducing poverty is produced because some pretransfer poor families receive enough to
move them well out of poverty, while other equally needy families
obtain little or no assistance. This phenomenon, and the nature of
the transfer system that generates it, is a subject of Chapter 6.

Another thread in our explanation of the persistence of poverty
despite massive government aid lies in the fact that many social
welfare programs affecting the poor may produce results not fully
evident until far into the future. The benefits from regular public
education, special education efforts for the disadvantaged, manpower
training, other human resources programs, and community-oriented

TABLE 3.6.   CASH TRANSFERS AND POVERTY REDUCTION

| | (1) | (2) Cash Transfers Received by | (3) | (4) |
	Pretransfer Poverty Gap[a]	Pretransfer Poor[a]	Posttransfer Poverty Gap[a]	Percentage Decline in Gap
1965	22.13	21.01	10.40	53
1968	23.79	24.58	10.18	57
1972	34.29	42.72	12.48	64

Sources: Columns 1 and 3 are from tabulations of the Survey of Economic Opportunity and Current Population Survey data tapes. Columns 2 and 4 are from Tables 3.2, 3.3, and 3.4.

[a] In billions of dollars.

programs are not direct substitutes for the current cash or in-kind income of a poor household. About 20 percent of the pretransfer poor's SWE has come from such programs, but these benefits do not reduce income poverty immediately. Rather, outlays on these activities may help prevent poverty in future years, though evidence to support this hope is inconclusive.[18]

While SWE may help reduce poverty, other government decisions and activities (which fall among the indirect social welfare activities that this study has excluded) may have helped perpetuate low-income status for many Americans, thus offsetting the positive gains from SWE. The federal government's refusal to extend the protection of labor union laws to groups such as farm workers may have impeded severely the chances of these workers to escape poverty. Similarly, more vigorous enforcement of laws against race and sex discrimination and protection of the rights of minorities at all government levels might have done more to overcome poverty than providing increased job counseling and training. Macroeconomic policy more sympathetic to low-income families might also have helped the poor more than large increases in SWE.

III. CHANGING PATTERNS OF AID TO THE POOR

Broad trends in the public sector's pattern of aid to the poor are often obscured when discussion is narrowly concentrated on the income-support system or policies administered by OEO. The relative impact of different policies on the poor's welfare may not be noticed behind the cloud of rhetoric, debate, and controversy that accompanies welfare and antipoverty spending and legislation. The antipoverty budgets, however, place the full range of social programs in perspective relative to one another and permit easy comparison of their actual outlays, allowing the study of several general tendencies.

The Changing Composition of Benefits

Analysis of the antipoverty budgets reveals that a profound transformation of the structure of aid to the poor in the United States occurred during 1965–1972 (see Table 3.7). While cash payments provided more than two-thirds of the pretransfer poor's SWE in 1965, this share had fallen to 54 percent by 1972 despite the large absolute increases indicated in Table 3.6. The introduction of Sup-

TABLE 3.7.   COMPOSITION OF SOCIAL WELFARE EXPENDITURES TO PRETRANSFER POOR FOR 1965, 1968, AND 1972, BY FUNCTIONAL CATEGORIES

| | SWE to Pretransfer Poor | | |
	1965	1968	1972
Total dollars (in billions)	31.1	43.9	78.7
Composition (in percentages)			
Cash transfers	67.6	56.0	54.2
Payments to farmers	.7	.5	.2
Nutrition	1.1	.9	3.3
Housing	.5	.7	1.3
Health	10.0	17.5	17.6
Welfare and OEO services	2.9	4.3	4.9
Employment-manpower	1.4	3.6	3.6
Education	15.8	16.5	14.9
Total	100.0	100.0	100.0

Source: Computed from Tables 3.2, 3.3, and 3.4.

plemental Security Income and more generous Social Security payments may halt this decline, but, barring the enactment of a universal cash income-maintenance plan, a reversal seems unlikely. The explanation for the downward movement lies in the surge of in-kind transfers and other noncash SWE that have been channeled to the poor in recent years. Between 1965 and 1968, as most great society programs became well-established, these forms of benefits rose from 32 to 44 percent of public spending on the poor. After four more years and a change of administration, their share stood at 46 percent. The gain is probably permanent.

Nutrition programs, led by food stamps, provided more than 3 percent of the poor's benefits in 1972, compared to around 1 percent in earlier years. Continued growth in food stamp enrollment since 1972 has probably pushed this figure to more than 4 percent for 1974, and it may go well beyond that in a few years.

Housing programs have never been an important source of benefits for low-income people, although their contribution has grown from .5 to 1.3 percent. For those families living in public housing or receiving other housing subsidies, the increase in welfare from these programs can be considerable.[19] But the limited supply of funds and publicly operated apartments has meant simply that benefits have been unavailable to most poor households. In 1972, for example, the number of pretransfer poor families with two or more members exceeded 11 million; public housing projects contained about one-half million dwelling units, and some of these were occupied by nonpoor. If a far-reaching "rent stamp" or housing allowance program were to be enacted, housing benefits would assuredly provide a much greater fraction of the poor's SWE than at present.

Health outlays jumped sharply from 10 to 17.5 percent of the poor's SWE between 1965 and 1968, reflecting the strong effect of Medicare and Medicaid upon the mix of SWE. Since then, in the absence of other major structural changes in the public provision of health care, the share from health programs has held steady. Adoption of a national health insurance plan would probably push the percentage slightly higher.[20]

Welfare and OEO services have grown from 3 to 5 percent of public expenditures directed at the poor. The change during the 1965–1968 period marks the impact of Community Action; the growth since 1968 is largely due to rising costs of public assistance social services. The Community Action Program will be continued, but at somewhat lower levels of funding than in 1972. This will lead to a modest decline in this program area's share of SWE unless offset by rapid expansion of other social service programs.

Employment and manpower expenditures also have provided a substantially larger portion of the poor's benefits after 1965. The rise from 1.4 to 3.6 percent mirrors the massive federal attempt, which began in 1966, to offer job training to large numbers of disadvantaged workers. Increased public-service-employment funding in response to the 1974–1975 recession will cause total federal manpower outlays to rise about $1 billion over the 1972 figure. Since the pretransfer poor receive only about 30 percent of these benefits, this recent development will not produce any large increase in the share of the benefits to the poor provided by employment–manpower spending.[21]

The final functional area, education, has consistently accounted for about 15 percent of public outlays to the poor. Cutbacks in educational expenditures relative to other program categories in response to ebbing enrollments should cause this percentage to drop gradually. Rising postsecondary school attendance by students from low-income families may partly offset this, however.

Special Antipoverty Programs

Looking at the budgets from a slightly different approach, one is struck by the relative unimportance to the pretransfer poor (in dollar terms) of the direct benefits from special war on poverty programs created by OEO and other federal agencies in the 1960s (see Table 3.8). In the bitter debate and careful scrutiny of their objectives, methods, and costs, these programs—primarily educational, manpower, and Community Action activities—came to be popularly regarded as a major element of the nation's effort to assist its poorest members. In fact, the poor were obtaining the overwhelming portion of their government benefits elsewhere. As Table 3.8 shows, the innovative programs in 1965 cost only $359 million and delivered $266 million in aid to low-income people, a tiny .9 percent of direct government benefits to the poor. By 1968, when funding for these central war on poverty activities was channeling $2.6 billion to the poor, this sum was only 6 percent of their SWE. Four years later, benefits to the poor from these sources reached nearly $4 billion, up 51 percent. However, the relative importance of these programs had actually declined to 5 percent of the poor's benefits.[22]

A complete assessment of the importance of these activities cannot be gained solely by examining dollar amounts, but must also consider the symbolic and political effect of OEO programs and their influence upon other social programs. For example, increased benefits to the pretransfer poor from AFDC, food stamps, and other transfer

TABLE 3.8.   EXPENDITURES FOR SPECIAL ANTIPOVERTY PROGRAMS COMPARED TO TOTAL SOCIAL WELFARE EXPENDITURES
(in millions of dollars)

	Total Funds			Benefits to Pretransfer Poor Only		
	1965	*1968*	*1972*	*1965*	*1968*	*1972*
OEO Programs[a]	129	1,881	2,443	126	1,835	2,365
Related Antipoverty Programs[b]	230	1,430	2,252	140	780	1,588
Total	359	3,311	4,695	266	2,615	3,953
All SWE	74,481	109,224	184,871	31,052	43,914	78,653
OEO and related programs as a percentage of all SWE	0.5	3.0	2.5	0.9	6.0	5.0

Source: Appendix A.

[a] Includes Community Action, OEO health and nutrition, Legal Services, Action, VISTA, Head Start, Follow Through, Upward Bound, Adult Education, Neighborhood Youth Corps, Job Corps, Public Service Careers, JOBS, Concentrated Employment Program, Operation Mainstream, Work Experience, Migrant Farmworkers Aid, and Community Economic Development. Programs are listed under OEO if originally administered by OEO.

[b] Includes MDTA, Work Incentive (WIN), Employment for Disadvantaged Youth, Model Cities, Title I of Elementary and Secondary Education Act, Talent Search, and higher education remedial services.

programs may, in part, be traced to efforts of Legal Services and Community Action workers, as was discussed earlier.[23]

Low-Income–Conditioned Benefits

Extending the preceding observations, we ask how the division of SWE into low-income–conditioned and non-low-income–conditioned categories has changed in recent years. Low-income–conditioned programs are those for which persons qualify specifically because of their small incomes: public assistance, public housing, or most manpower activities, for example. All the OEO and related programs discussed above are, of course, included. Programs reserved for low-income areas are also placed in this grouping. Social welfare expenditures not conditioned on low income encompass the remaining programs, for which eligibility is a right—elementary education, for example—or depends directly on criteria other than one's current income—for example, Medicare (age) or Workmen's Compensation (work injury). Table 3.9 summarizes our findings.

In 1965, low-income–conditioned programs comprised about 12 percent of all SWE (column 2). During the next seven years, this set of programs grew relatively fast as new ones, like Medicaid and rent supplements, began operation and older ones, such as food stamps, expanded. By 1972, the distribution of 18 percent ($33.8 billion) of public social expenditures was tied to some kind of low-income criterion. This upward trend may continue for several more years, especially if a housing allowance or universal income-support program is enacted.[24]

Throughout these years, about 80 to 85 percent of the benefits from income-tested programs went to the pretransfer poor, compared to around 35 percent of the other expenditures. This share was not higher for three reasons. During this period, eligibility limits for public assistance, public housing, food stamps, Medicaid, other social services, and some forms of college student aid, which account for a large portion of income-tested spending, have exceeded federal poverty lines in some states. Second, because eligibility for public assistance, food stamps, and some other benefits is determined by monthly family income, some recipients may obtain aid in one or several months when their incomes are low, yet have an annual income greater than the poverty level. Third, funds flowing to low-income areas, such as in Model Cities or Title 1 of the Elementary and Secondary Education Act, have aided both poor and nonpoor residents alike.

TABLE 3.9. LOW-INCOME-CONDITIONED AND OTHER SOCIAL WELFARE EXPENDITURES

	(1) All SWE	(2) All SWE	(3) SWE to Pretransfer Poor[a]	(4) SWE to Pretransfer Poor[a]	(5) Percentage Spent on Pretransfer Poor
	amount	percentage	amount	percentage	
1965					
Low-income—conditioned expenditures[a]	8,857[b]	12[c]	7,506[b]	24[c]	85
Other expenditures	65,624	88	23,546	76	36
Total	74,481	100	31,052	100	42
1968					
Low-income—conditioned expenditures[a]	16,388	15	12,988	30	79
Other expenditures	92,846	85	30,926	70	33
Total	109,224	100	43,914	100	40
1972					
Low-income—conditioned expenditures[a]	33,803	18	27,129	34	80
Other expenditures	151,068	82	51,524	65	34
Total	184,871	100	78,653	100	43

Source: Appendix A.

[a]Includes public assistance cash and social services, part of veterans' income maintenance and medical care, food stamps, school breakfast, special and nonfood cash assistance, donated food, surplus commodities, public housing, rent supplements, homeowner and rental housing assistance, Model Cities, Neighborhood Facilities, Medicaid and MAA, special projects and dental health under maternal and child health, all OEO-initiated programs, all manpower training, work-study and cooperative education, Educational Opportunity Grants, health and nursing professions, ESEA I, VII, VIII, Talent Search, Upward Bound, and higher education remedial services.

[b]In millions of dollars.

[c]In percentages.

Because of the rising volume of low-income–conditioned outlays relative to other types of SWE, this type of aid has formed a steadily rising fraction of the poor's total benefits. In 1965, 24 percent of their aid was means-tested, while in 1972, 34 percent was means-tested (column 4). At the same time, these benefits have contributed $19.6 billion to the $47.6 billion gain in SWE to the poor over this period (column 3). Hence, while low-income–conditioned benefits have formed a substantial and increasing share of the poor's SWE, well over one-half of their total aid has been derived from programs that have *not* been aimed specifically at low-income households.

Source of Dollar Increases

The preceding three sections have been concerned with changes in the percentage of the poor's total benefits coming from different sets of programs. Here we shall look at actual dollar changes in the total benefits to the poor and ask which public programs were responsible for boosting SWE to the pretransfer poor from $31.1 billion in 1965 to $43.9 billion in 1968 and $78.7 billion in 1972.

Table 3.10 (columns 1 and 2) indicates that $7.4 billion (57 percent) of the $12.9 billion difference between 1965 and 1968 was accounted for by benefits not conditioned on low income. Twenty-five percent of the rise was provided by Social Security and railroad and government pension benefits, which increased payments to the poor by $3.2 billion. Medicare, nonexistent in 1965, added $2.1 billion. These large increases were primarily obtained by elderly pretransfer-poor persons. Primary and secondary education outlays on poor children rose $.8 billion, and the remaining $1.3 billion were widely scattered among small programs.   ·

Low-income–conditioned benefits provided the other $5.5 billion of the increase during 1965–1968. Medicaid, replacing and expanding Medical Assistance for the Aged, accounted for $2 billion; OEO and closely related antipoverty spending raised benefits $2.3 billion. Little of the gain is owed to public assistance received by the poor, which rose only $292 million in three years.

During the years from 1968 to 1972, government benefits to the pretransfer poor rose $34.7 billion. Spurred by large increases for Social Security voted in 1970, retirement and disability payments to the poor alone represented $11.1 billion—one-third—of this jump. Medicare benefits climbed $1.3 billion. Local elementary and high school expenditures added $2.3 billion. A strong surge in other non-low-income–conditioned cash transfer programs, reflecting in-

TABLE 3.10.   SOURCES OF GROWTH OF SOCIAL WELFARE EXPENDITURE
BENEFITS TO THE PRETRANSFER POOR

	(1)	(2)	(3)	(4)	(5)	(6)
	1965-1968		1968-1972		1965-1972	
Total growth	$12.9[a]	100[b]	$34.7[a]	100[b]	$47.6[a]	100[b]
Non-poverty- conditioned programs	7.4	57	20.6	59	28.0	59
Social Security, railroad, and govern- ment pensions	3.2	25	11.1	32	14.3	30
Other cash transfers[c]	.1	-1	1.6	5	1.5	3
Medicare	2.1	16	1.3	4	3.4	7
Local primary and secondary schools	.8	6	2.3	7	3.1	6
All other	1.4	11	4.3	12	5.7	12
Poverty-conditioned programs	5.5	43	14.1	41	19.6	41
Public assistance cash	.3	2	5.0	14	5.3	11
Food stamps	.1	1	1.4	4	1.6	3
Public housing and other low-income housing programs	.1	1	.5	1	.6	1
Medicaid (and MAA)	2.0	16	3.1	9	5.2	11
Special OEO and related antipoverty efforts	2.3	18	1.3	4	3.7	8
Public assistance social services	.2	2	1.3	4	1.5	3
Veterans' pensions	.2	1	.5	1	.7	1
All other	.1	1	1.1	3	1.2	3

Source: Appendix A.

Note: Entries may not sum to total due to rounding.

[a]In billions of dollars.

[b]In percentages.

[c]Excludes public assistance and veterans' pensions (but not veterans' compensation).

creased participation and payment levels, raised aid to the poor by
$1.6 billion. Altogether, non-low-income—conditioned benefits pro-
vided $20.6 billion—59 percent—of the total increase. As in the
earlier period, most of these gains were shared by the needy elderly
and disabled.

Low-income—conditioned SWE to the poor grew by $14.1 billion
between 1968 and 1972. The well-publicized expansion of welfare

rolls brought the poor $5 billion; AFDC accounted for three-quarters of this gain. The boom in low-income–conditioned in-kind transfer programs beginning in the late 1960s led to a $5.0 billion increase in these four years, which was divided in this way: (1) $1.4 billion for food stamps; (2) $0.5 billion for public housing and other low-income housing programs; (3) $3.1 billion for Medicaid. Public assistance social services, expanding, like Medicaid, as the welfare population grew, devoted $1.3 billion more to the poor in 1972 than in 1968. Special antipoverty efforts by OEO and other federal agencies added $1.3 billion. All other low-income–conditioned program benefits rose by $1.5 billion during these years. This growth of conditioned aid was, we suspect, more widely shared among the pretransfer poor than were the nonconditioned benefits.

Federal Versus State–Local Benefits

Different levels of government tend to provide different mixes of SWE. The responsibility, direction, and major funding for the war on poverty have always rested in Washington. Comparing federal to state–local SWE, therefore, can be expected to uncover marked differences.

Table 3.11 shows that total outlays by both levels of governments were about equal in 1965. During the next seven years, state–local

TABLE 3.11.   FEDERAL AND STATE-LOCAL SOCIAL WELFARE EXPENDITURES

	Total Outlays[a]	Benefits to Pretransfer Poor[a]	Percentage Received by Pretransfer Poor
Federal			
1965	37,774	19,952	53
1968	58,572	29,703	51
1972	105,016	54,757	52
State–local			
1965	36,708	11,099	30
1968	50,652	14,211	28
1972	79,856	23,896	30

Source: Appendix A.

[a]*In millions of dollars.*

spending expanded 11.7 percent a year. This growth was powered by increases in the costs of traditional state–local services, especially education, and by state contributions to Medicaid. Federal SWE, in contrast, grew at 17.6 percent annually and exceeded state–local outlays by 32 percent in 1972. This more rapid growth reflected both heavy increases in long-standing programs such as Social Security and new and costly expenses authorized in the new social legislation of the mid-1960s.[25]

Slightly more than one-half the output of federal SWE has consistently gone to pretransfer poor households. Only about 30 percent of the transfers and services provided by state–local agencies has reached this group (column 3 of Table 3.10). As a result of this fairly constant difference and the more rapid increase in federal SWE, the central government's contribution to benefits to the poor rose from 64 to 70 percent during these seven years. Because further expansion of social programs is likely to come from federal initiative, this upward trend should continue.

The fraction of federal SWE benefiting the poor exceeded the state–local percentage because of the considerably different mixes of social welfare programs funded by the two governmental levels.[26] Table 3.12 presents evidence to support this contention. Columns 4

TABLE 3.12.   PERCENTAGE OF FEDERAL AND STATE-LOCAL EXPENDITURES, BY PROGRAM AREA

	(1)	(2)	(3)	(4)	(5)	(6)
				Percentage of Program Area's Funds Going to Poor		
	Percentage of All SWE					
	1965	1968	1972	1965	1968	1972
Federal						
Cash transfers	79.9	65.3	64.1	58	54	53
Education	3.9	8.5	7.8	21	32	35
Health	5.3	14.0	14.0	40	50	53
All other categories	10.9	12.2	14.1	30	46	58
Total	100.0	100.0	100.0	53	51	52
State-local						
Cash transfers	16.3	14.5	16.0	57	52	56
Education	69.8	70.3	67.7	18	16	16
Health	10.0	11.5	12.3	63	62	61
All other categories	3.9	3.7	4.0	55	58	58
Total	100.0	100.0	100.0	28	30	28

Source: Appendix A.

through 6 indicate that about the same high fraction of cash transfers has been given to the poor at both levels, while the poor have received relatively small percentages of federal and state–local outlays on education. From columns 1 through 3 we see that the bulk of federal money (more than 60 percent in all years) has been directed into cash transfers—a program area that gives a large fraction of its funds to the poor—while two-thirds of state–local SWE has been spent on education, an activity that gives relatively less to low-income groups.

A more complicated test may be used to check thoroughly this explanation. Suppose the composition of state–local SWE were identical to the federal pattern: that is, in 1965, state–local governments had spent 79.9 percent on cash transfers, 3.9 percent on education, and so forth. Further, assume that the share of benefits going to the poor were as given in the state-local part of column 4. (That is, 57 percent of transfers, 18 percent of education programs, and so forth, were still received by the poor.) Then, under these assumptions, how high a portion of total state–local SWE would have reached the poor? For 1965, 1968, and 1972, the answers respectively would be 54, 49, and 53 percent. These are comparable to the federal percentages in Table 3.11.[27] Hence, to restate our finding, it is mainly the different distribution of funds *among* program areas that has been responsible for the relative generosity of federal SWE, not the higher fraction of funds given to the poor *within* program areas.

IV. SUMMARY AND CONCLUDING COMMENTS

Examination, from an antipoverty perspective, of public spending for social welfare purposes uncovers a number of findings:

• The enormous seven-year increase in government social welfare expenditures, their rising share of the public sector's "budget," and the shifts in their composition are changes with important implications. Total SWE rose from $74 billion to $185 billion and from 39 to 46 percent of all public outlays in the seven years between 1965 and 1972. Cash transfers and payments to farmers declined as a proportion of SWE, while all other program categories became more important.

• The pretransfer poverty population, which has included about one-quarter of all households, has received slightly more than 40 percent of these outlays in every year. Benefits per poor household have grown quite rapidly and have surely contributed substantially to the level of well-being of this group.

● Poverty remaining after transfers are added to household incomes has not disappeared, however. This state of affairs has persisted, in part because cash and in-kind transfers have not been distributed in a way that has maximized poverty reduction, and because expenditures on human capital and community-oriented programs that may produce long-run antipoverty effects do not reduce income poverty in the short run.

● Cash transfers have accounted for more than one-half of the poor's benefits, but a marked shift toward in-kind transfers and services, especially in health, has occurred and will probably continue.

● Federal aid to the poor has exceeded state–local aid, partly because of the division of fiscal responsibility and partly due to federal antipoverty initiatives.

● A rising fraction of the poor's SWE has been derived from low-income–conditioned programs. By 1972, 35 percent of their benefits were based on some form of low-income criterion. However, special antipoverty expenditures have never accounted for more than 6 percent of total assistance to the poor and their relative importance has declined since 1968.

● About 60 percent of the dollar growth in SWE for the poor has stemmed from non-low-income, non-OEO-sponsored programs and has accumulated quietly behind the controversies over OEO and welfare reform during these years. Most of this aid has been concentrated on the elderly and disabled pretransfer poor. The lesson from this observation may be that certain special groups among the poor can receive substantial government assistance without substantive opposition as long as the benefits are not explicitly based on an antipoverty, redistributive rationale and the groups enjoy general political support.

● Poverty-conditioned aid for the poor increased nearly $20 billion during the years studied. This gain was largely attributable to the growth of public assistance and three major in-kind transfer programs. Special OEO and related antipoverty activities have also been important, though they have accounted for a smaller portion of total SWE to the poor than one might have anticipated. The worth and desirability of many poverty-conditioned types of assistance have been hotly debated both politically and academically. And the rapid expansion of benefits has escaped neither public nor congressional attention. Yet, despite the often hostile political atmosphere, considerable new benefits have been obtained for the pretransfer poor. Not enough aid, or not enough of the right sort of aid, has been provided to eliminate poverty. But we may safely conclude that some progress in assisting the poor has been made in recent years.

NOTES

[1] Income before public transfers is the sum of wages, salaries, property income, and private transfers, such as alimony or private charity. The federal government's definition of poverty is a set of income lines that attempts to represent equivalently low levels of economic welfare for families of different sizes, with an adjustment for farm residents, adjusted annually by the Consumer Price Index. In 1972, the poverty line for a nonfarm family of four was $4247. For a discussion of this and other definitions of poverty, see Chapter 2. A relative approach would yield results similar to those reported in this chapter, however.

[2] We acknowledge our debt to Robert Lampman's important early work in this area. See Robert Lampman, "Transfer Approaches to Distribution Policy," *American Economic Review* 60 (May 1970): 270–279, and "Public and Private Transfers as Social Process," in *Redistribution to the Rich and the Poor: The Grants Economics of Income Distribution,* ed. Kenneth Boulding and Martin Pfaff (Belmont, Calif.: Wadsworth, 1972), pp. 15–40.

[3] A related set of estimates that measures the benefits from *federal* programs only to the *posttransfer* poor has been prepared by Gordon Fisher of the Department of Health, Education, and Welfare (formerly of OEO). The list of programs covered in those estimates differs somewhat from ours. We wish to acknowledge our gratitude to Mr. Fisher for kindly allowing us to examine his work and use it in preparing our estimates.

[4] Two important exceptions to this guideline are the Community Action and Model Cities programs, which, though community oriented and often indirect in their effects on persons, are included because of their special antipoverty objectives.

[5] See, for a similar approach, Ida Merriam and Alfred Skolnik, *Social Welfare Expenditures Under Public Programs in the United States, 1926–1966* (U.S., Department of Health, Education, and Welfare, Social Security Administration, Office of Research and Statistics, Research Report No. 25 (Washington, D.C.: U.S. Government Printing Office, 1968), (HE 3.49:25). We have drawn heavily on this work and updated revisions for expenditure data. The major differences between our budgets and the Merriam–Skolnik series is that we exclude all research and all funds spent on active military men and their families, including those for health and education. The second exclusion is justified on two grounds—such spending can be regarded as a cost of defense and, moreover, our data sources generally include only civilian families. Also, we include farm subsidies and price supports since these payments, in our judgement, can be satisfactorily assigned to households. Other producer subsidies, however, are excluded.

[6] The implicit assumptions behind this approach is that persons who earned income working on government projects could have obtained other jobs with (approximately) the same wage in other sectors of the economy. Thus, their earnings from the government are

not transfer benefits, but rather a competitively determined payment in return for services rendered.

[7]It should be noted that all studies of the impact of government activity on the distribution of economic welfare suffer from this defect.

[8]Conversely, some benefits may be worth more to the recipient than they cost governments to provide, though examples of this are not readily apparent. For further discussion on this general issue of recipient evaluation of transfers, see Maria Schmundt, Eugene Smolensky, and Leanna Stiefel, "When Do Recipients Value Transfers at Their Costs to Taxpayers?" in *Integrating Income Maintenance Programs,* ed. Irene Lurie (New York: Academic Press, 1975).

[9]This omission is not serious since we estimate that the total value of interest subsidies for social welfare loan programs has been less than 2 percent of total SWE between 1965 and 1972. The poor receive few of these subsidies (roughly, between 10 and 15 percent).

[10]The poor pay little in taxes in an absolute sense (since their incomes are so low). But they pay an equal or larger *proportion* of their incomes for taxes than do many in the middle-income groups. See Joseph Pechman and Benjamin Okner, *Who Bears the Tax Burden?* (Washington, D.C.: The Brookings Institution, 1974).

[11]For a detailed discussion of changes in pretransfer poverty, see Chapter 5. The dollar figures in this paragraph are not adjusted for inflation. If they all had been expressed in 1972 dollars, the pretransfer poverty gap would have been $29.3 billion in 1965 and $28.7 billion in 1968. The average gap would have been $1880 and $1915 for these two years. Hence, the numbers in Table 3.1 overstate the real changes during this period. See Chapter 6 for additional related statistics in constant 1972 dollars and a longer discussion of the trends in the pretransfer gap.

[12]Detailed tables for each year and full documentation are in Appendix A.

[13]Total public expenditures used to compute this figure and succeeding ones are from U.S., President, *Economic Report of the President Together with the Annual Report of the Council of Economic Advisers,* transmitted to the Congress, February 1974, Table c-65, C-70 (Washington, D.C.: U.S. Government Printing Office, 1974), (74:PR37.9:74).

[14]For 1967, Robert Lampman estimates that about 40 percent of SWE went to the pretransfer poor. He uses a slightly different set of programs to define SWE and the estimates are not so detailed as ours. See Lampman, "Transfer Approaches to Distribution Policy," and "Public and Private Transfers."

[15]We should note that while SWE aiding the poor grew rapidly during the period since 1965, total SWE for the *nonpoor* remained greater than SWE for the pretransfer poor in every year. Hence, the popular impression that most of the major increases in SWE have gone to the poor is unfounded.

[16]See p. 85 and 180–181. See also Timothy Smeeding, "Measuring the Economic Welfare of Low Income Households, and the Anti-Poverty Effectiveness of Cash and Non-Cash Transfer Programs" (Ph.D. diss., University of Wisconsin-Madison, 1975).

[17]Cash transfers to the pretransfer poor were, as shown in Table 3.6, $21.0, $24.6, and $42.7 billion according to the antipoverty budgets for 1965, 1968, and 1972, respectively. However, on our Survey of Economic Opportunity and Current Population Survey data tapes the pretransfer poor reported total transfer income of $16.9 billion in 1965, $19.5 billion in 1968, and $34.3 billion in 1972. The difference between the antipoverty budget estimates and the data source statistics reflects the well-known underreporting of transfer income in household surveys. Comparing antipoverty budget results with poverty gap statistics is, therefore, not fully appropriate. Nonetheless, we did so in the text for simplicity. The reported transfer income from the data tapes could not have filled the pretransfer poverty gap in 1965 or 1968, though they could have reduced the gap by 80

percent in 1965 and 82 percent in 1968. In 1972, reported cash transfers could have filled the entire gap. The reason for the difference between these potential decreases in the gap and the actual ones of 53, 57, and 64 percent is as explained in the text that follows.

[18]Spending on these programs may not lead to lower levels of poverty. This point is forcefully argued in Henry M. Levin, "A Decade of Policy Developments in Improving Education of Low-Income Children," in *A Decade of Federal Antipoverty Policy: Achievements, Failures, and Lessons,* ed. Robert H. Haveman (New York: Academic, forthcoming).

[19]Eugene Smolensky and J. Douglas Gomery, "Efficiency and Equity Effects in the Benefits from the Federal Housing Program in 1965," in U.S., Congress, Joint Economic Committee, *Benefit–Cost Analyses of Federal Programs* (Washington, D.C.: U.S. Government Printing Office, 1973), (Y4.Ec7:B43).

[20]This point may need further elaboration, since recent insurance proposals have carried large price tags compared to current federal health expenditures. Insurance plans *completely* paid by participants' premiums would not be considered a federal SWE. In such a case, the government would simply be serving as intermediary, collecting premiums and paying medical bills (much like a nonprofit, privately run insurance company). Now, suppose that part of the costs came out of general revenues or that some group's insurance premiums were subsidized by other participants (making the insurance an in-kind transfer much like Medicare). Then the general revenue funds or the subsidies would appear as SWE. Benefits obtained by the poor under such an arrangement would probably be more than what is currently received from Medicaid and Medicare. Hence, health benefits would increase as a fraction of the poor's total benefits, but probably by a small amount.

[21]Thirty percent of the projected $1 billion rise is $300 million. And $300 million is 0.4 percent of the poor's SWE in 1972. Hence, even with no increase in SWE to the poor between 1972 and 1974 except in this one area (which is clearly not the case), manpower and employment benefits would rise only to 4.0 percent of all SWE to the poor.

[22]As a percentage of the poor's *federal* benefits from SWE, the OEO and related expenditures (all federally funded) were 1.3, 8.8, and 7.2 percent for the three years. While these are somewhat greater than Table 3.8 figures, they still show the small role these programs played in assisting the poor.

[23]For in-depth discussions of these issues and related material concerning the growth of the poor's benefits, see Frank N. Jones, "The Development of the Law and Legal Services Affecting Low-Income Families since the Early 1960s," in Haveman, *A Decade of Federal Antipoverty Policy.*

[24]Further discussion of the role and implications of the increasing volume of income-conditioned benefits may be found in Robert Lampman, "Scaling Welfare Benefits to Income: An Idea That is Being Overworked," *Policy Analysis* 1 (Winter 1975).

[25]Federal programs that existed in 1965 grew at a rate of 12.7 percent, nearly the same as state–local spending. Hence, responsibility for the relatively quick growth of federal SWE rests with the new social initiatives of the Johnson Administration.

[26]The different program mixes detailed in Table 3.11 may be partly explained by economic theories of fiscal federalism and partly by American historical conditions. We shall not pursue these issues here.

[27]These results are based on a division of federal and state–local SWE into the eight program areas shown in Table 3.5.

4 The Changing Character of Poverty

Between 1964 and 1974, major changes occurred in the poverty population. In this chapter, we describe these changes, concentrating particularly on the period 1965 to 1972. However, no explanation is offered for why the changes took place; Chapters 5 and 6 address aspects of this important question.

We begin this chapter by introducing several concepts and providing some information to establish a framework for our discussion. Next, the principal trends are presented in a series of tables, with commentary. Finally, because simple tables cannot adequately capture the complex interrelationships among the many social and economic variables related to poverty, the results of multivariate statistical analyses are reported.[1]

The two definitions of poverty previously discussed—that is, the absolute and relative definitions—are used to examine changes in poverty population. The two groups identified by these definitions contrast with each other both in numbers and in characteristics.

In this chapter, we will look solely at changes in the *posttransfer* poverty population. The posttransfer poor include all households remaining below the poverty line *after* government and private cash transfers are added to their labor earnings and poverty income.[2] Later chapters will look at the pretransfer poor and the relationship between pretransfer and posttransfer poverty.

In our examination of the posttransfer poor, although we present a few statistics on the official poverty population in 1962 and 1973, nearly all the discussion focuses on the period from 1965 to 1972. The emphasis was determined by the pragmatic reason that 1965 was the earliest year and 1972 the most recent for which adequate data were available.[3] Fortunately, 1965 serves well as the base period since it was during that time that national attention turned squarely to the poverty problem and the war on poverty was mobilized into full operation.

These statistics, on which the results in the next section are based, are of the number of poor *persons* in the country.[4] We also discuss poverty among *families* and *unrelated individuals* in parts of this study. As defined by the Bureau of the Census, a family is "a group of two or more persons related by blood, marriage, or adoption and residing together," while unrelated individuals are "persons 14 years old and over (other than inmates of institutions) who are not living with any relative."[5]

From these data we have developed information about the *incidence* and *composition* of the poverty population. Because these concepts are central to our discussion, we describe them here.

Differences in the *incidence* of poverty among subgroups and over time form a major interest of this study. "Incidence" refers to the fraction or percentage of persons, families, or unrelated individuals with a particular characteristic that falls below the poverty threshold. For example, in 1972 there were 175 million persons in households headed by males,[6] and 12.9 million of them were poor. The incidence of poverty for this group, therefore, was 12.9/175 = .073 or 7.3 percent. In contrast, of the 31.2 million persons in female-headed families, 11.6 million were poor; the incidence for this group was 11.6/31.2 = .372 or 37.2 percent. These statistics help identify the characteristics that have been most strongly associated with poverty, and they automatically adjust for differences in the population of various groups and for growth of the population over time.

Statistics of incidence tell us what fraction of households having a given characteristic is poor. We are also interested in knowing what fraction of the poor possesses a given characteristic. Such questions concern the *composition* of the poor. Suppose we wished to see if the proportion of poor persons living with male heads had changed in recent years. The data reveal that there were 29.9 million poor persons in 1965, of which 20.3 million—68 percent—lived in households with male heads. In 1972, absolute poverty affected 24.5

million persons, of which 12.9 million—53 percent—were in house-holds with male heads. Hence, the composition of the poor had shifted toward those in female-headed units.

I. TRENDS IN POSTTRANSFER POVERTY

This section begins with broad summary statistics of the changes in the incidence of poverty and the number of poor persons, families, and unrelated individuals. A description of trends in the income gap is also included. We then examine how the composition of the poor has varied with respect to such socioeconomic characteristics as the head's race and sex, age, education, and work experience. Because these dimensions of poverty have been of greatest interest, we discuss the findings in detail. The distributions of poverty among geographic regions and metropolitan and nonmetropolitan locations are also treated, but less thoroughly.

Patterns produced by the official, absolute, poverty definition are presented first and followed by a comparison with the trends based on the relative definition that we introduce in this volume. As we noted earlier, the relative poverty line rises as the median level of economic welfare rises. Persons are viewed as poor or nonpoor based on their position in the overall distribution of welfare. Our definition was selected so that the 1965 relative poor were identical to the absolute poor. But after that year, the two definitions trace out different patterns (see the last section of Chapter 2 for more detail).

The Broad Changes in Incidence

Absolute Poverty

Table 4.1 provides summary estimates of the poverty population in recent years. The extent of absolute poverty greatly diminished over the eleven-year period 1962 to 1973. The percentage of persons in poverty fell from 21 to 11 percent; the incidence for families declined from 17 to 9 percent; and for unrelated individuals it dropped from 45 to 26 percent. In the same period, the actual number of poor persons fell from 38 to 23 million; the number of poor families declined from 8 to 5 million; and poor unrelated individuals totaled 5 million in 1962 and 4.7 million in 1973. Most of this progress had occurred by 1968. Declines in poverty continued

TABLE 4.1. POSTTRANSFER POVERTY

	Poor Persons		Poor Families		Poor Unrelated Individuals	
	Number (in thousands)	Incidence (in percentages)	Number (in thousands)	Incidence (in percentages)	Number (in thousands)	Incidence (in percentages)
Absolute poverty						
1962	38,265	21.0	8,077	17.2	5,002	45.4
1965	29,900	15.6	5,989	12.4	4,460	36.7
1968	25,055	12.8	5,051	10.0	4,699	34.0
1970	25,516	12.6	5,221	10.1	5,044	32.8
1972	24,494	11.9	5,075	9.3	4,896	29.2
1973	22,973	11.1	4,828	8.8	4,674	25.6
1974 estimate[a]	25,100	11.8	—		—	
1975 estimate[a]	27,100	12.7	—		—	
Relative poverty						
1962	—		—		—	
1965	29,900	15.6	5,989	12.4	4,460	36.7
1968	28,657	14.6	5,846	11.6	5,067	36.7
1970	30,443	15.1	6,286	12.1	5,759	37.5
1972	32,287	15.7	6,802	12.5	6,096	36.3
1973	—		—		—	

TABLE 4.1.—(continued)

Sources: *For 1965-1972, tabulations of Survey of Economic Opportunity and Current Population Survey tapes. For 1962, U.S. Department of Commerce, Bureau of the Census, "Poverty in the United States, 1959 to 1968,"* Current Population Reports: Consumer Income, Series P-60, No. 68 *(December 31, 1969) (Washington, D.C.: U.S. Government Printing Office, 1969) (C3. 186: P60/68). For 1973, same series, "Characteristics of the Low-Income Population, 1973,"* Current Population Reports, Series P-60, No. 98 *(January 1975) (Washington, D.C.: U.S. Government Printing Office, 1975) (C56. 218: P60/98).*

[a] *Estimates based on the following equation (t-ratios in parentheses)*

$$LP_t = 7.518 - 1.590LY + .017LU_t - .044A_{66} \qquad R^2 = .997$$
$$\quad (23.3) \quad (19.2) \quad (0.6) \qquad (4.5)$$

where LP_t = *logarithm of poverty incidence in year t,*

LY_t = *logarithm of median family income in year t, in 1971 dollars,*

LU_t = *logarithm of national unemployment rate in year t, and*

A_{66} = *dummy variable equal to one for 1966 and each year thereafter (to capture effect of a change in the Census Bureau technique for counting income).*

The unemployment rate for 1975 is assumed to be 8.7 percent, the Administration's prediction as of June 1975. The figures for median family income are our estimates and were $10,684 for 1974 and $10,273 for 1975. We assumed that median family income would fall by the same rate as per capita gross national product (GNP) in both 1974 and 1975. Per capita GNP fell by 2.8 percent in 1974 and the Administration as of June 1975 predicts a 3 percent fall in GNP in 1975, which is equal to approximately a 4 percent decline in per capita GNP.

For further detail on this prediction, see I. Garfinkel and R. Plotnick, "Poverty, Unemployment, and the Current Recession," 33 Public Welfare *(Summer 1975).*

83

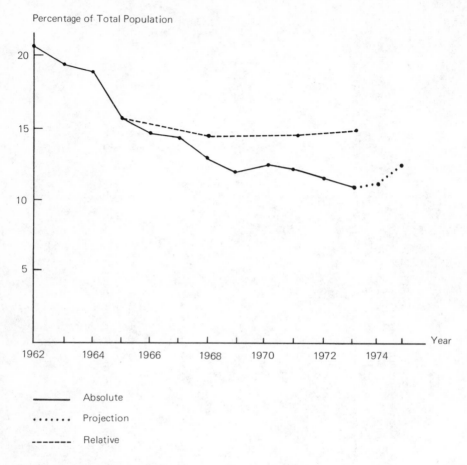

Figure 4.1. Incidence of Poverty

in 1969, but the changes since that year have been much smaller. This can be seen easily in Figure 4.1. Such gains, of course, did not reduce absolute poverty to a rare condition in America. Twenty-three million persons still endured extremely low income in 1973. Moreover, we estimate that the depressed economic environment of 1974–1975 led to a rise in the number of poor persons to 25.1 million (11.8 percent of the total population) in 1974, and 27.1 million (12.7 percent) in 1975. If these projections are correct, the nation will have made no progress in eliminating absolute poverty since the mid-1960s.

Relative Poverty

The estimates of relative poverty in the lower half of the table tell a completely different story. Relative poverty did *not* decline between 1965 and 1972 but remained fairly constant. Figure 4.1 displays this lack of change. The incidence of poverty among persons was 15.6 percent in 1965 and dipped slightly over the next three years to 14.6 percent (a change, we shall see in Chapter 5, that can be traced to the tight labor market of 1966–1968). Relative poverty then increased. By 1972, about the same fraction of the population was poor as in 1965. The fractions of families and unrelated individuals in poverty showed similar patterns. Since the total population grew, the number of relative poor persons, families, and individuals actually rose.

The sharp contrasts between the findings based on absolute and relative approaches indicate the crucial role played by the choice of definition in assessing changes in poverty. These differences will reappear throughout this and later chapters and, taken together, become an important theme of this volume. The official (absolute) measure of poverty shows gradual progress in reducing poverty (at least until 1974) through a combination of economic growth and increasingly generous government transfer programs. The relative perspective indicates little or no progress in eliminating poverty.

Accounting for In-Kind Transfers, Taxes, and Underreporting

The data and definitions from which the preceding statistics were derived reflect standard approaches to measuring income and poverty. Hence, they do not adjust income for taxes paid and in-kind transfers. Also, cash transfer income is underreported in the household surveys upon which the analysis is based.[7] A recent study has attempted to correct for these deficiencies in the data.[8] It was determined that in 1968, 1970, and 1972, the fractions of all persons below the official poverty lines were, respectively, 8.7, 8.0, and 5.4 percent.[9] Compared to the results in Table 4.1, this approach shows a lower incidence of poverty and much greater progress in reducing poverty during these four years.

Trends in the Income Gap

Measuring changes in the total and average income gap, or poverty gap, supplements in an important way the data we just discussed.

TABLE 4.2.   TOTAL AND AVERAGE INCOME GAP OF POSTTRANSFER
POOR PERSONS
(in constant 1972 dollars)

	Total (in millions)	Average per Posttransfer Poor Person
Absolute poverty		
1965	13,794	461
1968	12,241	489
1970	12,375	485
1972	12,484	510
Relative poverty		
1965	13,794	461
1968	14,851	518
1970	16,598	545
1972	19,265	597

Source: Tabulations of Survey of Economic Opportunity and Current Population Survey
tape files. Some tabulations in this study vary slightly from those of the Census Bureau but
not enough to affect conclusions.

Instead of considering trends in the number or fraction of households below either the absolute or relative poverty line, this approach
examines changes in the total and average *dollars* needed to bring all
poor persons up to the poverty threshold. This measure, therefore,
provides a valuable alternative indicator of the financial magnitude of
the poverty problem. Table 4.2 presents statistics on the total and
average poverty gap. To facilitate comparison across years, all dollar
amounts are expressed in 1972 dollars.

Absolute Poverty

In 1965, total incomes of absolute poor persons fell $13.8 billion
short of the poverty lines. After three years, this gap had been
reduced to $12.2 billion, a decline of 9 percent. Since 1968, how-
ever, there has been no progress; the gap was $12.4 billion in 1970
and about the same in 1972 (even though there were 1 million fewer
persons in 1972 than in 1970).

The average gap per poor person has gradually risen from $461 to
more than $500 throughout these years. Thus, though the incidence

of absolute poverty has been reduced, the average degree of poverty has been slowly increasing for those suffering from it.[10]

Relative Poverty

A relative perspective uncovers a considerably different trend. While the incidence of relative poverty stayed fairly steady over this period, the dollar gap between incomes and the poverty cutoff greatly increased. The total gap rose steadily from $13.8 billion to $19.3 billion—40 percent—in seven years. In part, this growth simply reflected the increases in the number of relative poor. But the mean gap also grew from $461 to $597, or about 30 percent. Thus, even at the individual level, the poverty gap sharply increased.

Accounting for In-Kind Transfers, Taxes, and Underreporting

Adding in-kind transfers and subtracting taxes from household incomes and adjusting for underreporting of transfer income again yields a considerably different view of progress in reducing the poverty gap.[11] Using this approach, the total incomes of all poor households fell $8.3 billion below the official poverty lines in 1968. Two years later, the absolute income gap was $8.2 billion. By 1972, it had fallen to $5.4 billion. In comparison, the unadjusted data—also using the official poverty threshold—show larger gaps in each year and a slight upward trend over this time period. Because of the recent rapid growth in in-kind transfers, the difference in perspective between the data in Table 4.2 and this third view may well be even greater in 1975 than in 1972.

The Changing Composition of the Poverty Population

Having considered the overall changes in the incidence of poverty, we now examine shifts in the demographic composition of the poor. Composition statistics indicate the distribution of the poverty population by important socioeconomic characteristics. Such information helps us understand what the poor "look like" and, thereby, how different policies or economic changes might affect them. Of course, the enormous diversity of economic and social situations among the poor cannot be fully captured by simply demographic categories. Rather, they present only a broad picture, which may require additional detail for specific purposes.

Changes in the composition of poverty are first analyzed when the absolute perspective is used. Because findings based on the relative measure were quite similar, we have included only a short discussion of them. Statistics on relative poverty may be found in Appendix B.

The composition of the poor is determined by the interaction of two factors. Persons who are members of a group with an incidence of poverty greater (less) than the average incidence will be found more (less) frequently in the poverty population than in the general population. Second, groups that include a large portion of the *total* population will tend to be heavily represented among the poor, unless the first factor acts to offset this.[12]

Extending this analysis, we see that changes in the composition of poverty can be traced to two similar factors. First, the incidence of poverty of each group may not be changing at the same rate. If the overall incidence falls but the incidence for a particular group declines more slowly than average (or remains constant or rises), this group will become a larger component of the poverty population. Conversely, groups whose incidence drops faster than the average will form a smaller fraction of the poor. Second, and equally important, the demographic composition of the entire population—poor and nonpoor alike—may be shifting. For example, as the whole population becomes better educated, the average level of education in the poverty population will also tend to rise (unless the first factor counteracts this). In the next several pages, we shall use these relationships to understand better the observed compositional changes within the absolute poverty population.

Race and Sex of Head

In 1965, 48 percent of all poor persons—nearly one-half—lived in households with white male heads (line 1, Table 4.3).[13] Another 20 percent were living with nonwhite male heads. Households with white female heads contained 19 percent of the poor. Those with nonwhite female heads accounted for 13 percent. Female-headed households were much more heavily concentrated among the poor than among the general population (only 12 percent of *all* persons lived in such households) because the incidence of poverty for these households was far above the average (see line 3 of Table 4.3). Conversely, while the incidence of poverty was well below average

TABLE 4.3.   PERSONS IN ABSOLUTE POVERTY ACCORDING TO RACE
AND SEX OF HEAD OF HOUSEHOLD
(in percentages)

	White Male	Nonwhite Male	White Female	Nonwhite Female	All
Composition of the poor					
1965	48.0	20.1	18.6	13.3	100
1972	39.1	13.5	27.5	19.9	100
Incidence of poverty					
1965	9.5	35.8	31.9	66.2	15.6
1972	6.1	19.5	29.7	57.4	11.9
Composition of total population					
1965	79.0	8.8	9.1	3.2	100
1972	76.6	8.2	11.0	4.1	100

Source: Tabulations of Survey of Economic Opportunity and Current Population Survey tape files.

for persons living with white male heads, they were almost one-half of the poverty population because 79 percent of the nation's people fell into this category.

By 1972, a dramatic shift in the race–sex composition of the poor had occurred. Only 39 percent were living with white male heads and only 14 percent with nonwhite male heads (line 2, Table 4.3). Persons in female-headed units represented 47 percent of the poor. Households with white and nonwhite female heads contributed equally to this large increase. If this trend continues, the poverty population will become dominated by female-headed living units.

This important change reflects the effects of both factors discussed above. The proportion of *all* persons living in female-headed households steadily rose from 12 to 15 percent over this period (lines 5 and 6 of Table 4.3). This accounted for part of the change. Second, the incidence of poverty among people in units with female heads declined very little compared to the average incidence of absolute poverty (compare lines 3 and 4 of the table). The average incidence dropped from 15.6 to 11.9 percent—24 percent of the way to zero. But the incidence for persons living with white (nonwhite) females heads only fell 7 (14) percent, despite the increasing labor force participation of women and rising transfer benefits during these years.

The slower-than-average decline in incidence for persons in female-headed units meant, of course, that the incidence for persons in male-headed households fell at a faster rate. For people living with nonwhite male heads, poverty incidence dropped from 36 to 20 percent—45 percent of the way to zero. This rate of decline was faster than the white male rate. This suggests that while various factors have caused a higher portion of persons in nonwhite male-headed households to be poor in any year, these factors have not prevented this group from escaping poverty faster than the white one.

Age of Head

Persons living in households where the head was young—age twenty-two or less in Table 4.4—accounted for 5.2 percent of the poverty population, but only 2.7 percent of the total population in 1965. In that year, members of households with aged (over sixty-five years of age) heads were 19.6 percent of the poor but only 11.1 percent of the entire populace. People living with heads who were in the three middle age-groups, in turn, were less prevalent among the poor than among all persons, though they still accounted for 75 percent of the poor. This age composition reflected the relatively high incidence of poverty among persons in units with young and elderly heads. More than 30 percent of the young group and about 28 percent of the aged were poor, while the average level of poverty was 15.6 percent.

These above-average levels of poverty accord with our expectations. Young household heads are either attending school or just beginning their careers. Earnings opportunities for students are limited to summer or part-time work. Young workers are distinguished by their low levels of experience and seniority, high unemployment, and rapid job turnover—characteristics that tend to produce lower-than-average earnings. At the other end of the age scale, a combination of social mores, the career structure, and reduced stamina dictates full or partial retirement for most persons over sixty-five. The resulting loss of income is often not completely replaced by private pensions and Social Security. Moreover, the elderly who continue to work tend to receive lower wages than middle-aged employees.[14]

TABLE 4.4.   PERSONS IN ABSOLUTE POVERTY ACCORDING TO AGE
OF HEAD OF HOUSEHOLD
(in percentages)

	Years of Age					
	14–22	23–36	37–50	51–64	65 and Above	All
Composition of the poor						
1965	5.2	29.3	28.5	17.5	19.6	100
1972	8.1	31.5	25.5	16.4	18.7	100
Incidence of poverty						
1965	30.4	15.7	12.0	13.6	27.6	15.6
1972	27.2	12.2	9.0	9.4	19.2	11.9
Composition of total population						
1965	2.7	29.2	37.0	20.0	11.1	100
1972	3.5	30.7	33.6	20.6	11.6	100

Source: Tabulations of Survey of Economic Opportunity and Current Population Survey
tape files.

Between 1965 and 1972, the age composition of the poor varied
only marginally. The share of the poor in the youngest category rose
to 8.1 percent. This largely reflected the slower-than-average decline
in incidence for this group, but a rise in the fraction of all persons
living in such households also played a role. Persons in living units
with elderly heads became a smaller proportion of the poor. Because
these households contained a slightly greater share of the *whole*
population in 1972 than in 1965, the decrease indicates that this
group's incidence fell faster than average. This relatively rapid gain
can be attributed to the growth of Social Security benefits in the
early 1970s (see Chapter 6 for more discussion of this point).

Education of Head

In 1965, persons in living units with poorly educated heads (zero to
eight years of school) formed 60 percent of the poor but only 30
percent of the entire population (Table 4.5). In contrast, less than 7

TABLE 4.5.   PERSONS IN ABSOLUTE POVERTY ACCORDING TO
EDUCATION OF HEAD OF HOUSEHOLD
(in percentages)

	Years of Schooling			
	0–8	*9–12*	*13 or More*	*All*
Composition of the poor				
1965	59.5	34.0	6.5	100
1972	42.5	47.3	10.3	100
Incidence of poverty				
1965	30.8	11.1	4.7	15.6
1972	23.0	10.8	4.4	11.9
Composition of total population				
1965	30.2	48.0	21.8	100
1972	21.6	51.3	27.1	100

*Source: Tabulations of Survey of Economic Opportunity and Current Population Survey
tape files.*

percent of the poor came from households whose heads attended or
graduated from college, while such households contained 22 percent
of the population. The other 34 percent of the poor were found in
households in which the head had received some high school education. This pattern appeared because heads with low levels of schooling have tended to earn less than the better educated and, therefore,
have been more likely to be poor (see line 5 of Table 4.5).

Seven years later, only 43 percent of the poor were found in living
units where the head received only zero to eight years of education.
About 47 percent lived with heads who attended postsecondary
schools. This enormous shift in the educational composition of
poverty can be principally traced to the marked change in the
educational composition of *all* households' heads. Persons in households with poorly educated heads represented only 22 percent of the
population in 1972, versus 30 percent in 1965. Thus, as suggested
earlier, a large drop in the percentage of poor persons who lived with
such heads would be expected. This tendency was reinforced by the
faster-than-average decline in the incidence of poverty for the zero to
eight years of school group (compare lines 3 and 4 of Table 4.5).

Work Experience of Head

One-eighth of the nation lived with heads who did not work at all during 1965 (Table 4.6, line 5). But one-third of the poverty population lived in such households because the likelihood of poverty was rather high (41.4 percent) for this category compared to the average (15.6 percent). That the head did no work did not guarantee poverty, of course. Property and transfer income and earnings of other family members kept out of poverty more than one-half of the people in households in which the head did not work.

Less than 6 percent of the total population lived with heads who worked between one and twenty-six weeks in 1965, but, because the incidence of poverty was so high for this group, it contained 16 percent of the poor. Indeed, poverty was slightly *more common* among this group than among the group working zero weeks. This surprising finding reflects the nature of the American transfer system. Many people in the zero-weeks-worked class live with heads who are retired, disabled, female, or otherwise entitled to transfer income that, combined with their property income, is enough to keep them out of poverty. In contrast, a large fraction of those in the group that worked one to twenty-six weeks are likely to be ineligible for most transfer benefits and, through a combination of factors like low wages, illness, and sporadic unemployment, cannot earn enough to avoid poverty. They, along with the poor persons with heads who worked more than twenty-six weeks, fill the ranks of the "working poor."

The incidence of poverty was lowest among persons whose heads labored throughout 1965. Nonetheless, 35 percent of the poor were in this class because it contained such a large share (69 percent) of the total population.

By 1972, the composition of the poverty population with respect to the work experience of household heads had greatly changed (compare lines 1 and 2 of Table 4.6). Persons whose heads worked all year made up less than one-quarter of the poor. Still, this meant that even in 1972, nearly 6 million persons lived in households in which a full year's earnings of the head were not sufficient to maintain a minimally decent standard of living. Almost one-half of the poor were found in living units in which the head did not work. The trend has been toward a poverty population whose heads-of-households are attached less and less to the labor market and, hence, are less able to earn their way out of poverty.

This conclusion should not be interpreted as saying that a hard core of poor families whose heads have not been working for many years is becoming a larger fraction of all poor families. A recent

TABLE 4.6.   PERSONS IN ABSOLUTE POVERTY ACCORDING TO WEEKS
WORKED BY HEAD OF HOUSEHOLD
(in percentages)

| | Weeks Worked | | | | |
	0	1–26	27–49	50–52	All
Composition of the poor					
1965	33.1	15.9	19.5	35.1	100
1972	47.2	17.4	12.0	23.5	100
Incidence of poverty					
1965	41.4	44.3	19.4	7.9	15.6
1972	37.3	33.7	12.8	4.2	11.9
Composition of total population					
1965	12.5	5.6	12.8	69.1	100
1972	15.2	6.2	11.2	67.4	100

Source: Tabulations of Survey of Economic Opportunity and Current Population Survey
tape files.

study has shown that such a group is very small.[15] Rather, we are
making the point that in any given year, those who fall into poverty
have been more weakly attached to the labor market in recent years
than in the mid-1960s. This trend is consistent with our earlier
observations on the shift toward female-headed families in the poverty population.

This compositional shift mainly reflected unequal rates of decline
in the incidence of poverty of the different work-experience groups.
Persons living with heads working a full year exhibited the largest
percentage decline in incidence (from 7.9 to 4.2 percent, 47 percent
of the way to zero). The group that worked twenty-seven to forty-
nine weeks showed the second biggest decrease, while the zero-
weeks-worked category had the smallest. In short, rising real wages
during 1965–1972 brought the greatest reduction in poverty to those
who worked the most.

Region of Residence

The preceding discussion has revolved around the relationship between poverty and the personal characteristics of household heads.

We now switch the emphasis to the association between geographic variables and poverty.

Poverty has been concentrated in the South. This region contained 48 percent of the poor in 1965, but only 31 percent of the entire populace (Table 4.7, lines 1 and 5). All three other geographic areas had smaller shares of the poor than their shares of total population. This relationship resulted from the high level of poverty in the South relative to the rest of the nation. For example, while 25 percent of southern residents were poor, only 10 percent of those living in the Northeast and 12.9 percent of those in the West were below the poverty line. The difference in incidence was but a reflection of the lagging pace of industrialization and economic growth in the South.

Between 1965 and 1972, incidence of poverty fell fastest in the South (though it still remained well above average). Hence, the concentration of poverty in this region dropped to about 45 percent. The decline would have been greater, except that the percentage of all people that lived in the South had risen slightly. Incidence declined more slowly than average in the West, where there was actually an increase after 1968 (not shown), and in the Northeast. As a result, a larger share of the poor lived in these two regions in 1972 than seven years earlier.

TABLE 4.7. PERSONS IN ABSOLUTE POVERTY ACCORDING TO REGION OF RESIDENCE
(in percentages)

	Northeast	Northcentral	South	West	All
Composition of poor					
1965	15.7	22.4	48.0	13.9	100
1972	17.4	21.5	44.6	16.5	100
Incidence of poverty					
1965	10.0	12.5	24.5	12.9	15.6
1972	8.8	9.3	17.0	11.2	11.9
Composition of total population					
1965	24.4	28.2	30.6	16.8	100
1972	23.6	27.5	31.3	17.6	100

Source: Tabulations of Survey of Economic Opportunity and Current Population Survey tape files.

Location of Residence

Table 4.8 shows that in 1965 more than one-half of the poor lived in nonmetropolitan areas; about 31 percent lived in the central city of a metropolitan area (SMSA), and 16 percent were found in the surrounding communities. This distribution largely resulted from the differentials in poverty incidence among these locations—about 24 percent of all persons living in nonmetropolitan areas, were poor, 16 percent in the central city, and only 7 percent in the suburbs.

The economic forces behind such differences are easily described. The nature of American economic development has created more employment opportunities and higher wages in SMSAs than elsewhere. Inside metropolitan areas a variety of mutually reinforcing factors—among these, changing transportation systems, the desire of the more affluent to own homes, steep central-city taxes, and migration from rural areas—have combined to concentrate low-income households in the central city and generate a steady flow of upper-income ones to the suburbs.[16]

TABLE 4.8.   PERSONS IN ABSOLUTE POVERTY ACCORDING TO LOCATION OF RESIDENCE
(in percentages)

	Central City	Suburban	Non-metropolitan	All
Composition of the poor				
1965	30.9	15.8	53.3	100
1972	37.3	21.9	40.8	100
Incidence of poverty				
1965	15.7	7.2	23.8	15.6
1972	14.7	6.8	15.4	11.9
Composition of total population				
1965	30.7	34.3	35.1	100
1972	30.2	38.3	31.5	100

Source: Tabulations of Survey of Economic Opportunity and Current Population Survey tape files.

The locational composition of poverty was quite different by the early 1970s. Only about 40 percent of the poor had homes outside of SMSAs, while the concentration of poverty in both central cities and suburbs increased sharply. Though a small shift toward suburban location contributed to this change, it was caused mainly by the rapid reduction in poverty outside of SMSAs. Incidence in these locations declined 35 percent, while poverty in central cities and suburbs barely fell. Indeed, in cities the trend has been upward since 1968 (not shown).

The Changing Composition of the Relative Poverty Population

Up to this point, the discussion of changes in composition has focused solely on the absolute poor. When the relative poor were studied, we discovered that changes in demographic composition formed the same overall patterns and trends as those revealed when the absolute approach was used. However, for the race–sex and work-experience variables, the shifts were smaller than those outlined above. For example, persons in households with female heads rose from 32 to 44 percent of the relative poor between 1965 and 1972. The corresponding absolute figure in 1972 was 48 percent. Composition changes along age, education, and location dimensions were virtually identical under the two approaches. The regional distribution of relative poverty changed more than did that of absolute poverty, but in the same direction. (See Appendix B for the tables on relative poverty).

II. A MULTIVARIATE ANALYSIS OF POVERTY

The tables presented above have been helpful for uncovering some general changes in the incidence and composition of poverty and for comparing the changes under two different poverty definitions. However, restricting one's attention to these tables may lead to faulty inferences regarding which variables have been most closely associated with poverty and the extent to which the associations have changed over time. For example, Table 4.5 reveals that the incidence of absolute poverty among persons with poorly educated heads was always above the average. But the table gives no indication of the *independent* contribution of low education to the likelihood of being poor, nor of how the contribution changed over time. It may be that poorly educated heads are older than average, live more often in the South, or more often have some other characteristics associated with a higher incidence of poverty. The independent effects, therefore, can be captured only by addressing the question, How do the chances of being in poverty differ for households with, say, one level of education (of head) versus those with another level of education, holding constant other characteristics related to poverty?

Technical Notes

A number of statistical techniques are available for estimating the independent relationship of various family characteristics to the chances of being poor. While ordinary multiple regression analysis is often used for similar problems, special technical considerations argue against its use here. Instead, we have chosen another approach that yields more accurate estimates.

The technique estimates the change in the *odds* of being poor associated with, for example, being a family with a female head versus being one with a male head, holding other characteristics constant. The odds of being poor are not the same as the probability of being in poverty, but the two concepts are closely related. If the number of poor families with a given characteristic is a and the number of nonpoor families is b then, with respect to the characteristic in question, the odds of being poor are a/b, while the probability of poverty is $a/(a + b)$. If the odds are x, the corresponding probability is $x/(1 + x)$. Hence, as the odds rise, so does the probability. Consider Table 4.9. We observe that the odds of a male-headed family being poor were $4340/39,213 = .11$. The corresponding probability was $4340/43,553 = .10$. Similarly, the odds of poverty for female-headed families were $1648/3284 = .50$ and the probability was $.33$ $[= .50/(1 + .50)]$.

TABLE 4.9. POVERTY STATUS OF FAMILIES, IN 1965, BY SEX OF HEAD (in thousands)

	Male	Female
Poor	4,340	1,648
Nonpoor	39,213	3,284
Total	43,553	4,932

Source: Tabulations of Survey of Economic Opportunity and Current Population Survey tape files.

We have estimated the independent relationships of seven demographic variables to the odds of being poor.[17] Limitations of the data that arise when this technique is used permit the inclusion of only a limited number of variables. We have selected those that are usually regarded as having the most important influence on poverty status. The seven variables are age of head (categorized as under thirty, thirty—sixty-four, sixty-five and over), sex, race (white and other nonblack, or black), education (divided into zero—eight, nine—twelve, and thirteen or more years of schooling), type of household (family or unrelated individual), region (South or elsewhere), and location of home (in an SMSA or not in one).

The estimates produced by our method represent the *multiplicative* effect of each variable on the odds. The predicted odds of being poor for a given household are found by multiplying the coefficients associated with its demographic traits, as will be shown.[18] In this situation, a variable whose coefficient is estimated to equal one has no effect on the odds, since multiplying the odds by a factor of one does not change them. Coefficients greater (less) than one increase (decrease) the odds. From this, it follows that the coefficients of those variables most closely related to poverty will be furthest away from one.

Odds of Being in Absolute Poverty

With these technical preliminaries established, let us consider the results. Table 4.10 gives estimates based on the definition of absolute poverty for 1972. (Results for 1965 and those based on the relative measure are in Appendix C, along with greater technical discussion.) Because the type of household, sex of its head, and region of residence crucially affect the odds, we separate the findings for each region, for families and unrelated persons, and for each sex.

The findings can be readily summarized and, for the most part, do not contradict the patterns shown in the preceding tables. Being black, having little education, being female, living as an unrelated individual, living in the South, or living outside a major urban area were all *independently* associated with increased chances of poverty. We shall comment briefly on the findings for several variables.

With all other characteristics held fixed, the odds are higher for blacks to be poor than for the rest of the population. Being a black family head increases the odds by a factor of 1.81; in contrast, for whites the odds are lowered by a multiple of .55. The same general relationship holds for unrelated individuals.

TABLE 4.10.   THE EFFECT OF DEMOGRAPHIC CHARACTERISTICS ON
THE ODDS OF BEING POOR IN 1972
(absolute poverty definition)

	(1)	(2)	(3)	(4)	(5)	(6)	(7)	(8)
			Non-South				South	
	Families		Unrelated Individuals		Families		Unrelated Individuals	
	Male	Female	Male	Female	Male	Female	Male	Female
Constant	.10	.45	.34	.70	.13	.57	.43	1.05
White and other	.55	.55	.70	.70	.55	.55	.70	.70
Black	1.81	1.81	1.43	1.43	1.81	1.81	1.43	1.43
Age 14-29	1.23	3.52	1.66	1.49	1.23	3.52	1.66	1.49
Age 30-64	.79	.86	.69	.65	.79	.86	.69	.65
Age 65 or over	1.03	.32	.87	1.03	1.03	.32	.87	1.03
0 8 years school	2.14	2.17	1.85	1.88	3.04	3.08	2.62	2.66
9-12 years school	.86	1.13	.68	.89	.90	1.19	.71	.94
13+ years school	.55	.41	.80	.60	.37	.27	.53	.40
Lives in SMSA	.73	.73	.73	.73	.73	.73	.73	.73
Lives outside SMSA	1.37	1.37	1.37	1.37	1.37	1.37	1.37	1.37

Source: See Appendix C for description of our methods

Note: Observation of this table shows that the effects of race on the odds of poverty are
identical for males and females, and between non-South and South, but differ for families
and unrelated individuals. Similarly, the age coefficients differ for males and females and for
families and unrelated individuals, but are constant across regions. The education estimates
differ for all region-sex-household-type categories, while the location ones are uniform.

These patterns reflect the presence or absence of interactions between demographic
variables identified by our analysis. The pattern for race indicates that one's race and
household type had a joint effect on the odds as well as separate effects. We combined the
three effects to obtain the displayed coefficients. The race effect, we see, is more
pronounced for families than for unrelated individuals. The age variable interacts with both
sex and type of household, but not with region, in influencing the odds. Education interacts
with sex, region, and household type. In contrast the effect of location on the odds was
independent of other demographic variables.

Turning to the age variable, we find for male and female individuals a pattern similar to that in Table 4.3—higher odds in young and old age brackets compared to the middle ones. For families with female heads, this is not the case. Apparently, the independent effects of age decrease the odds of poverty as age rises for this group.

The pattern for education is as we expect. Within each region—sex—household-type category, higher levels of schooling are strongly associated with lower chances of being poor. Residing outside an SMSA is independently associated with increased chances of being poor. This last effect is constant across regions, sexes, and household types.[19]

The figures in Table 4.10 refer to the year 1972. When we tested to see if any of the demographic associations with poverty were weaker or stronger back in 1965, we found only one significant difference: The age effect was a little stronger then. The 1965 constant terms for the eight categories were all higher by 45 percent, however. (The meaning of this change will be clarified later.)

The unchanging coefficients of the demographic variables mean that the odds did not change more rapidly for one subgroup than for another over the seven years. For example, we could not reject the hypothesis that the independent effect of education on poverty had not changed. Therefore, the unusually rapid decline in poverty that we observed among families with poorly educated heads (see Table 4.5) did not reflect a decrease in the independent association of poor education with poverty. Rather, to produce the pattern in Table 4.5, the distribution of the other socioeconomic characteristics of poorly educated heads must have been changing in a way that promoted less poverty—by 1972, a greater fraction of them may have been male or white or living outside the South, for example. The same conclusion holds for the independent relationship between poverty and race—it did not change. So the faster decline in poverty among persons in households with black male heads compared to those with white male heads (see Table 4.3) was accounted for by differing changes in the distribution of nonracial factors across these two groups, not by a decline in the "pure" race effect. For example, the level of education among black males shifted up more quickly than that among white males.

Odds of Being in Relative Poverty

Using the relative poverty measure produces estimates very similar to Table 4.10 for each demographic variable. In the relative analysis, no change over time in *any* coefficient was observed. The major difference from the absolute results is that the constant terms also did not change significantly. Hence, for all groups in the population, the odds of relative poverty did not vary in a statistically meaningful direction between 1965 and 1972. Appendix C may be consulted for the numerical results.

Illustrative Predictions of the Chances of Being Poor

An example will demonstrate how the estimates can be used to predict the odds of being poor for any particular group in the population. Consider a *family* headed by a *black female,* aged *twenty-seven,* with *ten years of education,* living in a *major city not in the South.* To determine the odds that such a family would be officially poor in 1972, we use Table 4.10, column 2. The constant term .45 is multiplied by 1.81 for the race effect, 3.52 for age, 1.13 for education, and .73 for SMSA residence. The resulting odds are 2.37. The predicted probability that such a household was poor in 1972 equals 2.37/(1 + 2.37) = .70.

The larger constant term for 1965 means that the odds of poverty were uniformly higher for all households in 1965 than in 1972. In the preceding example, if we had computed the odds for the same household in 1965, we would have used the same numbers, except the constant would have been .65 instead of .45, and the coefficient on age would have been 3.45 instead of 3.52 (see Appendix C). The resulting odds would have been 3.35 and the corresponding probability, .77.

The above example could be thought of as representing the stereotypical family with a black female head on welfare. The probability that such a family would be poor in 1972 under the official definition, even if it received public assistance, was quite high. Table 4.11 compares this finding to the results for fourteen other representative types in the population in both 1965 and 1972. The patterns in the table, of course, are only rough illustrations that depend on the choice of demographic variables used to define each group.

Two conclusions are clear. First, the probabilities spanned a wide range in both years. In 1972, for example, several groups had quite small chances of poverty compared to the average (see lines 10, 12, 13, 14). One would expect poverty to be rare among middle-aged nonmetropolitan families (line 12) and well-educated young ones (line 13). But it is surprising to see how low the probability was for urban, white elderly couples (line 10). Other demographic categories had probabilities of .5 or higher (lines 1, 2, 11).

TABLE 4.11. PREDICTED PROBABILITY OF BEING POOR FOR
REPRESENTATIVE GROUPS
(absolute poverty definition)

		1965	1972
1.	Black, female head with children[a]	.77	.70
2.	Southern, poorly educated black family[b]	.64	.55
3.	Black, urban elderly woman[c]	.55	.40
4.	White, urban elderly woman[d]	.37	.25
5.	Young, well-educated white male[e]	.38	.30
6.	Young black male[f]	.36	.29
7.	Middle-age female head[g]	.29	.25
8.	Black, male head[h]	.13	.11
9.	Poorly educated, white male head[i]	.14	.11
10.	Elderly couple I—metropolitan white[j]	.06	.04
11.	Elderly couple II—nonmetropolitan black[k]	.65	.51
12.	Middle-age nonmetropolitan family[l]	.08	.07
13.	Well-educated young family[m]	.03	.02
14.	Single, middle-age man[n]	.10	.09
15.	Single, middle-age woman[o]	.14	.12

Note: All calculations based on tables in Appendix C (which are more detailed than Table
4.10).

[a]black, female, family, age 14-29, 9-12 years school, non-South, in SMSA
[b]black, male, family, age 14-29, 0-8 years school, South, not in SMSA
[c]black, female, individual, age 65+, 9-12 years school, non-South, in SMSA
[d]white, female, individual, age 65+, 9-12 years school, non-South, in SMSA
[e]white, male, individual, age 14-29, 13+ years school, non-South, not in SMSA
[f]black, male, individual, age 14-29, 9-12 years school, non-South, in SMSA
[g]white, female, family, age 30–64, 9–12 years school, non-South, not in SMSA
[h]black, male, family, age 30-64, 9 12 years school, South, in SMSA
[i]white male, family, age 30-64, 0-8 years school, South, in SMSA
[j]white, male, family, age 65+, 9-12 years school, non-South, in SMSA
[k]black, male, family, age 65+, 0-8 years school, South, not in SMSA
[l]white, male, family, age 30-64, 9-12 years school, South, not in SMSA
[m]white, male, family, age 14-29, 13+ years school, South, in SMSA
[n]white, male, individual, age 30-64, 13+ years school, non-South, in SMSA
[o]white, female, individual, age 30-64, 13+ years school, non-South, in SMSA

Second, the probabilities declined for all groups between 1965 and
1972.[20] Thus, the concern expressed by advocates of antipoverty
policies in the mid-1960s that a sizeable core of low-income households—especially those with aged or female heads—would hardly be
touched by economic growth was, in retrospect, unwarranted. The
benefits of economic growth, which led to higher earnings and larger
transfer payments, decreased the odds of poverty among all segments
of society.

Several of the examples in Table 4.11 provide interesting contrasts
with each other. Consider lines 3 and 4. The characteristics defining

these two sets of women are identical except for race. The effect of being black, therefore, increased the probability from .25 to .40 in 1972. Examples 8 and 9 present male-headed families living in similar areas. One—line 8—has a black head with a high school education; the other had a white head who completed only eight years of school or less. The probabilities are nearly identical—the positive effect of better education was offset by being black. Lines 10 and 11 compare two elderly couples. Metropolitan white ones enjoy small chances of being poor, while nonmetropolitan black ones, who are likely to be trapped in the economic backwaters, have a very high likelihood of suffering poverty. Finally, the last two cases examine single men and women with similar demographic characteristics. The economic barriers facing females, it can be surmised, increased the chances of poverty from .09 to .12 in 1972.

III. SUMMARY

In this chapter, various recent trends in posttransfer poverty have been presented. Our findings can be summarized as follows:

- Absolute poverty affected 15.6 percent of the population in 1965. By 1972, the incidence had fallen to 11.9 percent. Most of this improvement occurred in the sixties; very modest gains have been made since then.

- The absolute income gap declined from $13.8 billion in 1965 to $12.2 billion in 1968 (both in 1972 dollars). By 1972, however, the gap had risen to $12.5 billion. The average gap per poor person rose by $50 in this period.

- A relative definition of poverty yields very different findings. Relative poverty among persons, families, and unrelated persons has been virtually constant since 1965. Those on the bottom have not improved their economic status relative to the general standard of living.

- The relative income gap steadily grew from $13.6 billion to $19.3 billion. And the per person gap moved up by $130.

- In contrast, a third view, which incorporates adjustments in the income measure for taxes, in-kind transfers, and underreporting, suggests a sizeable reduction in poverty and the poverty gap—as defined by the SSA—between 1968 and 1972.

● The composition of absolute poverty changed substantially along several important dimensions. Compared to the 1965 poor, those below the poverty line in 1972 were more frequently living in households with female heads, with young heads, with heads who did not work during the year, and with heads who had high school or college educations. Nonetheless, in 1972 a majority of the poor still lived with male or middle-aged heads, and a substantial fraction resided with poorly educated heads or ones who had worked a full year. A higher proportion of the poor lived outside the South and in metropolitan areas in 1972 than seven years earlier. Shifts in the demographic composition of relative poverty were similar.

● A multivariate analysis of the socioeconomic characteristics associated with absolute poverty was conducted. The independent effects of variables such as education, age, or location on the chances of being poor were generally in agreement with the patterns displayed in the simple cross tabulations. There was a wide range for various household types in the predicted probability of being poor.

● This analysis further showed that the odds of absolute poverty declined between 1965 and 1972 at essentially the same rate for each detailed demographic subgroup. Hence, the cross tabulations that reveal unusually rapid declines in absolute poverty for a very broad group (families with poorly educated heads, for example) must have arisen primarily from shifts in the composition of that group with respect to other variables.

● A similar statistical analysis of relative poverty yielded the same associations between demographic variables and the chances of poverty but found that the odds of relative poverty did not decline over time.

NOTES

[1] For an excellent analysis of changes in poverty from 1967 to 1971, see *Five Thousand American Families—Patterns of Economic Progress,* volumes I and II, by James N. Morgan et al., (Ann Arbor, Michigan: Institute for Social Research, 1974). This study uses different data and takes a different analytical approach than we do.

[2] Published government statistics on poverty always refer to the posttransfer poor.

[3] For 1965, the data come from the Survey of Economic Opportunity, a special survey conducted for OEO. Because of sampling variability and methodological differences, the figures differ from those published by the Bureau of the Census, in U.S., Department of Commerce, Bureau of the Census, "Poverty in the United States, 1959 to 1968," *Current Population Reports: Consumer Income.* Series P-60, No. 68 (December 31, 1969) (Washing-

ton, D.C.: U.S. Government Printing Office, 1969), (C3.186:P60/68). These were derived from the Current Population Survey (CPS). For 1968, 1970, and 1972, our data bases are the CPS computer tape files. There are published tabulations describing the official poverty population of 1973. However, because the raw data are needed to estimate statistics on pretransfer poverty and on relative poverty, and we want to compare relative to absolute poverty over time, 1972 is the last year in our analysis.

[4]We have chosen to discuss persons in order to simplify the exposition of the next section. For each topic in that section, we need present only one table, while if families and unrelated individuals were analyzed, two tables would be necessary. Generally, the results we obtain are very similar to the patterns found when families and unrelated persons are examined separately. However, complete tables using family and unrelated-individual data are in Appendix B.

The distinction between families and unrelated persons is often used to prevent any distortion produced by lumping the two groups together, because poverty has been much more prevalent among unrelated persons than among families. By weighting all poor living units by the number of members in them to yield poor persons, our approach carries this reasoning to its logical conclusion. (After all, large families are more likely than couples to be poor, so counting each family as one unit produces distortion.)

[5]U.S., Department of Commerce, Social and Economic Statistics Administration, Bureau of the Census, "Characteristics of the Low-Income Population, 1972," *Current Population Reports: Consumer Income,* Series P-60, No. 91 (December 1973) (Washington, D.C.: U.S. Government Printing Office, 1973), pp. 143, 144, (C56.218: P-60/91).

[6]"The head of a family is usually the person regarded as the head by members of the family. Women are not classified as head if their husbands are resident members of the family at the time of the survey." "Poverty in the United States, 1959 to 1968," U.S. Department of Commerce, Bureau of the Census.

[7]Cash transfers as reported by households that were interviewed have fallen about 20 percent below total benefits paid according to government records.

[8]Timothy M. Smeeding, "Measuring the Economic Welfare of Low Income Households, and the Anti-Poverty Effectiveness of Cash and Non-Cash Transfer Programs," (Ph.D. diss., University of Wisconsin-Madison, 1975). He provides empirical results only for 1968, 1970, and 1972. In determining poverty status, this study uses a different notion of the reporting unit than we do. We distinguish between families and unrelated individuals as defined by the Bureau of the Census. If a census-defined family and unrelated individual reside in the same dwelling unit (a live-in maid and her employer, for example), Smeeding combines them into one larger unit, arguing that there is probably income sharing between the family and individual and, hence, they should be considered as one economic unit.

[9]Ibid. Smeeding does not report data on poor persons. To convert his figures on poor living units into the number of poor persons, we multiply his estimate of poor units by the average number of persons per poor household as measured by our data.

[10]See Appendix B for corresponding tables for families and unrelated persons.

[11]Smeeding, "Measuring the Economic Welfare."

[12]More formally, consider a total population $P = \sum_{i=1}^{n} p_i$, where the p_i are groups in the population, and a poverty population $R = \sum_{i=1}^{n} r_i$, where the r_i are groups of poor people corresponding to the p_i. We have the identity $r_i/R = (p_i/P) \cdot (r_i/p_i) \cdot P/R = (p_i/P) \cdot [(r_i/p_i) \div (R/P)]$. Now, r_i/R is the share of the poor found in Group i and p_i/P is the share of the total population in Group i. Also, r_i/p_i is the incidence of poverty for Group i and R/P is the overall incidence of poverty. Hence, the share of the poor in Group i is higher, the higher the total population in the Group (p_i/P), and the higher the incidence for Group i is in relation to the overall, average incidence $[(r_i/p_i) \div R/P]$.

[13]The *number* of persons in households with white male heads may be found by multiplying the total number of poor persons in 1965 (29.9 million) by .480, the fraction living with white male heads. The same may be done for any other group in this table and in Tables 4.4 to 4.8.

[14]Older workers tend to be less educated and in poorer health than persons of prime working age. Labor market discrimination against the aged also contributes.

[15]James N. Morgan et al., *Five Thousand American Families.*

[16]See Edwin S. Mills, *Urban Economics* (Glenview: Scott, Foresman and Company, 1972).

[17]While we hesitate to attribute much causal significance to this model, the estimates at least measure the relative strengths of these seven correlates of poverty and determine if they changed over time. The results provide useful descriptive statistics.

[18]The interpretation of the coefficients generated by our approach differs somewhat from the usual practice. In most applications, coefficients represent the *additive* impact of the independent variables upon the dependent one.

[19]Identifying the relationships between sex, household type, region, and the odds of poverty is not as easy as seeing the patterns for the variables discussed in the text. To see that living in the South raises the chances of poverty, note that the constant term for each sex—household-type category (male-head—family, for example) is higher in the "South" columns. As the example in the text will show, a higher constant leads to greater odds. Similarly, within each region—household-type category (non-South—family, for example), the male constant is less than the female one. And within each region—sex grouping (such as the non-South male), the constant for families is smaller than the one for unrelated individuals.

[20]We observe that the decrease in the probability of poverty, whether measured by the difference between the two predictions or the percentage decline, was not the same for all groups. This does not contradict our finding that the odds of poverty decreased uniformly (except for a shift in the age effect) for all groups. To see this, suppose the odds of poverty in 1965 were .5 for one group and 1.0 for a second. The corresponding probabilities would be .33 and .50. Now, assume that by 1972 the odds had declined by 40 percent for each group to .3 and .6 respectively. The new probabilities are .23 and .38. The percentage decline is greater for group 1 and the arithmetic difference is bigger for group 2, even though the odds dropped equally. The "paradox" arises because of the mathematical

relationship between a probability, p, and the corresponding odds, $x : x = \dfrac{p}{1-p}, p = \dfrac{x}{1+x}$.

5

The Effect of Macroeconomic Conditions on the Poor

Chapter 4 has presented the changing character of American poverty. The next step is to ask, How did these changes occur? This chapter and Chapter 6 take steps toward answering this question.

One approach to analyzing changes in posttransfer poverty over time begins with the observation that, in any given year, the economy generates a set of earnings, property incomes, and private transfers among households. The magnitude and distribution of this money determines the level of poverty that exists before government transfers are added to incomes. Many of these persons who are poor before government transfers receive cash (and in-kind) transfers from public funds that raise them over the poverty line, so that posttransfer poverty will be less common than pretransfer poverty.[1]

As time passes, posttransfer poverty can be changed by two forces. First, economic fluctuations and structural or demographic changes in the society may generate a different level of pretransfer poverty. Second, changes in the system of transfers—new benefit schedules, revised eligibility rules, changing numbers of recipients—can then eliminate a larger or smaller amount of poverty to reach a new level of posttransfer poverty. Hence, the observed difference in posttransfer poverty from one time to another can be divided into a pretransfer component and a transfer component.

Admittedly, it is an oversimplification to divide the forces that affect poverty into two kinds: those that change pretransfer poverty and those that attack posttransfer poverty. The level of pretransfer income clearly helps determine the volume of transfers. Benefits from Unemployment Insurance, public assistance, and Social Security respond to changes in earned income. Conversely, virtually all studies of labor supply show that income-maintenance programs affect labor supply decisions and, hence, earnings, especially among female and elderly workers.[2] Despite this problem, it is useful for expository purposes to consider these two components separately.

The major aim of this chapter is to analyze the relationship between pretransfer poverty and macroeconomic conditions in the 1960s and early 1970s. We first describe the history of overall economic conditions during these years to place the succeeding discussion in a wider context. Second, summary statistics on pretransfer poverty between 1965 and 1972 are presented. Third, we examine the effects of macroeconomic conditions on the poor. As in Chapter 3, results based on both absolute and relative viewpoints are discussed. Fourth, other important findings on several related issues are summarized. A review of the major points in this chapter is contained in the last section.

I. THE AMERICAN ECONOMY, 1961–1975—
AN OVERVIEW

In 1961, when President Kennedy assumed office, the economy was performing sluggishly. Unemployment stood at 6.7 percent, while real GNP had risen less than 2 percent above the 1960 level. The new Administration was committed to active government management of the economy, and took several steps to counter this recession. Government spending was increased; taxes were cut in 1962 and 1964. The policies seemed effective. Annual growth rate of real GNP averaged about 5.8 percent until 1966, while unemployment dropped to 3.8 percent. Seven million more jobs were created in this five-year period. During this expansion, inflation averaged a modest 1.6 percent per year.

Between 1966 and 1969, the unemployment rate remained below 4 percent, but real output climbed more slowly than in the early sixties. Expansion of social welfare expenditures and the war effort in Indochina, unaccompanied by tax increases, led to federal deficits of almost $9 billion in 1967 and $25 billion in 1968. These deficits, coming when the economy was already booming, created inflationary pressures. Prices rose 2.9 percent in 1967, 4.2 percent in the next year, and 5.4 percent during 1969.

The Nixon Administration attempted to counter the price rise in 1969 and 1970 with traditional deflationary tools, but only succeeded in raising the unemployment rate to 4.9 percent in 1970 and 5.9 percent in 1971. Real GNP fell slightly in 1970, then resumed an upward path in 1971. Despite the 1970 recession and rising joblessness, prices climbed 6 percent in 1970, and had risen another 2.5 percent by August 1971, when wage and price controls were declared.

During Phases I and II of Nixon's anti-inflation campaign, which lasted until January 1973, the annual rate of inflation dropped to 3.3 percent. Economic expansion was robust during this period. Unemployment declined steadily to 5 percent by January 1973, while real output jumped 6 percent. The boom continued in early 1973 but weakened as the year progressed. A combination of poor crops, rising oil prices, the oil embargo, the relaxation of Phase II controls, and other factors led to a strong burst of inflation, and the rate of price increase rose to more than 6 percent.

The economy continued to decline throughout 1974 and early 1975. Real output fell by 2.2 percent in 1974—the largest drop since 1947. Unemployment climbed steadily from about 5 percent in early 1974 to more than 8 percent by January 1975, while prices soared at an 11 percent per year rate. The overall health of the economy had not been this poor in the past twenty-five years.

II. TRENDS IN PRETRANSFER POVERTY

Broad Changes

Absolute Poverty

Absolute pretransfer poverty affected households that included 40.8 million persons—21.3 percent of the U.S. population—in 1965 (Table 5.1, upper section). After three years of strong economic growth and falling unemployment rates, 18.2 percent of the population was poor before public transfers. This rate of progress disappeared by 1970, a recession year. At that time, about 18.8 percent of all persons lived in households that did not receive enough income from private sources to lift them out of poverty. This upward trend continued

TABLE 5.1.   PRETRANSFER POVERTY, 1965-1972

	(1) Poor Persons		(2) Poor Families		(3) Poor Unrelated Individuals	
	Number (in thousands)	Incidence (in percentages)	Number (in thousands)	Incidence (in percentages)	Number (in thousands)	Incidence (in percentages
Absolute						
1965	40,790	21.3	9,445	19.5	6,164	50.7
1968	35,770	18.2	8,403	16.6	6,530	47.3
1970	37,840	18.8	8,973	17.3	7,258	47.2
1972	39,440	19.2	9,607	17.7	8,033	47.9
Relative						
1965	40,790	21.3	9,445	19.5	6,164	50.7
1968	38,650	19.7	9,024	17.9	6,714	48.7
1970	41,970	20.8	9,860	19.0	7,611	49.5
1972	45,600	22.2	11,020	20.3	8,537	50.9

Source: Tabulations of the Survey of Economic Opportunity and the Current Population Survey tapes.

into 1972, when 19.2 percent of the population was pretransfer poor. During these seven years, when average pretransfer income per household rose 15 percent, this broad indicator of absolute pretransfer poverty declined very little.

The pattern of absolute pretransfer poverty among families parallels the one just described for persons. The fraction of families that were pretransfer poor dropped from 19.5 to 16.6 percent between 1965 and 1968, then slowly rose for four years. Pretransfer poverty among unrelated individuals has been very widespread. More than 50 percent of these persons had sub-poverty-line incomes from private sources in 1965. The incidence fell to slightly more than 47 percent in 1968, remained there through 1970, then rose to nearly 48 percent by 1972.[3]

Relative Poverty

Statistics based on our relative poverty definition uncover a more discouraging pattern.[4] Between 1965 and 1968, relative pretransfer poverty dipped; it rose in the next two years; and, by 1972, a higher fraction of persons—22.2 percent—were pretransfer poor than in 1965. The incidence of relative pretransfer poverty among the population remained at this higher level in 1972. While the trends for families and unrelated individuals are slightly different, they also show that relative pretransfer poverty increased between 1965 and 1972. In other words, over these years the distribution of private incomes changed in such a way that more and more households fell so far below the median level of well-being that the incidence of relative pretransfer poverty rose.

Pretransfer Poverty Among Major Demographic Groups

These figures give a broad view of recent changes in pretransfer poverty but do not illuminate different experiences of important groups in the population. These are presented in Table 5.2, which disaggregates the family statistics according to sex, race, and age of the head, and in Table 5.3, which examines pretransfer poverty among unrelated persons classified by age and sex.

Absolute Poverty

Families with white male heads under sixty-five years of age have always had the lowest incidence of pretransfer poverty. In 1965, 8.5 percent of such families were poor before transfers. By 1972, this had fallen to 6.8 percent (20 percent of the way to zero). Families with nonwhite prime-age male heads have endured much higher levels of pretransfer poverty than their white counterparts, but the decline in incidence has been considerably faster. Over these seven years, incidence dropped from 29.5 to 17.3 percent or 41 percent of the way to zero (twice the white rate). Most of the gain occurred in the mid-1960s, but, unlike any of the other groups in the table, the downward trend continued through 1970 and 1972. This finding suggests that minority families with male heads under sixty-five have been able to earn their way over the absolute poverty line more easily than similar white families.

The patterns for nonelderly female heads sharply differ from these. For both whites and nonwhites, the incidence of pretransfer poverty greatly exceeds the corresponding male figures. This is not surprising, given the lower labor force participation rates and lower wages of women with families. For families with nonwhite female heads, incidence of pretransfer poverty has stood between 62 and 69 percent. It fell between 1965 and 1970, then returned to the 1968

TABLE 5.2. INCIDENCE OF PRETRANSFER POVERTY AMONG DEMOGRAPHIC SUBGROUPS OF FAMILIES (in percentages)

	Characteristics of Family Head						
	White Males <65	Nonwhite Males <65	White Females <65	Nonwhite Females <65	Males >65	Females >65	All
Absolute poverty							
1965	8.5	29.5	36.1	68.5	57.4	44.7	19.5
1968	6.4	19.2	36.5	66.0	51.1	42.9	16.6
1970	6.8	18.4	37.6	62.4	51.7	41.0	17.3
1972	6.8	17.3	40.1	65.7	51.4	45.1	17.7
Relative poverty							
1965	8.5	29.5	36.1	68.5	57.4	44.7	19.5
1968	7.4	21.8	38.7	68.6	52.9	43.7	17.9
1970	8.0	21.7	40.4	64.9	54.1	43.3	19.0
1972	8.7	21.5	44.4	69.6	55.9	48.0	20.3

Source: Tabulations of the Survey of Economic Opportunity and the Current Population Survey tapes.

TABLE 5.3.   INCIDENCE OF PRETRANSFER POVERTY AMONG
DEMOGRAPHIC SUBGROUPS OF UNRELATED INDIVIDUALS
(in percentages)

	Sex and Age of Unrelated Individual				
	Males <65	Females <65	Males >65	Females >65	All
Absolute poverty					
1965	25.7	38.1	75.2	81.9	50.7
1968	21.7	34.5	76.9	77.3	47.3
1970	26.1	31.7	70.4	77.7	47.2
1972	25.2	35.0	73.6	79.8	47.9
Relative poverty					
1965	25.7	38.1	75.2	81.9	50.7
1968	23.5	35.8	78.3	78.4	48.7
1970	27.9	34.2	73.6	80.0	49.5
1972	27.5	38.6	77.6	82.7	50.9

Source: Tabulations of the Survey of Economic Opportunity and the Current Population
Survey tapes.

level in 1972. This meager advance looks favorable only in comparison to the trend for families with white female heads under sixty-
five. Pretransfer poverty among this group steadily climbed from 36
to 40 percent.

Turning to families with aged heads, we observe a large decline in
pretransfer absolute poverty during 1965–1968, followed by little
change. Slightly more than one-half of these households have been
poor before transfers in recent years. Surprisingly, families headed by
females have had lower levels of pretransfer poverty. Between 41 and
46 percent of such families were pretransfer poor in these years.

Patterns of absolute pretransfer poverty among groups of unrelated
persons are shown in Table 5.3. In 1965, pretransfer poverty affected
25.7 percent of all unrelated men under sixty-five. This fraction
dipped sharply in 1968; in the early 1970s it rebounded to the 1965
level. Among unrelated females under sixty-five, the incidence of
pretransfer poverty decreased until 1970, then rose. In 1972, 35
percent of these women were pretransfer poor. Poverty before transfers among elderly unrelated persons has always been very high, since
most of them are retired or semiretired and depend largely on Social

Security and savings to provide most of their income. About 74 percent of elderly single men and 79 percent of the women have been pretransfer poor during 1965–1972.

Relative Poverty

Trends in relative pretransfer poverty for the ten groups in Tables 5.2 and 5.3 can be quickly summarized. As in the absolute statistics, families with nonwhite male heads under sixty-five made the greatest gains, though since 1968 little has changed. Indeed, over the seven years, this was the only group that exhibited a marked decline (and only one other category showed any decline). Pretransfer poverty among nonelderly white male heads fell from 8.5 to 7.4 percent in the mid-1960s, then rose to 8.7 percent by 1972. A similar pattern of change appeared for families with aged male heads. Incidence of pretransfer poverty increased substantially for families with white female heads under sixty-five, while remaining fairly constant, though at a much higher level, for the nonwhites.

Each of the four classes of unrelated persons made no net progress in reducing the level of relative pretransfer poverty during 1965–1972. The incidence in 1972 exceeds the 1965 figure in all cases, though the differences are small.

Interpretation of Trends

While the above observations are not conclusive in themselves, in our view they cast considerable doubt on any belief that economic growth, by itself, will cause poverty to wither away fairly quickly. Rather, at least during 1965–1972, a time of rising real pretransfer income per household and, by American standards, low or moderate unemployment rates, only two major demographic groups—families with white and nonwhite male heads under sixty-five—experienced a noticeable reduction in the incidence of absolute pretransfer poverty. All other groups show little or no improvement when the official poverty definition is used, and even less if we judge progress from a relative viewpoint.

III. ECONOMIC GROWTH, UNEMPLOYMENT, AND PRETRANSFER POVERTY

The preceding discussion highlighted the differences in pretransfer poverty among demographic groups, but merely described the recent changes. This section attempts to assess the relationship between the observed changes and variations in macroeconomic conditions.

While a thorough description of the economy's health involves numerous variables, it is generally agreed that a useful summary is provided by four key ones: real per capita GNP (or some other broad measure of output), the growth rate of this indicator, the unemployment rate, and the inflation rate. Because both poverty definitions center on family income, average pretransfer family income (or average unrelated-individual pretransfer income, where appropriate) adjusted for price changes will be used instead of per capita GNP as our output measure.[5] Table 5.4 displays data on income, unemployment, and inflation for recent years.

Average Income and Absolute Pretransfer Poverty

The level of average pretransfer income has been inversely related to the fraction of families below the official poverty line. Our estimates indicate that a rise in average pretransfer family income of 1 percent was associated with a decline in the incidence of absolute pretransfer poverty of approximately .97 percent. For unrelated persons, the response to economic growth has been somewhat weaker. Pretransfer poverty has fallen by about .63 percent for every 1 percent rise in the mean pretransfer unrelated individual income.[6] Clearly, the growth rate of average family income is a vital factor in determining how quickly absolute poverty is reduced. A rapidly growing economy generates increases in income that pull large numbers of families over the poverty line; a sluggish economy does not.

For example, suppose mean pretransfer family income rose from $10,000 to $10,300 (3 percent) between years A and B. The level of absolute poverty would be predicted to fall by .97 × 3 = 2.9 percent. If pretransfer poverty were 18.0 percent in year A, it would fall to about 17.5 percent (that is, a drop of 2.9 percent) in year B. This calculation assumes that all other economic conditions remained constant.

We observe from Table 5.4 that mean pretransfer real income steadily rose between 1965 and 1972, yet the incidence of poverty did not steadily fall. And over the entire period, mean family income jumped 18 percent while absolute pretransfer poverty dropped only 9 percent (the drop from 19.5 to 17.7 is 9 percent of the way to zero). This conflict with the estimated effect of rising output on pretransfer poverty reported earlier is resolved when one recognizes that other important economic conditions—in particular, the unemployment rate—had not remained stable over these years.

TABLE 5.4.   SUMMARY MEASURES OF ECONOMIC PERFORMANCE
IN RECENT YEARS

Year	Average Real Pretransfer Income of Families[a]	Average Real Pretransfer Income of Unrelated Individuals[a]	National Unemployment Rate[b]	Annual Inflation Rate[b]
1964	—	—	5.2	1.3
1965	9,822	3,521	4.5	1.7
1966	—	—	3.8	2.9
1967	—	—	3.8	2.9
1968	10,876	4,039	3.6	4.2
1969	—	—	3.5	5.4
1970	11,240	4,025	4.9	5.9
1971	—	—	5.9	4.3
1972	11,596	4,191	5.6	3.3
1973	—	—	4.9	6.2
1974	—	—	5.6	11.0

[a] In 1972 dollars. Computed from the Survey of Economic Opportunity and Current
Population Survey tapes.

[b] In percentages. From U.S., President, Economic Report of the President Together with
the Annual Report of the Council of Economic Advisers, transmitted to the Congress,
February 1975 (Washington, D.C.: U.S. Government Printing Office, 1975) (PR38.9:975).

Unemployment and Absolute Pretransfer Poverty

The unemployment rate exerts a strong, direct, and independent
effect on the level of pretransfer poverty. That is, even if the average
pretransfer family income does not change, a drop in the unemployment rate will decrease the number of poor persons. Our statistical
estimates suggest that a 10 percent fall in this rate (a fall from 5 to
4.5 percent, for example) is, in itself, associated with a decline in the
incidence of family pretransfer poverty by about 2.7 percent and,
among unrelated persons, by about .6 percent.[7]

In 1972, for example, 9.6 million families were pretransfer poor
and the unemployment rate was 5.6 percent. If the economy had
been operating at a 4.5 percent unemployment rate (20 percent less),
pretransfer poverty would have affected 5.4 percent fewer families,
or only 9.1 million of them.

Understanding the economic interactions that underlie this finding is essential to perceiving the nature of poverty in a market economy. Low-income workers tend to come from the least-educated, least-skilled, and most-discriminated-against groups in the nation. When economic activity slackens, these laborers are among the first to be laid off and the least able to find new jobs. Those who retain jobs often must suffer underemployment by involuntarily accepting part-time work. And the worsening job market discourages many low-income persons who otherwise would seek work because they had been recently laid off or were reentering the labor market after being housewives. Unable to find jobs, these people drop out of the labor force entirely. Neither unemployed nor underemployed, these "discouraged" workers nonetheless form a third group of poor persons who are victims of rising unemployment. Since labor earnings provide the bulk (on average, 70 percent[8]) of most pretransfer poor and near-poor households' incomes, the outcome of a depressed labor market is that some near-poor households fall below the poverty threshold, while the destitution of the working poor who lose jobs or retain only part-time work is increased.

On the other hand, in an expanding economy, labor markets tighten and the real wages of low-income earners rise. Employers are induced by the market to recruit and train low-skill and nonwhite workers who previously were left jobless, while their low-wage employees are given increased full-time work and promotion opportunities. And, as the employment situation brightens, discouraged workers regain interest in seeking jobs. The higher wages and longer work hours of the newly hired, newly full-time, and newly promoted workers produce increased earnings that often are sufficient to pull their families out of the poverty population. And even if some households remain poor after their heads find new or better jobs in the growing economy, they will be less poor than before.

A fall in unemployment tends to be accompanied by an increase in the growth rate of average family income. Hence, the direct effect of a reduction in the unemployment rate—the escape from pretransfer poverty of families because their heads obtain new jobs, wage hikes, or longer work hours—is complemented by an indirect effect—the generally faster rise in incomes. Reducing the level of unemployment, then, has a doubly beneficial antipoverty impact.

Preventing cyclically heavy unemployment by maintaining a tight labor market induces a third antipoverty response from the economy that is more long-term in character than the previous two. Such unemployment harms young entrants into the work force, who fail to obtain jobs: They, thereby, miss opportunities for the on-the-job training necessary for occupational advancement. It also hurts older

TABLE 5.5.   EFFECT OF MACROECONOMIC CONDITIONS ON THE
INCIDENCE OF PRETRANSFER POVERTY

	Percent Change in the Incidence of Pretransfer Poverty Associated with a 1 Percent Rise in Average Family Pretransfer Income (Average Unrelated Individual Pretransfer Income for Unrelated Individuals)		Percent Change in the Incidence of Pretransfer Poverty Associated with a 10 Percent Rise in the National Unemployment Rate	
	Absolute	*Relative*	*Absolute*	*Relative*
Families:				
All families	− .97*	− .30	2.7*	2.7*
White male head under 65	−2.14*	− .90	5.8*	5.8*
Nonwhite male head under 65	−2.97*	−1.79*	3.4*	2.1
White female head under 65	.29	.84*	2.3*	2.2*
Nonwhite female head under 65	− .33	− .02	0.1	−0.1
Male head over 65	− .84*	− .50*	1.2*	1.4*
Female head over 65	− .48	− .23	2.0	2.5
Unrelated individuals:				
All unrelated individuals	− .63*	− .50*	0.6	0.8
Males under 65	− .48*	− .70	5.2*	4.7*

workers laid off during a recession, who find it difficult to regain
employment in jobs paying wages equal to those received previously.
These effects of cyclical unemployment not only increase the current
incidence of poverty, but also contribute to higher levels of poverty
in the future.[9]

Effects of Growth and Unemployment on
Absolute Pretransfer Poverty among Demographic
Groups

Various demographic groups of the population do not uniformly
benefit from the antipoverty impacts of rising income and decreasing
unemployment rates. This is clearly shown by the very different
patterns of change in pretransfer poverty across the ten categories of

TABLE 5.5—(continued)

	Absolute	Relative	Absolute	Relative
Females under 65	- .47	- .34	1.4	1.9
Males over 65	- .33	- .16	0.3	0.3
Females over 65	- .29*	- .23*	0.5	0.6

Note: The equation used to provide these estimates was

$$\ln P_i = a + b \cdot \ln U + d \cdot \ln Y + c \cdot D + e,$$

where P_i = incidence of pretransfer poverty among the ith demographic group,
   Y = mean pretransfer income of families (or unrelated individuals were appropriate),
   U = unemployment rate,
   D = a dummy equal to 1 if observation is from the South, 0 otherwise, and
   e = error term.

The data for these regressions are observations of pretransfer poverty, mean income, and the unemployment rate in the four Census regions—Northeast, Northcentral, South, and West. We used four tape files (for years 1965, 1968, 1970, and 1972) to generate these data. Hence each regression has sixteen observations. The dummy variable for South was needed to obtain any meaningful results. We would have preferred to use regular time series data for this analysis, but the needed numbers have not been published by the Census Bureau and our own data could provide only four points. Hence, we were forced to use the pooled cross-sections and must hope this has not yielded distorted estimates. All estimates used the weighted least squares technique, with weights equal to the square root of the population upon which the P_i numbers were computed.

*Statistically significant at .05 level. All other estimates failed to be significant at the .1 level.

households in Tables 5.2 and 5.3. In this section, we shall examine the different response of each group to fluctuations in average income and the unemployment rate.

One would predict that economic growth and falling unemployment rates would have the strongest effect on pretransfer poverty among those groups who are most likely to earn their way out of poverty. As suggested in Table 5.5, pretransfer absolute poverty among families with male heads under sixty-five, who are generally firmly oriented toward the labor market, reacts most strongly to economic conditions. A 1 percent rise in mean pretransfer family income was associated with a fall in the incidence of poverty of 2.1 percent for families with prime-age white male heads and 3.0 percent for families with nonwhite male heads in the same age group. For these two groups, a 10 percent reduction of the unemployment rate has been associated with a decline in absolute pretransfer poverty of 5.8 and 3.4 percent, respectively.

In contrast, families with working-age female heads have responded rather feebly to general economic conditions. Neither changes in unemployment nor changes in mean pretransfer income have been highly correlated with the incidence of absolute pretransfer poverty among white and nonwhite female heads. This result reflects the lower labor force participation rates of women with families and the smaller and more slowly rising wages paid to those women who did work.

Family heads over age sixty-five are much less likely to be in the labor force than younger heads, which leads to higher levels of pretransfer poverty (as shown in Table 5.2). This fact also suggests that macroeconomic fluctuations should have a smaller effect on changing the incidence of pretransfer poverty among the elderly, since a smaller portion of them directly benefit from rising wages and employment. Among families with elderly male heads this expectation is borne out. A drop of .84 percent in pretransfer absolute poverty has been associated with a 1 percent rise in mean pretransfer income. This is about one-third of the estimate for under-sixty-five male heads. Variations in the unemployment rate also have lesser impacts for older than for younger heads. Families with female heads over sixty-five responded better to rising mean income than those with working-age female heads. However, the estimates for all three groups of female heads are statistically insignificant, so this finding may not be reliable.

Different groups of unrelated individuals also exhibit a range of responses to changing economic conditions. Comparing unrelated men and women under sixty-five, we see from Table 5.5 that pretransfer poverty among the men has been more strongly associated with changes in the unemployment rate and level of pretransfer income per unrelated person. Absolute pretransfer poverty among elderly unrelated males and females, as expected, has been much less sensitive to macroeconomic conditions.

Macroeconomic Conditions and Relative Pretransfer Poverty

With the preceding discussion for background, the relationships between relative pretransfer poverty and economic conditions can be readily summarized and contrasted with results based on the absolute definitions.

When a relative approach is used, the antipoverty benefits of rising average income still exist but are considerably smaller. This difference is expected because the relative poverty lines increase at about the same rate as real average income rises, while the absolute ones remain fixed. A 1 percent increase in mean family pretransfer income was associated with a .30 percent fall in the incidence of pretransfer poverty among all families (versus .97 percent for the absolute case). Not surprisingly, the effect of growth, as measured by the coefficients, is also smaller for each of the six demographic categories. Indeed, for families with white female heads under sixty-five years of age, growing average income has been significantly associated with *rising* levels of relative pretransfer poverty (the absolute result actually was also positive, but the estimated relationship was not statistically significant). Economic growth was most strongly associated with declining relative pretransfer poverty among families with nonwhite male heads under sixty-five, followed by those with working-age white male heads and elderly male heads. This pattern parallels the one described earlier. For unrelated persons the findings are similar: Increasing income still helps reduce relative pretransfer poverty, but not as effectively as it did for absolute poverty.

The correlations between changes in unemployment and relative pretransfer poverty, in contrast, are nearly identical to those derived from the absolute approach. This is true whether we look at all families and unrelated individuals or focus on one particular subgroup. It follows, once again, that moving toward full employment will have varying degrees of success in helping to reduce relative pretransfer poverty among different groups in the population.

Some Implications of These Findings

The policy implications that flow from these findings are important. If all groups gained substantially from declining joblessness and rapid economic growth, government action that directly promoted these macroeconomic goals would steadily reduce pretransfer poverty by letting the benefits of a strong economy "trickle down." In fact, only part of the poverty population appears to benefit substantially from such a trickle-down approach. Thus, speedily reducing the level of pretransfer poverty, that is, increasing the number of households that earn their way over the poverty line, could not be accomplished solely by maintaining a vigorous economy. An appropriate set of policies would also be required to compensate for differential anti-poverty effects of growth and tightening labor markets among demographic subgroups.

While such policies are one option for reducing poverty, they would involve explicit government interference with the market processes that generate the distribution of earnings and property income. Consequently, they currently enjoy little political support. Moreover, a high level of pretransfer poverty among the elderly generally is not viewed as a serious problem. There is clear political and social consensus that members of this group need not earn their way out of poverty, but rather should be able to depend on adequate transfer incomes to prevent poverty. For these reasons, attempting to prevent pretransfer poverty among all segments of the population would not be a sound strategy for reducing poverty.

The preceding analysis lends substance to the early assertion that macroeconomic conditions exert a major influence on poverty problems. It follows that policies affecting the performance of the economy are among the most potent antipoverty weapons. However, because these policies are shaped by macroeconomic conditions and not out of concern for the poverty population, their impact on poverty has been in the nature of a side effect of efforts to manage the economy. Indeed, the determinants of economic policy range far beyond an interest in how the changes they produce will affect the poor. Concern with a favorable balance of payments, low unemployment, and growth, as goals in themselves, the welfare of the nonpoor or certain sectors of the economy, political strategy, and many other such factors are all vital considerations shaping the choice of national economic policy. Some argue that in choosing among these goals, the consequences for the poor receive the lowest priority by decision-makers.[10] Hence, while broad economic policies undoubtedly have important impacts on the extent of poverty, they cannot be viewed as antipoverty policies per se.

IV. EFFECTS OF MACROECONOMIC CONDITIONS ON THE WELL-BEING OF THE POOR—FURTHER EVIDENCE

The empirical relationships and trends presented so far provide useful information for assessing the effect of macroeconomic variables upon poverty. However, our treatment has neglected a number of important related issues: most notably, the impact of inflation upon the well-being of the poor. Also, the effectiveness of the public transfer system in cushioning the adverse impact of unemployment upon the incomes of the low-income population has not been explored. This section summarizes the major findings of several research studies that assess these topics.[11]

The reader should note two differences between the approach used here and the approach of these other studies. First, their results are based on the official definition of poverty only. (Using a relative definition would not have greatly altered their conclusions.) Second, for reasons that will be apparent, their findings concern the *post-transfer* poor instead of the pretransfer poor.

Effects of Inflation on the Poor

Changes in inflation, unemployment, and the level of output occur simultaneously in response to the complex interactions of persons, business, government bodies, and international circumstances. The precise connection between inflation and the other variables, especially unemployment, has been widely debated and currently remains poorly understood. In the 1950s and 1960s, rising prices were generally associated with falling unemployment rates. Since 1969, the experience has been one of rising prices and steady or increasing unemployment. Whatever the true relationship between these crucial macroeconomic variables, it is important to separate conceptually and analytically the effect of inflation from the impact of unemployment upon the poor.

Inflation alters the welfare of the poor primarily by

- Changing the prices of products purchased by low-income households;
- Reducing the worth of the poor's wealth; and
- Eroding the real value of transfers and other nonlabor incomes, which account for a large share of the incomes of many post-transfer poor families.

Inflation may also affect real wage and salary income of the poor if wage increases lag behind price increases in some or all labor markets. Occupational wage differentials may change during inflation. The existence of these effects has not been firmly established, and, compared to the strong impact of unemployment, they are not likely to be very important determinants of changes in the earnings of the poor. Hence, we will not discuss them.

Cost of Living and Low-Income Households and Inflation

The measure of inflation most often used is the Consumer Price Index (CPI). This index is based on the prices of a combination of goods and services typically bought by families headed by an urban wage earner or clerical worker. Consequently, it is largely determined by the consumption patterns of middle-income families. On average, the poor spend a larger share of their incomes on food and housing, and a smaller share on clothing, transportation, and recreation, than do middle-income families. Thus, the CPI does not accurately measure the true impact of inflation on the cost of the set of commodities usually purchased by the poor.

To examine changes in the cost of living at low-income levels, several economists have constructed a "Poor Person's Price Index"

TABLE 5.6.   COMPARATIVE PRICE INDICES, 1960-1974
(1970 = 100)

	Poor Person's Price Index (PPI)	Consumer Price Index (CPI)
1960	76.9	76.3
1961	77.7	77.0
1962	78.4	77.9
1963	79.5	78.8
1964	80.4	79.9
1965	81.5	81.2
1966	84.1	83.6
1967	85.8	86.0
1968	89.3	89.6
1969	94.3	94.4
1970	100.0	100.0
1971	104.0	104.3
1972	107.8	107.7
1973	116.0	114.4
June 1974	128.7	126.5

Sources: Poor Person's Price Index from Robinson G. Hollister and John L. Palmer, "The Impact of Inflation on the Poor," in Redistribution to the Rich and the Poor: The Grants Economics of Income Distribution, ed. Kenneth E. Boulding and Martin Pfaff (Belmont, Cal.: Wadsworth, 1972). Consumer Price Index from U.S., Department of Health, Education, and Welfare, Office of the Assistant Secretary for Planning and Evaluation, Office of Income Security Policy, "The Impacts of Inflation and Higher Unemployment: With Emphasis on the Lower Income Population," by John L. Palmer, Michael C. Barth, et al., Technical Analysis Paper No. 2 (Washington, D.C.: HEW Office of Income Security Policy, 1974).

(PPI) based upon the average expenditure patterns of households with official poverty-line incomes.[12] The results of their effort and, for comparative purposes, the CPI are displayed in Table 5.6 for the period 1960–1974. Between 1960 and 1972, the two indices moved at about the same rate—the poor's purchasing power did not suffer relative to other groups. In sharp contrast, during the period of rapid inflation beginning in early 1973, the cost of living rose faster for the poor than for the rest of society. Between 1972 and June 1974, the PPI rose 19.4 percent, while the CPI gained 17.4 percent. The difference can be traced to the large price increases for food and housing (including utilities), two consumption categories that absorb relatively high fractions of the poor's budget.

This recent trend may or may not continue during future inflationary periods. The actual pattern will depend on which sectors of the economy experience the greatest price changes. Nonetheless, the fact remains that in part of the early 1970s the loss of buying power was most severe among those households least able to afford it.

Inflation and Net Worth

The net worth of a household may be divided into four components:

- Fixed dollar assets, like cash, bonds, and bank accounts;
- Physical assets, like houses, cars, and real estate;
- Intangible ownership assets, stocks and mutual funds; and
- Liabilities, mortgages and other debts.

As prices rise, fixed dollar assets decline in real value, while the real burden of liabilities becomes lighter. Physical assets and intangibles tend to rise in value at about the same rate as prices.[13] Thus, households whose net worth is most strongly weighted toward fixed-value assets suffer the greatest proportional losses of wealth during inflation, while those with heavy debts gain.

The poor generally hold a high proportion of their assets in fixed-value forms and have low levels of debt (mortgages, the major liabilities of most families, are seldom held by the poor). Inflation, therefore, leads to declines in the real net worth of the poor.[14] In contrast, among middle- and upper-middle-income groups, where debts (mainly mortgages) are often fairly large and many assets are tangibles (mainly houses), net worth rises in inflationary times. Like the poor, the very rich (incomes over $50,000 in 1968) tend to have losses of real net worth during periods of inflation because they hold substantial amounts of fixed-value assets.

Though the real net worth of most poor households declines during inflation, the losses are fairly small. After all, most of the poor have very little wealth for inflation to erode. In 1961 (the only year for which suitable data were available), more than one-half the families with incomes below the absolute poverty line had less than $425 of their wealth in the form of cash, bonds, or other fixed-value assets, vulnerable to inflation. Hence, if there had been a rate of inflation of 5 percent in that year, the net worth of a typical poor family would have fallen less than 5 percent of $425, or $21.50.

The impact of inflation on the real income received by poor people from their assets is also quite small. Suppose the $425 in vulnerable assets were to yield about $43 of income per year, a sizeable rate of return of 10 percent. If prices had been rising 5 percent, the real value of $43 would drop by $2.15. Since the median family income of the poor was $1164 in 1961, the loss of real income due to inflation's effect on asset yields was negligible.[15]

These small estimates of the "wealth effects" of inflation have been based upon the median values of wealth and income of the poor. However, there is a minority of the poor, especially among the aged, whose situations diverge from the median and instead accord more with the stereotype of a family living on a meager income derived in large part from fixed-value assets. Recent inflation has surely created severe economic difficulties for such households. Similarly, some poor households depend on dividends or rents for a major share of their income. Over the long run, income from these sources would be expected to rise at least as fast as prices. But over a short period, it may not, and these families would suffer temporary, but very real, losses from inflation.

Transfer Income and Inflation

Transfer income has formed an important portion of the total incomes of many poor households. In 1972, for example, about 83 percent of all poor households with heads over sixty-five received Social Security, which accounted for an average of 80 percent of their total income. About 22 percent of all poor aged households obtained public assistance payments that provided, on average, one-half of the recipients' cash income. Similarly, public assistance income was given to 42 percent of all poor households with non-aged female heads and was 77 percent of these families' income. Unemployment Insurance benefits were received by about 7 percent of poor households with male heads under sixty-five and was 26 percent of their income.[16] Because the poor so heavily depend upon transfers, we here examine the degree to which average transfer benefits have kept pace with inflation in recent years.

Throughout the 1960s and early 1970s, neither private nor government transfer payments were automatically adjusted for price rises. Increased public benefits required specific legislative approval. Only since 1974 have automatic cost-of-living increases been mandated for Social Security, Supplemental Security Income (SSI), and food stamps.[17] Benefits from other government transfer programs—AFDC, Unemployment Insurance, Workmen's Compensation, and veterans' benefits—have never been formally indexed to the cost of living. Thus, the adverse impact of inflation on the real value of these latter transfer payments must be offset by conscious policy decisions.

Table 5.7 presents the average payment of several transfer programs for several years. All figures are expressed in constant 1970 dollars to correct for inflation.[18] In the 1960s and early 1970s, the growth rate of average benefits for nearly all transfer programs

TABLE 5.7.   AVERAGE PAYMENT PER RECIPIENT FROM SELECTED TRANSFER PROGRAMS
(in constant 1970 dollars)

	Social Security to Retired Workers	Old Age Assistance	AFDC	Unemployment Insurance	Black Lung
1960	96	77	37	43	—
1962	97	79	37	44	—
1964	96	79	39	45	—
1966	100	81	43	47	—
1968	111	78	47	49	—
1970	118	78	50	50	112
1971	127	74	50	52	113
1972	151	74	50	52	117
1973.	143	66	49	51	119
June 1974	145	—[a]	46	49	108

Source: Unadjusted payment data is from Social Security Bulletin 38 (January 1975), Tables M-13, M-35, and M-36.
Note: Price index used to deflate payments is the PPI of Table 5.6.
[a]Replaced by Supplemental Security Income.

exceeded the slow or moderate rise in prices and, as the table indicates, grew in real terms. The one exception—Old Age Assistance—has disappeared with the introduction of SSI, the payments of which will be adjusted for inflation.

Since 1972, this trend has been broken. The real value of the mean Social Security benefit has been fairly constant. Between 1972 and mid-1974, real average payments from AFDC, Unemployment Insurance, and black lung disability all fell about 7 percent. In the past few years, therefore, the adverse effect of inflation on *aged* poor persons, who receive the bulk of Social Security and SSI going to the poor, has been offset, though benefits have not grown in real terms. Among poor families dependent on other transfer programs for a substantial share of their income, who tend to have *non-aged* heads, inflation has been eroding the value of their transfers.

The Response of the Transfer System to Unemployment[19]

To complement the preceding discussion of inflation and the transfer system, this section focuses on how successfully the transfer system cushions the poor's real income losses resulting from unemployment. Several income-support programs are intentionally designed so that the number of persons they benefit and the size of their budgets automatically respond to changes in the economy. When the unemployment rate rises, Unemployment Insurance payments also rise and, in countercyclical fashion, offset part of the income loss for those who were laid off and eligible for this benefit. The amount of cash public assistance and food stamp benefits to which a family is entitled is determined by its money income. Also, it has been found that private transfers and the portion of Social Security that benefits the non-aged (mainly the disabled) tend to help offset income losses. Hence, macroeconomic changes, by influencing the average level of income and its distribution, greatly influence total expenditures on transfers.

Edward Gramlich has demonstrated that, in 1971, for low-income[20] families with a female head, transfer income from all sources rose an average of fifty-six cents for every dollar that earned income declined. This provided a substantial cushion against income losses due to cyclical factors. Among poor families with male heads, about 31 percent of any loss in earned income was replaced by transfers. It should be noted that these cushions are averages across the entire population. They overstate the effect of transfers in reducing hardship for those who are ineligible for one or more of the programs and understate the protection against loss for those who participate.[21]

These findings are based on 1971 data. Because of the rapid growth of the food stamp program since then, the protection by transfer programs currently available to the poor is probably somewhat higher (despite the decline in the real value of transfer payments). In the 1960s, on the other hand, the replacement percentages would have been smaller.

V. SUMMARY

This chapter has explored the relationships between poverty and the state of the economy during the past ten to fifteen years. We observed these points:

• The reduction of absolute pretransfer poverty has been rather small between 1965 and 1972, except for families (especially non-white families) with male heads under sixty-five.

• Relative pretransfer poverty rose for nearly every demographic group.

To better understand these findings, statistical estimates were used to examine the changes in pretransfer poverty associated with changes in the average income per family and the unemployment rate.

• We generally found that the overall incidence of pretransfer poverty declined when average income rose and unemployment decreased, but the strength of these relationships varied greatly across different demographic groups. Growth in average income was in all cases associated with a smaller reduction of relative pretransfer poverty than of absolute pretransfer poverty.

The impact of inflation on the welfare of the poor was also treated in this chapter. In this discussion, the focus was upon the post-transfer poor instead of the pretransfer poor. Inflation was seen to affect the poor in the following three ways:

• Since 1972, prices of a typical bundle of commodities purchased by low-income households rose faster than the average rate of inflation as measured by the CPI.

● Inflation has been eroding the real value of many poor households' net worth, but the losses have not been large except for a small minority dependent on fixed-value assets for most of its income.

● The real value of the average transfer payment rose throughout the 1960s and until 1972, but during the recent time of rapid inflation, it has decreased. Consequently, many of the poor who depend heavily on transfers for the bulk of their income have suffered real-income losses.

● Lastly, we saw that the loss of earnings resulting from unemployment was partially offset by transfers. Poor families with female heads generally had higher levels of replacement than those with male heads. The degree of protection provided by the transfer system has gradually increased in the past decade.

NOTES

[1]"Pretransfer" poverty is defined in this report as poverty before public transfers are included in income, but after private transfers have been added. The term is more convenient than the more correct "pre-government-transfer."

[2]See Glen G. Cain and Harold W. Watts, *Income Maintenance and Labor Supply,* (Chicago: Rand McNally, 1973); and *Journal of Human Resources* 9 (Spring 1974), which contains a summary of the major results of the New Jersey Income-Maintenance Experiment.

[3]There were more pretransfer poor families and unrelated persons in 1972 than in 1965 even though the incidence figures were lower. This, of course, reflects the growth in the total number of families and unrelated individuals.

[4]Recall that a household is defined to be relatively poor if its welfare ratio (income divided by official poverty line) is less than .44 of the median ratio.

[5]We recognize that median income is the preferred measure in a study such as this. However, our data posed serious obstacles to obtaining this figure easily. The correlation between median and mean income is quite high, so our use of means should not yield misleading results.

[6]See Table 5.5 for explanation of how these numbers were obtained.

[7]See Table 5.5 for explanation of how these numbers were obtained.

[8]Property income provides 17 percent and private transfers 13 percent. For absolute pretransfer poor households with heads under 65, labor income provides 86 percent. For the elderly, it contributes only 33 percent. (All figures based on 1972 CPS data.)

[9]Harry Johnson, "Unemployment and Poverty," in *Poverty Amid Affluence,* ed. Leo Fishman (New Haven, Conn.: Yale University Press, 1966).

[10]Matthew Holden, "The Politics of Poor Relief," Institute for Research on Poverty Discussion Paper 161-73 (University of Wisconsin-Madison, 1973), p. 2.

[11]This entire section draws heavily on these studies. Robinson G. Hollister and John L. Palmer, "The Impact of Inflation on the Poor," in *Redistribution to the Rich and the Poor: The Grants Economics of Income Distribution,* ed. Kenneth Boulding and Martin Pfaff (Belmont, Calif.: Wadsworth, 1972), pp. 240–270. Thad Mirer, "The Distributional Impact of Inflation and Anti-Inflation Policy," Institute for Research on Poverty Discussion Paper 231-74 (University of Wisconsin-Madison, 1974). John L. Palmer, *Inflation, Unemployment and Poverty* (Lexington, Ky.: D.C. Heath and Company, 1973). U.S., Department of Health, Education, and Welfare, Office of the Assistant Secretary for Planning and Evaluation, Office of Income Security Policy, *The Impacts of Inflation and Higher Unemployment: With Emphasis on the Lower Income Population,* Working Paper by John L. Palmer, Michael Barth, et al., Technical Analysis Paper No. 2 (Washington, D.C.: Office of Income Security Policy, 1974). Edward M. Gramlich, "The Distributional Effects of Higher Unemployment," *Brookings Papers on Economic Activity* 2 (1974): 293–336.

[12]Hollister and Palmer, "The Impact of Inflation on the Poor."

[13]Sometimes, as in the case of stock prices, there is a lag in the speed of adjustment, but over the long run the value of these assets rises enough to offset any inflation that occurs.

[14]This conclusion holds rigorously only to the extent that inflation is unanticipated, so that funds were not transferred into assets with higher yields that would compensate for inflation. Still, even if the poor anticipate inflation, there are serious limitations on their ability to adjust fully for inflation. The poor do not deal in the major money markets, where interest rates freely move in response to expected inflation. Instead, their money is held in savings accounts, and legal controls prevent interest rates on these accounts from rising enough to offset inflation.

[15]See Note 13 for a minor qualification.

[16]These figures are from Technical Analysis Paper Number 2, cited in Note 11.

[17]Increases are tied to the CPI which, we saw, has recently understated the real rate of inflation among the poor, and they occur after a long lag, during which time the real value of the payment is falling.

[18]We have used the more appropriate PPI to adjust the payments, not the CPI.

[19]This discussion is almost entirely drawn from Gramlich, "The Distributional Effects of Higher Unemployment."

[20]In the Gramlich paper (ibid.), a low-income family is one whose average yearly income over the period 1967–1972 was below the official poverty line. This is somewhat different than the usual approach, which considers income only in the current year.

[21]The calculations ignore other in-kind benefits—notably Medicaid—that would increase the average cushion. The results also are not adjusted to correct for the considerable underreporting of transfer income in surveys.

Poverty and the Public Cash Transfer System, 1965-1972

Income poverty can be reduced in various ways. We have grouped these into three broad analytic categories. The "macroeconomic approach" relies upon rising affluence and modest levels of unemployment to generate more jobs and rising wage rates that, in turn, lead to higher incomes for the poor. This "approach," we have seen, has had important effects on the size and composition of the pretransfer poverty population. A second strategy looks to manpower, education, and retraining programs to help low-income workers obtain better jobs and earn their way above the poverty line. This labor supply approach, which formed one of the cornerstones of the war on poverty, has been both praised and condemned as an antipoverty weapon.[1] We have not attempted another assessment of its worth in this study and merely wish to remark here that, like the first approach, its impact is essentially confined to reducing *pretransfer* poverty. Redistribution through private and public transfers is the third way to prevent low incomes. This method simply provides some of the pretransfer poor with cash or in-kind income, which, when added to their earned incomes, may raise total posttransfer incomes above the poverty line or, at least, may lower the income gap.

As observed in Chapter 5, dividing antipoverty strategies into those that strictly affect pretransfer poverty versus those that attack only posttransfer poverty is not entirely correct. The level and distribution of pretransfer income partly determine the flow of transfers. Unemployment Insurance, public assistance, food stamps, and even Social Security benefits may vary if earned income changes. Conversely, virtually all studies of the determinants of labor supply show that income-maintenance programs affect labor supply decisions and, hence, earnings, especially among female and elderly workers.[2] Despite this problem, we find it useful to break the reduction of poverty into these two components.

This chapter complements the macroeconomic studies of Chapter 5 by focusing upon the public *cash transfer* system and its relationship to changes in poverty during the 1965–1972 period. Overall figures on the extent of pretransfer poverty are presented in section I. Section II examines the changing effectiveness of cash transfers in lifting families out of poverty. Attention is given to different programs and several important demographic groups. Inequities in the cash-transfer system during these years are studied in section III. The chapter concludes with a summary.

The discussion addresses these issues from the viewpoint of both absolute and relative poverty. As before, the absolute viewpoint is based on the Social Security Administration poverty lines, which remain fixed in real dollar terms over time. Our relative poverty threshold, in contrast, increases in real terms when the median level of affluence rises.[3] All dollar figures in this chapter are in constant 1972 dollars to permit ready comparison across years.

I. PRETRANSFER POVERTY, 1965–1972

Absolute Poverty

Chapter 5 discussed the pretransfer poverty population and its changing size and composition in detail. Here we shall review only the broad changes in this population. As revealed in Table 6.1, 15.6 million households (including both families and unrelated individuals), 25.7 percent, fell below the poverty line in 1965 when only pretransfer incomes were counted. The income gap for this group totaled $29.3 billion, an average of $1880 per household. From an absolute standpoint, pretransfer poverty declined by 1968, then rose over the next four years and affected 24.8 percent of all households in 1972. Surprisingly, the mean income gap did not fall during this era of rising affluence, but instead rose slowly to $1944.[4] In a period

TABLE 6.1.   PRETRANSFER POVERTY AND INCOME GAPS, 1965-1972

	(1)	(2)	(3)	(4)
	Pretransfer Poor Households		Total Pretransfer Income Gap (in millions of dollars)	Average Pretransfer Income Gap (in dollars)
	Number (in thousands)	Incidence (in percentages)		
Absolute poverty				
1965	15,609	25.7	29,349[a]	1,880[a]
1968	14,933	23.2	28,590	1,915
1970	16,231	24.1	31,237	1,930
1972	17,640	24.8	34,294	1,944
Relative poverty				
1965	15,609	25.7	29,349	1,880
1968	15,738	24.5	32,259	2,049
1970	17,471	26.0	37,439	2,143
1972	19,557	27.5	44,689	2,285

Source: Tabulations of Survey of Economic Opportunity and Current Population Survey tapes.

[a]Dollar amounts are in constant 1972 dollars.

when real pretransfer income per household rose 15 percent, the incidence of absolute pretransfer poverty barely fell, and the average gap between market income and minimum needs actually increased slightly.

Why, in a generally prosperous period, did the total and average pretransfer income gap fail to decline? The total pretransfer gap grew by $5 billion partly because the *number* of pretransfer poor living units rose by 2 million. So even if the average pretransfer gap per unit had remained constant, the total gap would have grown. The number of pretransfer poor households, in turn, increased because the national population grew, and the incidence of pretransfer poverty hardly fell between 1965 and 1972.

Two questions remain unanswered: Why did the incidence of pretransfer poverty decline only slightly, and Why did the average gap rise? Chapter 5 demonstrated that the level of pretransfer poverty has been directly related to the unemployment rate and inversely related to the level of average income. The unemployment rate was higher in 1972 than in 1965. Thus, the antipoverty influence of rising average pretransfer income was partly offset by the greater joblessness. This simple macroeconomic analysis does not tell the full story, however. The roles of demographic change and of transfer payments must also be noted.

During this period, the fastest growth in living units was among unrelated individuals and families with female heads. Increasing numbers of young and elderly persons and women with children have established independent households in recent years. Because these groups are more likely to be pretransfer poor than are families with prime-age male heads (see Tables 5.2 and 5.3), this change has increased the overall incidence of pretransfer poverty. This trend toward living apart from relatives has been encouraged by changing attitudes toward divorce, marriage, and nuclear and extended family and by rising incomes, including transfers, which enable persons to live independently by ensuring their financial security.[5] If these shifts in the living arrangements of Americans had not occurred between 1965 and 1972, we estimate that absolute pretransfer poverty would have affected about 23.7 percent of all households in 1972 (instead of 24.8 percent) and the income gap would have been about $2 billion lower.

Growth in the value of the average transfer benefit during these seven years may have contributed to a reduction in the work effort of the recipients. For example, the fraction of men aged 65 and above in the labor force fell from 28 to 24 percent between 1965 and 1972, while the average monthly Social Security payment to retired workers rose from $111 to $162. Rising benefits were not wholly responsible for the decline in labor force participation, but the two trends were, in all likelihood, related. Less work effort would lead to lower levels of earnings, thereby pushing the pretransfer income of more people below the poverty line and raising the incidence of pretransfer poverty. Also, reduced earnings by the poor in response to improved transfers would raise the average pretransfer income gap. However, in most cases the transfer income would more than replace the loss of earnings, so that even though pretransfer poverty might remain constant or rise, *posttransfer* poverty would become less serious.

Relative Poverty

A relative approach tells an even less encouraging story about pretransfer poverty. The incidence of relative pretransfer poverty inched gradually higher over these years, and affected 27.5 percent of the nation's households in 1972. Relative poverty, moreover, became more intense as time passed—the average gap moved from $1880 to $2285, while the entire gap jumped by more than $15 billion.[6] Though the nation prospered, the relative poor, on a pretransfer basis, got poorer.

II. PRETRANSFER POVERTY VERSUS POSTTRANSFER POVERTY: THE BROAD IMPACT OF PUBLIC TRANSFERS

This investigation covers the six major government cash-transfer programs that existed during 1965–1972. They are (1) Social Security and Railroad Retirement (considered jointly and hereafter referred to as just Social Security[7]), (2) public assistance, (3) government employee pensions,[8] (4) Unemployment Insurance, (5) Workmen's Compensation, and (6) veterans' pensions and compensation.[9] Social Security, unemployment, and veterans' payments are federally funded. The states provide the bulk of Workmen's Compensation, while the costs of pensions and public assistance are rather evenly divided. Eligibility for public assistance and veterans' pensions is determined by the recipient's current income; entitlements to the benefits from other programs are not conditioned in this manner.

In 1965, these programs provided a total of $38.1 billion in benefits; three years later, payments reached $42.4 billion. After 1968, cash transfers grew at a rapid rate of 10 percent per year. By 1970, $50.5 billion were distributed, and in 1972, benefits stood at $62.4 billion.[10]

Absolute Poverty and Cash Transfers

Progress in eliminating absolute poverty with cash transfers can be assessed with Table 6.2. The pretransfer poor received $22.4 billion in transfer income in 1965—59 percent of total benefits in that year. Their economic needs, as measured by the income gap, were $29.3 billion. This aid lifted 5.2 million—one-third—of the pretransfer poor households over the official poverty lines, while the poverty gap was reduced by 15.5 billion or 53 percent. Transfers steadily improved their antipoverty effectiveness in the following years. In 1968, 55 percent of all transfers—$23.4 billion—were given to the pretransfer poor. The income gap declined by 57 percent, and 35 percent of the pretransfer poor escaped poverty. By 1972, the poor were given

TABLE 6.2. CASH TRANSFERS TO PRETRANSFER POOR AND RESULTANT REDUCTION IN POVERTY AND POVERTY GAP (in constant 1972 dollars)

	(1) Transfers Received by Pretransfer Poor[a] (in billions of dollars)	(2) Pretransfer Income Gap (in billions of dollars)	(3) Posttransfer Income Gap (in billions of dollars)	(4) Households Taken Out of Poverty by Transfers (in thousands)	(5) Percentage of Pretransfer Poor Taken Out of Poverty by Transfers	(6) Percentage Fall in Total Gap	(7) Leakage Ratio
Absolute poverty							
1965	22.4[b]	29.3[b]	13.8[b]	5,161[b]	33	53	.31
1968	23.4	28.1	12.2	5,183	35	57	.32
1970	27.6	31.3	12.4	5,966	37	60	.31
1972	34.3	34.3	12.5	7,682	44	64	.36
Relative poverty							
1965	22.4	29.3	13.8	5,161	33	53	.31
1968	24.2	32.3	14.9	4,825	31	54	.28
1970	28.9	37.4	16.6	5,426	31	56	.28
1972	36.5	44.7	19.3	6,659	34	57	.30

Source: Tabulations of Survey of Economic Opportunity and Current Population Survey tapes.
[a]These figures are taken directly from the data tapes and are not corrected for underreporting.
[b]Dollar amounts in constant 1972 dollars.

$34.3 billion, $11.9 billion more than in 1965.[11] This income brought 44 percent of the pretransfer poor above minimum standards and reduced the absolute income gap, which had risen by $5 billion since 1965, by 64 percent.[12]

Viewed from the absolute perspective, the income-maintenance system has clearly become more adequate for reducing the financial needs of those who did not earn enough to be nonpoor. The improved adequacy reflected the higher benefits received by low-income households. Average payments of all the transfer programs have increased since 1965, especially for Social Security (where minimum payments rose substantially), and the poor have shared the gains. Increasing enrollment rates of low-income households in the programs, notably AFDC, have also contributed to the trend. The addition of SSI, which replaced and expanded non-AFDC public assistance in 1974, will further increase the fraction of the absolute pretransfer income gap filled by public transfers.

Transfers received by the pretransfer poor were not distributed in a manner designed to reduce the income gap by the greatest possible amount. Table 6.2 shows, for example, that in 1968 the absolute pretransfer gap was $28.1 billion. The poor obtained $23.4 billion. This sum could have cut the income gap to $4.7 billion, but, in fact, it fell to only $12.2 billion. This occurred because a subgroup of the pretransfer poor received $7.5 billion in transfers above what was needed to bring them to the poverty line, while other poor families received nothing. (The causes and extent of such inequities in the transfer system are examined later in this chapter.) In other words, of the $23.4 billion received, $7.5 billion—32 percent—did not contribute to reducing the income gap. If the transfer system is viewed strictly in terms of its effect on poverty, potential antipoverty effectiveness has been lost in such a situation.

A statistic that broadly measures this sort of ineffectiveness is the "leakage ratio." The difference between the pretransfer and posttransfer gaps is divided by total transfer income given to the pretransfer poor and the result is subtracted from one. A ratio of .25, for instance, implies that three-fourths of the poor's transfer income reduced the gap, while one-fourth was "leaked" since it provided some households with more money than they needed to escape poverty.[13] Stated in equation form:

$$\text{Leakage} = 1 - \frac{\text{pretransfer gap} - \text{posttransfer gap}}{\text{transfers received by pretransfer poor}}$$

When analyzed from an absolute perspective, leakage in the transfer system was fairly constant until 1970. Column 7 of Table 6.2 indicates that about 31 percent of the cash received by the pretransfer poor did not reduce the income gap, but instead went to recipients who already had enough transfer income to move over the poverty line. In 1972, leakage suddenly increased to 36 percent. We cannot tell at this time whether the jump is permanent or reflected peculiar circumstances.

This increased leakage carried important implications for the reduction of the poverty gap. If leakage from the $34.3 billion received by the poor in 1972 had remained at the 1970 level of 31 percent, the gap would have fallen to $10.7 billion. Instead, given the higher leakage, it stood at $12.5 billion. The additional drop of $1.8 billion, we estimate, would have resulted in roughly 1.7 million additional households being taken out of poverty.

The numbers in Table 6.2 further indicate that the pretransfer poor obtained $11.9 billion more in transfers in 1972 than in 1965. If this increase had been available in 1965 and had been distributed to maximize poverty reduction, the poverty gap could have been nearly eliminated (assuming no offsetting reduction in earned incomes of the poor). Yet, by 1972, after this growth had occurred, the posttransfer gap was $12.5 billion, only slightly lower than the 1965 level. Why?

Two phenomena explain this puzzle. First, the pretransfer poverty gap grew by $5 billion. Thus, the needs to be filled by the increased benefits had grown substantially. Second, like the transfers paid in 1965, a significant share of the increase was leaked. Between 1965 and 1970, the additional transfers must have leaked at about the 1965 rate, since the overall leakage ratio remained steady. Between 1970 and 1972, however, of the *additional* $6.7 billion obtained by the pretransfer poor, about 58 percent was leaked.[14] This reflected the impact of large, across-the-board increases in Social Security payments. Much of the increase was given to pretransfer poor households who already were receiving enough Social Security to escape poverty.

Relative Poverty and Cash Transfers

A relative analysis, as one might expect, shows that the cash transfer system has made much less progress in keeping households out of poverty. The lower half of Table 6.2 reveals that the fraction of the pretransfer poor brought out of poverty hovered around one-third throughout 1965–1972. However, cash aid did reduce the relative poverty gap by even greater percentages and filled 57 percent of it by 1972. Such mixed results reflect circumstances in which rising benefits obtained by many recipients did not permit them to cross the relative poverty line, though of course it helped reduce the income gap.

In contrast to the absolute pattern, leakage has fluctuated within a narrow range around 30 percent. Apparently, transfer income of the relative pretransfer poor has generally been distributed in such a fashion that the poverty gap has been reduced by about the same percentage each year.

A Note of Caution

The patterns just described must be qualified because of two important limitations of the data. These limitations may also have influenced other findings in this chapter.

First, transfer income has been underreported in the household surveys upon which the analysis is based. This means that the impact of transfers upon poverty is underestimated in all years. Total cash transfers, as reported by the households that were interviewed, have fallen about 20 percent below total benefits paid according to government agency records.[15] The degree of underreporting has been fairly constant in the surveys we used. Thus, while estimates of the antipoverty effects of transfers are suspect for any one year, the trend over time, which is our main interest, is probably captured fairly well.

Second, and more important, the impact of in-kind transfers upon low-income groups was not assessed because the surveys did not collect data on these income sources. In 1965, in-kind benefits for the pretransfer poor were less than $1 billion, so this omission created little distortion in our findings. But, in 1972, in-kind transfers provided more than $11 billion of aid to the pretransfer poor. The improvement since 1965 in the transfer system's ability to prevent poverty is, therefore, understated by measuring only cash benefits. Moreover, to the extent that the distribution of in-kind transfers across demographic groups differs from the distribution of cash benefits, differences in the treatment of various groups by the complete transfer system are imperfectly measured by examining only those created by cash transfers.[16]

However, even if these two problems were overcome, the contrast between the trends based on relative and absolute poverty measures would remain. The absolute approach would still show considerably greater progress in the antipoverty performance of the public transfer system than would the relative viewpoint.

Adjusting for In-Kind Transfers, Underreporting, and Taxes

A recent analysis attempted to correct for underreporting of transfer income and to estimate the antipoverty impact of in-kind transfers.[17] It also adjusted household incomes for the effects of taxes. Table 6.3 presents the results and, for comparative purposes, the unrevised statistics. According to this study, public transfers lifted 52 percent of all pretransfer poor households over the official poverty lines in 1968 and reduced the absolute poverty gap by 69 percent. Two years later, 55 percent of the pretransfer poor escaped poverty via transfers, and the income gap was reduced 73 percent. In 1972, transfer income brought 72 percent of the pretransfer poor above the official threshold and erased 83 percent of the poverty gap. Compared to the unadjusted results, this approach to determining the effects of transfers on poverty suggests a larger antipoverty impact in each year and a more rapid improvement in the adequacy of the transfer system for eliminating financial need.[18] Extrapolation of both the adjusted and the unadjusted figures to 1975 would probably show a greater disparity in the measured antipoverty effectiveness of public transfers.

TABLE 6.3.   GOVERNMENT TRANSFERS AND POVERTY REDUCTION: TWO MEASURES

	Percentage of Pretransfer Poor Households Taken Out of Poverty by Transfer System		Percentage of Pretransfer Poverty Gap Closed	
	(1) Official Figures	(2) Revised Figures	(3) Official Figures	(4) Revised Figures
1968	35	52	57	69
1970	37	55	60	73
1972	44	72	64	83

Source: Columns 1 and 3 from Table 6.2; Columns 2 and 4 from Timothy M. Smeeding, "Measuring the Economic Welfare of Low Income Households, and the Anti-Poverty Effectiveness of Cash and Non-Cash Transfer Programs," (Ph.D. diss.: University of Wisconsin–Madison, 1975).

Changes Across Demographic Groups and Types of Transfer Programs

Absolute Poverty

Table 6.4 disaggregates the absolute definition statistics in columns 4 and 5 of Table 6.2 for the years 1965 and 1972. It shows the shift over this period in the impact of different types of cash transfers upon the movements out of poverty of four demographic groups. The first column simply reports the number of pretransfer poor households within each group in 1965 and 1972. Column 2 presents the number and percentage of pretransfer poor households whose Social Security payments were enough to lift them over the absolute poverty line. Some pretransfer poor households obtained no Social Security income, while many of those receiving this transfer did not escape poverty (though, of course, their poverty gaps were reduced). Column 3 indicates the number of households that were poor after Social Security benefits were added to their pretransfer incomes, but that received enough cash from one or more of the four other nonpublic assistance transfers to be nonpoor. The effect of public assistance upon eliminating poverty is displayed in the fourth column. Eligibility for public assistance is based upon the level of household income after all other cash transfers are included. Hence, these columns show the number of living units that were poor after counting all other transfers, but that received enough welfare to move out of absolute poverty. Finally, column 5 summarizes the total impact of cash transfers upon reducing the poverty of each demographic group.

Social Security has been the most effective transfer for preventing poverty. In both 1965 and 1972 (and the intervening years not shown), the overwhelming majority of pretransfer poor households that escaped poverty were dependent upon Social Security to do so. And the fraction of households kept from poverty by this program rose sharply from 21 percent in 1965 to 30 percent in 1972. For obvious reasons, this impact has been mostly concentrated among the elderly—36 percent of the pretransfer poor aged households were made nonpoor by Social Security in 1965, 51 percent of them in 1972. For households without children or with male heads and children, Social Security also brought a higher fraction of households out of poverty in 1972 than in 1965. This was not the case for families with non-aged female heads and children.[19]

The four other non-public-assistance transfers, considered as a group, have played a much smaller role in reducing absolute poverty.

TABLE 6.4. NUMBER AND PERCENTAGE OF PRETRANSFER POOR HOUSEHOLDS TAKEN OUT OF ABSOLUTE POVERTY BY GOVERNMENT TRANSFERS, BY DEMOGRAPHIC GROUPS, 1965 AND 1972 (numbers in thousands)

| | (1) | (2) | | (3) | | (4) | | (5) | |
	Pretransfer Poor Households	Pretransfer Poor Households Made Nonpoor by Social Security		Additional Pre-transfer Poor Households Made Nonpoor by Other Nonpublic-Assistance Transfers[a]		Additional Pre-transfer Poor Households Made Nonpoor by Public Assistance Transfers[b]		Total Pretransfer Poor Households Made Nonpoor by All Cash Transfers	
		Number	Percent	Number	Percent	Number	Percent	Number	Percent
1965									
All households	15,609	3,258	21	1,454	9	449	3	5,161	33
Households with aged heads[c]	7,512	2,699	36	880	12	222	3	3,801	51
Households with non-aged male heads, with children	2,761	75	3	182	7	45	2	302	11
Households with non-aged female heads, with children	1,395	171	12	54	4	77	6	302	22
Households with non-aged heads, no children[d]	3,943	313	8	338	9	105	3	756	19

TABLE 6.4.—(continued)

1972								
All households	17,640	5,362	30	1,345	8	968	5	7,682	44
Households with aged heads^c	8,643	4,450	51	630	7	381	4	5,461	63
Households with non-aged male heads, with children	2,011	138	7	211	10	115	6	464	23
Households with non-aged female heads, with children	2,210	197	9	45	2	261	12	503	23
Households with non-aged heads, no children^d	4,776	581	12	461	10	212	4	1,254	26

Source: Tabulations of Survey of Economic Opportunity and Current Population Survey tapes.

Note: Percentages do not always sum to total because of rounding.

[a] Unemployment Insurance, Workmen's Compensation, veterans' benefits, and government employee pensions.

[b] Old Age Assistance, Aid to the Blind, Aid to the Permanently and Totally Disabled, and Aid to Families with Dependent Children.

[c] Includes unrelated individuals.

[d] Most are unrelated individuals, but childless couples are included.

About 9 percent of all pretransfer-poor households received enough from these sources to escape poverty in 1965. The corresponding figure for 1972 was only 8 percent; results for 1968 and 1970 (not shown) were similar. However, among pretransfer poor, non-aged childless households, these four programs and Social Security have been about equally important. For families with non-aged male heads and children, these transfers have been more important than Social Security in preventing poverty.[20] For the other two categories, the reduction in poverty attributable to these benefits decreased markedly over this period.[21]

Public assistance has had a mild effect on reducing the number of poor families. After other transfer income was counted, this aid raised about 3 percent of the pretransfer poor over the absolute poverty threshold in 1965. Welfare steadily became a more effective antipoverty weapon in later years as participation grew, but by 1972 it pushed only 6 percent of the pretransfer poor over the threshold.[22] A higher fraction of families with female heads and children have been made nonpoor by public assistance (mainly AFDC) than of any other group.

These low percentages reflect an important feature of the welfare system. The maximum income that a family can have and still qualify for public assistance and the maximum benefit paid (if the family has no nonwelfare income) have been below the official poverty line in many states. Hence, even though many needy families received welfare in the 1960s and 1970s, thereby increasing their income, most of them were not taken over the poverty line.

Column 5 of Table 6.4 shows the unequal and changing impacts of the entire transfer system upon the four demographic groups of the pretransfer poverty population. For instance, in 1965 transfers lifted out of poverty 51 percent of all pretransfer poor households with aged heads, but only 19 percent of households with working-age heads and no children. By 1972, these figures had risen to 63 and 26 percent, respectively. Cash transfers have always relieved more poverty among the aged than among the under-sixty-five groups. The difference has essentially been due to Social Security.

Over the seven-year span, transfers became more effective tools against absolute poverty for all four groups. The gains were not equally shared, however. They were fairly large for the aged, reflecting the large increases in Social Security benefits enacted in 1970 and 1971. The fraction of pretransfer poor families with both children and male heads under sixty-five escaping poverty also rose sharply from 11 to 23 percent. This improvement was attributable to the increasing antipoverty effectiveness of all three categories of transfers. Pretransfer poor families with working-age female heads and children, in contrast, made virtually no progress in escaping poverty with transfers. The percentage of such families made nonpoor by Social Security and other nonwelfare transfers declined; this was offset by the impact of public assistance.[23]

Relative Poverty

When the relative poverty measure is used, changes in the antipoverty impact of different types of transfers, and their effect on demographic subgroups, portray somewhat different patterns than those just described. They appear in Table 6.5, which may be interpreted the same as Table 6.4. Again, Social Security stands as the dominant antipoverty transfer, with the combined four far less important and public assistance at the bottom. But the growth of Social Security's and welfare's antipoverty impact was much less than measured by the absolute standard. In 1972, twenty-four percent of all households were taken out of relative poverty by Social Security benefits, a quite modest improvement over the 21 percent of 1965. With welfare, only 3 percent were taken out, no change from the 1965 figure.[24] The other four programs became less effective for preventing relative poverty during this period.

Changes in the antipoverty impact of transfers upon different demographic groups can also be assessed from a relative perspective with Table 6.5. In contrast to the absolute findings, the portion of elderly pretransfer poor made nonpoor by transfers rose very little. In 1965, fifty-one percent of these households escaped poverty; in 1972, it was 52 percent. Similarly, little improvement occurred for childless households with non-aged heads. The fraction of pretransfer poor families with male heads under sixty-five and children taken out of relative poverty was increased from 11 to 17 percent by the transfer system. As in the absolute case, this gain stemmed from the rising effectiveness of all three categories of transfers. Lastly, non-aged women with children were much less likely to be taken out of relative poverty by transfers in 1972 than in 1965, despite the surge in AFDC benefits during these years.

Transfer Recipients among the Pretransfer Poor and Average Benefits

Tables 6.2, 6.4, and 6.5, while broadly gauging the impact of transfers upon absolute and relative poverty, leave many questions untouched. They do not indicate the total number of households

TABLE 6.5. NUMBER AND PERCENTAGE OF PRETRANSFER POOR HOUSEHOLDS TAKEN OUT OF RELATIVE POVERTY BY GOVERNMENT TRANSFERS, BY DEMOGRAPHIC GROUPS, 1965 AND 1972
(numbers in thousands)

| | (1) | (2) | | (3) | | (4) | | (5) | |
| | Pretransfer Poor Households | Pretransfer Poor Households Made Nonpoor by Social Security | | Additional Pretransfer Poor Households Made Nonpoor by Other Non-Public Assistance Transfers[a] | | Additional Pretransfer Poor Households Made Nonpoor by Public Assistance Transfers[b] | | Total Pretransfer Poor Households Made Nonpoor by All Cash Transfers | |
		Number	Percent	Number	Percent	Number	Percent	Number	Percent
1965									
All households	15,609	3,258	21	1,454	9	449	3	5,161	33
Households with aged heads[c]	7,512	2,699	36	880	12	222	3	3,801	51
Households with non-aged male heads, with children	2,761	75	3	182	7	45	2	302	11
Households with non-aged female heads, with children	1,395	171	12	54	4	77	6	302	22
Households with non-aged heads,[d] no children	3,943	313	8	338	9	105	3	756	19

TABLE 6.5.—(continued)

1972							
All households	19,557	24	1,370	7	603	3	6,659	34
Households with aged heads[c]	9,158	42	611	7	243	3	4,730	52
Households with non-aged male heads, with children	2,682	5	231	9	100	4	460	17
Households with non-aged female heads, with children	2,395	7	45	2	148	6	371	15
Households with non-aged heads, no children	5,322	9	483	9	112	2	1,098	21

Source: Tabulations of Survey of Economic Opportunity and Current Population Survey tapes.
Note: Percentages do not always sum to total because of rounding.
[a]*Unemployment Insurance, Workmen's Compensation, veterans' benefits, and government employee pensions.*
[b]*Old Age Assistance, Aid to the Blind, Aid to the Permanently and Totally Disabled, and Aid to Families with Dependent Children.*
[c]*Includes unrelated individuals.*
[d]*Most are unrelated individuals, but childless couples are included.*

TABLE 6.6.   TRANSFER RECIPIENTS, AVERAGE BENEFITS, AND
AVERAGE NEEDS AMONG THE PRETRANSFER POOR, 1965-1972

	(1)	(2)	(3)	(4)	(5)
	Pretransfer Poor Households Receiving Transfers	Pretransfer Poor Households Made Nonpoor by Transfers	Average Recipient's Benefit	Average Pre-transfer Income Gap of Recipients	Ratio of (3) to (4)
Absolute					
1965	69%	33%	$2063	$1978	1.04
1968	74	35	2141	2003	1.07
1970	76	37	2234	2032	1.10
1972	78	44	2487	2023	1.23
Relative					
1965	69	33	2063	1978	1.04
1968	72	31	2144	2168	99
1970	74	31	2227	2270	.98
1972	75	34	2482	2415	1.03

Source: Tabulations of Survey of Economic Opportunity and Current Population Survey tapes.
Notes: The numbers in columns 1, 2, 3, and 5 would be higher if in-kind transfers were included.   Dollar amounts in constant 1972 dollars.

receiving cash assistance, including those that remained poor after receiving aid. Nor do they indicate changes in the average benefits. We now turn briefly to these matters. Inequities in the income-maintenance system are treated in the next section.

Table 6.6 shows that in 1965 about 69 percent of pretransfer poor families obtained some transfer income—excluding in-kind benefits—but less than half of these recipients got sufficient cash to escape poverty (columns 1 and 2). By 1972, 78 percent of the absolute pretransfer poor were given transfers. For well over one-half of them, this money brought their total income above the official poverty line. In contrast, figures on relative poverty show that a modest rise in the fraction of living units with transfer income has *not* been accompanied by a similar rise in the fraction that escaped relative poverty.

The average transfer payment has steadily risen in recent years (Table 6.6, column 3). In constant 1972 dollars, there was a $400 increase between 1965 and 1972. This 20 percent gain outpaced the growth of average household money-income, which rose 15 percent. The change was nearly identical under both absolute and relative approaches.

Table 6.7 expands column 3 of Table 6.6 to show changes in the average benefit for Social Security, public assistance, and the four other programs taken as a unit. Public assistance has always been the least generous and slowest growing. The slower growth reflects, in part, a decline in the average size of families receiving AFDC. The other two categories have paid about equal average amounts to pretransfer poor recipients.

TABLE 6.7   AVERAGE BENEFIT TO THE PRETRANSFER POOR ACROSS PROGRAMS

	Social Security	Public Assistance	Other Public Transfers[a]
Absolute:			
1965	$1655	$1399	$1683
1972	$2098	$1653	$2067
Annual growth rate	3.4%	2.4%	3.0%
Relative:			
1965	$1655	$1399	$1683
1972	$2112	$1633	$2056
Annual growth rate	3.5%	2.2%	3.0%

Source: Tabulations of Survey of Economic Opportunity and Current Population Survey tapes.

Note: Dollar amounts in constant 1972 dollars.

[a]*Government pensions, Unemployment Insurance, Workmen's Compensation and veterans' benefits. Our data sources do not allow us to separate satisfactorily the benefits from these programs.*

III. INEQUITIES OF THE TRANSFER SYSTEM

The Broad Evidence

We observe from column 5 of Table 6.6 that the average benefit received by pretransfer poor families has exceeded the average pretransfer poverty gap. If this average relationship had held uniformly (or with slight variation), we would expect to find a better match between columns 1 and 2—for example, in 1965, nearly 69 percent of the pretransfer poor would have escaped poverty instead of the 33 percent that, in fact, did so. The difference of 36 percentage points is evidence of a wide variation in benefits. Among households with equal pretransfer poverty gaps, some must have obtained enough money to move well beyond the poverty threshold, while other recipients were provided with little. (From column 1, we already know that 31 percent of the pretransfer poor received nothing.)

Evidence of unequal treatment by the transfer system also appears when demographic subgroups of the pretransfer poor population are examined. Tables 6.4 and 6.5 clearly demonstrated that age and sex of the household head and whether the household contained children are related to the chances of being taken out of poverty by transfers.

We do not claim novelty in discovering evidence of inequality in the transfer system—the phenomenon has been well documented in earlier work[25] and was featured prominently in welfare reform debates. Its causes have been thoroughly explored elsewhere. The contribution of this study is to examine its persistence during recent years. That inequities have persisted throughout the period 1965 to 1972 should not be surprising. Given the failure of significant welfare reform, and the recognition that several of the large transfer programs have not been specifically designed to meet the needs of the low-income population, could it have been otherwise?

Some Technical Notes

A household's welfare ratio is its cash income divided by its official poverty line. In this manner, incomes for families of varying size and location are transformed into a common unit. Households with equal welfare ratios are considered to be equally well-off. Under this logic, *horizontal* equity exists when households with the same pretransfer welfare ratio receive equal increases in welfare from transfers (this gain is similarly measured by dividing transfer income by the appropriate poverty line). Likewise, the criterion of *vertical* equity is satisfied when a household with a lower welfare ratio receives a bigger increase in welfare from transfers than does another with a higher ratio. Further, the gains of both parties must not reverse the original rankings of their welfare ratios.

Thinking about and analyzing effects of the transfer system in terms of welfare ratios may at first strike the reader as awkward, confusing, or unfamiliar. This we acknowledge. Yet, if the discussion were to be conducted in terms of earned income, income gaps, and dollars received from transfers, empirical findings would constantly carry the qualification that final conclusions on issues of equity and poverty require corrections for family size and location. Our approach eliminates this problem.

Objections may also be raised about our definitions of vertical and horizontal equity. It could be argued, for example, that equity in the Social Security program prevails when recipients are paid in proportion to their payroll tax contributions or their preretirement incomes and not according to their pretransfer incomes. Similarly, one could maintain that equity exists when equally disabled veterans receive equal disability compensation. While such alternatives may be plausible in some applications, our approach was chosen for two reasons. First, our notions of equity accord with the standard economic usage of the terms. Second, this study deliberately concentrates on *income* poverty, which is determined solely by household welfare ratios. Our definitions of equity reflect this orientation by letting us focus upon the cash transfer system's treatment of households ranked according to welfare ratios.

After the study of inequity and welfare ratios, we will consider inequities with respect to demographic characteristics. Here the focus centers on how such characteristics as the race, sex, or age of the family head affect the chances of escaping poverty via transfers.

Vertical and Horizontal Inequities of the Transfer System[26]

From an aggregate perspective, the transfer system has tended to promote vertical equity. The rows of Table 6.8 show that the higher a household's pretransfer welfare ratio is the less it is likely that the household received a transfer. The only exception to this rule has been among the small and unusual group of households whose pretransfer incomes were below zero. (These were mostly business losses.) This pattern existed in all years, though for simplicity only 1965 and 1972 appear in the table. Moreover, in all years the average

TABLE 6.8. PRETRANSFER WELFARE RATIOS AND TRANSFER BENEFITS, 1965 AND 1972

					Pretransfer Welfare Ratio							
	<0	0	.01-.25	.26-.50	.51-.75	.76-1	1-1.5	1.51-2	2.01-3	3.01-4	4+	Total
1965												
Percent receiving no transfer	55	14	19	32	42	52	63	71	75	76	81	63
Percent receiving transfer	45	86	81	68	58	48	37	29	25	24	19	37
Average benefit to recipient (as measured by rise in welfare ratio)	.75	.82	.88	.78	.70	.59	.53	.42	.40	.39	.44	.60
N = (in thousands)	184	3,722	3,393	2,861	2,709	2,740	6,214	7,156	12,981	8,582	10,097	60,643
1972												
Percent receiving no transfer	49	10	15	26	31	41	55	64	72	77	81	61
Percent receiving transfer	51	90	85	74	69	59	45	36	29	23	19	39
Average benefit to recipient	1.03	.94	.98	.96	.94	.93	.82	.69	.60	.60	.64	.79
N = (in thousands)	224	5,797	3,753	2,542	2,603	2,714	5,465	6,194	13,184	10,614	17,989	71,086

Source: Tabulations of Survey of Economic Opportunity and Current Population Survey tapes.

benefit received from transfers declined as economic well-being rose.

Underneath these broad tendencies toward vertical equity has lain a tangled set of vertical inequities at the individual level. In every year, many very poor households received no government transfers while a large number of rather well-off ones received quite substantial amounts. Table 6.8 reveals, for example, that in 1972, 31 percent of the households with pretransfer welfare ratios between .51 and .75 received no cash transfers, while 29 percent of those in the 2–3 range obtained aid, which, on average, raised their welfare ratios by .6 (for a nonfarm elderly couple, this would be equivalent to $1520). This aid was provided by all types of transfers except public assistance.

The continual presence of horizontal inequities among households with comparable pretransfer welfare ratios can also be observed in Table 6.8. In 1965, for example, among households with pretransfer welfare ratios within the band .26 to .50, 68 percent received cash transfers that, on average, raised their well-being substantially. The other 32 percent received nothing. By 1972, a higher fraction of the units within this welfare ratio class was receiving transfer income, but many equally poor households still were getting nothing.

Even if attention is restricted to transfer *recipients,* considerable horizontal inequity has been generated by cash transfer programs. Among recipients with approximately the same welfare ratio, some greatly increased their welfare due to transfer income, while others gained very little. In 1972, for example, 2 percent of the recipients with zero pretransfer income received aid that raised their welfare ratio to between .01 and .25, 25 percent reached the .76 to 1.00 bracket, and 9 percent had posttransfer welfare ratios above 1.50 and moved well out of poverty due to government aid.[27]

The explanation for these inequities lies in the eligibility requirements and benefit standards of the various cash transfer programs. Benefit levels and administrative policies for public assistance, which influence the number of households certified to receive welfare, vary from state to state. For Social Security, government pensions, Unemployment Insurance, Workmen's Compensation, and veterans' compensation (for service-connected disabilities), benefits are principally determined by past earnings (or degree of disability). Moreover, they are independent of the amount of property income. Hence, the recipient's *current* income, which determines his poverty status, does not strongly affect his benefits from these programs.[28] Because of this feature of the income-maintenance system, government can provide transfers to high-income households and deny them to poor ones, it can give cash income to one poor family and not to another equally needy one; and in no way does this behavior violate the purposes of the existing transfer legislation.

Numerous examples can be cited that illustrate how the normal operation of the transfer system creates vertical and horizontal inequity. An unemployed professional will receive Unemployment Insurance even though he may have already earned $10,000 in the year, while a steadily employed member of the "working poor" or a laid-off farmworker will generally be ineligible for any cash transfer.[29] Retired workers with different levels of property incomes could receive equal Social Security payments, while many young low-wage earners receive no transfers and must even pay Social Security taxes. Similarly, a disabled veteran would enjoy monthly compensation payments even if he earned high wages or was independently wealthy, while another veteran earning $4000 a year would not even qualify for the income-tested veterans' pension.

Another manifestation of vertical inequity, "leapfrogging," has been a continuing characteristic of the cash transfer system. Leapfrogging occurs if the welfare ratio of one family is lower than another's before transfers, but exceeds it after transfer income is counted. Its cause can also be traced to the eligibility and benefit rules of the income-maintenance programs. To cite but one possibility, a disabled veteran could receive $3000 a year in compensation while his wife earned another $2000 at part-time work. The couple would leapfrog over another family whose only income was the head's earnings of $4000.

Leapfrogging was widespread throughout the period 1965–1972. As a crude indication of the extent of this phenomenon, we can observe that in 1965, 21 percent of the pretransfer *poor* leaped over pretransfer *nonpoor* households. The corresponding figures based on the absolute definition for 1968, 1970, and 1972 were 22, 24, and 31 percent.[30] It appears that leapfrogging has been becoming a more common feature of the cash transfer system. This is as one would expect, given the absence of any structural change in the transfer system: As average payments rose during these years and little was done to modify or extend eligibility requirements, total incomes of transfer recipients became more likely to surpass those of nonrecipients.

Demographic Aspects of Inequity among the Pretransfer Poor

The evidence above testifies to widespread and continuing inequities in the transfer system. The combination of leapfrogging and unequal treatment of households with comparable levels of economic welfare has created a situation in which some families and individuals receive enough aid to escape poverty, while many others do not. As we observed in Table 6.2, about 33 percent of the 1965 pretransfer poor were lifted over the poverty line by cash transfers. By 1972, this had risen to 44 percent under the absolute definition and stood at 34 percent from the relative viewpoint. Different subgroups of the pretransfer poor population have had widely differing chances of escaping poverty, however. This was demonstrated with Tables 6.4 and 6.5. The goal of this section is to discover what demographic characteristics have been related to higher-than-average and lower-than-average chances of escaping poverty via transfers, and how these relationships changes over time.

Our method of resolving this question parallels the earlier treatment in Chapter 4 of the variables associated with posttransfer poverty. Using the same statistical technique, we have estimated the *independent* contributions of six important demographic variables to the *odds* of being lifted out of poverty by cash transfers (see Chapter 4 for further details). The six variables are age of head (categorized as under sixty-five, sixty-five and above), sex, race (white and other nonblacks, or black), education (zero—eight, nine—twelve, thirteen and above), type of household (family or unrelated individuals), and region of residence (South or elsewhere).

Absolute Results

From results based upon the official poverty definition, we find that households with heads over sixty-five-years old, other things remaining equal, are more likely to escape absolute poverty than are their younger counterparts.[31] Indeed, the direct effect of age is by far the largest of all estimated effects, a result of the nature and size of the Social Security program.

Among aged households, those with male heads are favored to escape poverty over those with female heads. For households with heads under age sixty-five, the odds are about equal for both sexes. The sex difference is much smaller than the effect of age.

Blacks are less likely than whites and other races to receive enough money to escape absolute poverty. The reason, we surmise, is that because blacks tend to earn less than otherwise similar whites, current payments to blacks from Social Security, government pensions, Unemployment Insurance, and Workmen's Compensation (all of which are tied to past earnings) are, on average, lower than benefits received by whites. Also, blacks have been disproportionately employed in occupations not covered by Social Security or Unemployment Insurance.[32] The racial difference is greater in the South than in the rest of the nation. Overall, the direct effect of race is stronger than the influence of sex.

The level of education of the household head bears a positive relationship to the odds of escaping poverty. More education tends to produce higher earnings. And higher earnings, as argued in the above paragraph, can lead to larger transfer payments.

Given otherwise identical pretransfer poor households, those living in the South will be less likely to receive enough transfer income to avoid absolute poverty. This presumably reflects two related conditions. First, transfer benefits determined by state governments— public assistance, Unemployment Insurance, and Workmen's Compensation—are lower in the South than elsewhere. This pattern partly results from political choices, but probably also exists because money incomes are lower in the region. Lower incomes, in turn, have led to smaller-than-average Social Security payments to retired or disabled southerners.

Transfers are more likely to bring families than individuals out of poverty. The AFDC program, of course, is restricted to families. And, for a variety of reasons, unrelated persons earn less than family heads.

Finally, the estimates show whether the associations between demographic characteristics and the odds of escaping absolute poverty changed between 1965 and 1972. We reach the conclusion that inequities across demographic categories *did not change* over the seven-year span.[33] The effect on the odds of escaping poverty of every socioeconomic variable was, for all practical purposes, identical for both years. The growth of transfer benefits over this period, however, did increase the odds for *all* demographic groups by about 80 percent. In other words, while the odds of escape rose for all types of absolute pretransfer poor households, the odds for any particular demographic group did not increase faster or more slowly than those for any other group.

This conclusion may seem to contradict the patterns of Table 6.4, which showed almost no change between 1965 and 1972 in the percentage of families with female heads under sixty-five that escaped poverty due to transfers, while the other household categories all made substantial gains. The statistical findings suggest that the observed lack of progress reflects a shift in the demographic composition of the female-headed families that unfavorably affected the odds. For example, by 1972, a higher proportion of these families were black. The simple table does not reveal this change.

Our explanation of the findings has emphasized that higher earnings in the *past* often lead to larger transfer payments in the current period. Thus, demographic traits associated with increased odds of escaping poverty are also those related to higher earnings. Earnings in the *current* year clearly affect the odds as well. A family with pretransfer income slightly below the poverty line is much more likely than one with zero pretransfer income to receive enough transfers to be nonpoor. The variables associated with higher past earnings are the same as those related to higher present incomes, so the previous interpretation of the statistical results is open to question.

To investigate this issue, we included a measure of the pretransfer welfare ratios of pretransfer poor households and reestimated the model.[34] The level of pretransfer welfare ratio had the strongest impact of all variables on the chances of escaping poverty—the higher the welfare ratio, the greater the odds. Nonetheless, inequities across demographic categories persisted, and their magnitudes were roughly the same as those found in the other analysis.

Relative Results

Analogous estimates have also been prepared for the relative pretransfer poor. The results (in Appendix D) form the same patterns and have very similar values as the absolute ones. Most importantly, a relative analysis also concludes that no change over time occurred in the effects of any demographic variable.

There is, however, one notable difference between the two sets of estimates. The odds for all groups increased by very little between 1965 and 1972 in the relative analysis. The change was *not* statistically significant and, in any case, was much smaller than the absolute results. This finding lends stronger empirical support to our earlier observation that transfers were not becoming much more effective in preventing relative poverty.

Illustrative Predictions of the Chances of Escaping Poverty

Using the statistical estimates discussed above, we have calculated the predicted odds of escaping absolute and relative poverty for a number of representative groups among the pretransfer poor. (A complete example of how such results are computed appears in Chapter 4.) The outcomes are converted into probabilities and presented in Table 6.9.

TABLE 6.9.   PREDICTED PROBABILITY OF ESCAPING POVERTY FOR
REPRESENTATIVE GROUPS AMONG THE PRETRANSFER POOR
(in percentages)

	(1)	(2)	(3)	(4)
	Absolute		Relative	
	1965	1972	1965	1972
Aged households:				
1. Elderly white couple I[a]	.79	.87	.77	.79
2. Elderly white couple II[b]	.83	.90	.83	.84
3. Elderly black couple I[c]	.57	.70	.56	.58
4. Elderly black couple II[d]	.33	.47	.32	.34
5. Widow (white)[e]	.34	.48	.31	.33
6. Widow (black)[f]	.22	.34	.21	.22
7. Widower (white)[g]	.55	.67	.54	.56
Non-aged households:				
8. Female family head I[h]	.19	.29	.20	.22
9. Female family head II[i]	.15	.25	.15	.16
10. Male family head I[j]	.18	.29	.20	.22
11. Male family head II[k]	.08	.13	.08	.09
12. Well-educated single white man[l]	.13	.22	.14	.15
13. Poorly educated single white man[m]	.09	.15	.09	.10
14. Moderately educated single black man[n]	.09	.15	.08	.09
15. Poorly educated single black man[o]	.03	.06	.04	.04

Notes:

	Age	Sex	Race	Education	Region	Household type
a	65+	M	W	9-12	Non-South	Family
b	65+	M	W	13+	Non-South	Family
c	65+	M	B	0-8	Non-South	Family
d	65+	M	B	0-8	South	Family
e	65+	F	W	0-8	Non-South	Individual
f	65+	F	B	0-8	Non-South	Individual
g	65+	M	W	0-8	Non-South	Individual
h	<65	F	W	9-12	South	Family
i	<65	F	B	9-12	Non-South	Family
j	<65	M	W	9-12	South	Family
k	<65	M	B	9-12	South	Family
l	<65	M	W	13+	South	Individual
m	<65	M	W	0-8	South	Individual
n	<65	M	B	9-12	Non-South	Individual
o	<65	M	B	0-8	South	Individual

Ideally the probabilities computed from the absolute and relative estimates would be
identical for 1965 because the relative definition was chosen in such a manner that the
relative poor 1965 were the same group as the absolute poor. However, because the
estimates do not fit the data perfectly, there are slight differences for most examples.

Looking at the predictions based on either approach, we observe a wide range of probabilities. Elderly couples in pretransfer poverty have had generally high chances of escaping poverty with cash transfers. The probabilities have exceeded .75 for those with white heads-of-households (lines 1 and 2)—these families typically enjoyed middle-class incomes before retirement and, in their later years, then received enough Social Security to remain nonpoor. Elderly black couples have had lower chances of escape. This has been especially true for old, poorly educated black couples living in the South (line 4), many of whom have remained in the rural backwaters. Aged widows and widowers were less likely to be taken out of poverty by transfers. Non-aged families and unrelated persons have had considerably smaller probabilities of escape. Female-headed families I and II, which could represent typical AFDC families, had lower-than-average chances of escaping poverty. Pretransfer poor families with male heads under sixty-five (lines 10 and 11)—the "working poor"—also had rather low likelihoods of escape. Finally, the probabilities for unrelated men under sixty-five have been comparatively smaller. Predictions for similar unrelated women (not shown) were about the same. Some categories of unrelated persons enjoyed better chances of escape than did some family types.

The probabilities of being taken out of absolute poverty improved markedly for all demographic groups between 1965 and 1972 (compare columns 1 and 2). Results based on the relative approach indicate little or no change over this period (columns 3 and 4).

Several of the examples in Table 6.9 provide interesting contrasts with each other. Consider lines 3 and 4. The characteristics defining these two couples are identical except for the region of residence. Living in the South, therefore, lowered the probability from .57 to .33 in 1965. Lines 5, 6, and 7 present elderly single persons who differed only by race (5 and 6) or sex (5 and 7). In 1965, the effect of being black reduced the chances of escape from .34 to .22, while being male raised them from .34 to .55. Examples 8 and 9 compare two families with equally educated female heads. One—line 8—had a white head and lived in the South; the other head was black and resided in another region. The predictions indicate that the positive impact of living outside the South, where transfers were greater, was more than offset by being black. The two male-headed families (lines 10 and 11) differ only by race; so do examples 13 and 15, which are unrelated males. Being black, it can be surmised, lowered the probability in 1965 from .18 to .08 for the families and from .09 to .03 for the unrelated men. Lastly, the effect of education on the chances of escape can be seen with cases 12 and 13, which are demographically identical except that the former is more highly schooled than the latter.

IV. SUMMARY

This chapter has examined the impact of government cash transfers upon poverty in a number of ways. The findings and any inferences one might draw from them must be tempered by the recognition that the omission of in-kind transfers may have distorted the results.

- The fraction of absolute pretransfer poor households lifted over the official poverty lines by transfers steadily increased from .33 in 1965 to .44 in 1972. Cash transfers reduced the absolute pretransfer income gap by 53 percent in 1965; they had erased 64 percent of it by seven years later.

- This upward trend did not appear when a relative definition of poverty was used. About one-third of the relative pretransfer poor received enough transfer income to escape poverty each year. Although transfers received by the relative poor rose by more than 60 percent, the relative poverty gap grew nearly as fast, leading to only a minor increase in the percentage of the gap that these transfers filled.

- In comparison, an analysis that attempted to adjust measured incomes for in-kind transfers, underreporting, and taxes indicated that cash and in-kind transfers raised 72 percent of the pretransfer poor over the official poverty lines in 1972 and filled 83 percent of the income gap.

- The antipoverty effect of transfers has varied greatly across demographic subgroups. Among the pretransfer poor, the elderly have been heavily favored over other households to receive enough aid to be made nonpoor. This reflects the importance of Social Security in the American transfer system. Among non-aged families with children, those with female heads were more likely to escape poverty than those with male heads in 1965. By 1972, this was no longer true.

- Substantial horizontal and vertical inequities have been created by the eligibility rules and benefit standards of the various transfer programs. However, it must be recognized that these programs have not been designed principally to minimize such inequities or to meet the needs of the low-income population.

• Demographic aspects of inequity generated by the transfer system were explored. Six socioeconomic variables also were found to be significantly associated with a household's odds of escaping poverty. Characteristics that were positively related to the odds included being a family, having a head age sixty-five or above, having a male household head, having a white (or other nonblack) head, having a head with above-average education, and living outside the South. The effects of these demographic variables did not change between 1965 and 1972. Such patterns appeared in both the absolute and the relative analyses.

NOTES

[1] See Chapter 1 for further discussion.

[2] See Glen G. Cain and Harold W. Watts, *Income Maintenance and Labor Supply* (Chicago: Rand McNally, 1973); and *Journal of Human Resources* 9 (Spring 1974), which contains a summary of the major labor supply results of the New Jersey Income-Maintenance Experiment.

[3] See Chapter 3 for a description of the relative measure.

[4] The absolute pretransfer poverty gap per poor *person*—not household—was $720 in 1965, $799 in 1968, $807 in 1970, and $870 in 1972. The upward trend in the average gap is more pronounced when we focus on persons than on households because the average size of pretransfer poor households was falling in this period.

[5] See Alice Rivlin, "Income Distribution—Can Economists Help?" *Papers and Proceedings of the American Economic Association* (May 1975), p. 5. Rising earnings and transfers may help change attitudes toward the family, while shifting attitudes simultaneously may influence government transfer policies. The process by which these factors develop and interact is not well understood at present.

[6] The relative pretransfer gap per person was $720 in 1965 and $980 in 1972.

[7] The data sources combine these two programs, which are parallel in many respects.

[8] We include these pensions because some government employees are not covered by Social Security.

[9] Only one public cash transfer is omitted, temporary disability insurance, which has accounted for less than 1 percent of all transfer payments and was not included in our data sources.

[10] These figures are taken directly from the data tapes and were not corrected for underreporting (see later discussion in text). Hence, they are lower than the corresponding numbers in Chapter 3, which are based on official government expenditure records.

[11] The comments in Note 10 apply here as well.

[12] The fraction of pretransfer poor persons brought out of absolute poverty with transfers in these years was 27, 30, 34, and 38 percent.

[13] This ratio (and our use of the percentage fall in the poverty gap as a measure of antipoverty effectiveness) places zero weight on transfers accruing to the pretransfer nonpoor, even if some of these recipients are barely above the poverty threshold. These two measures also ignore payments to the pretransfer poor *beyond* what is needed to reach the

poverty line. Such approaches are somewhat artificial. Transfers to the near-poor and money that raises pretransfer poor households above the poverty cutoff surely raise the welfare of the recipients and deserve some weight in policy considerations. Further, the goals of programs like Unemployment Insurance and Workmen's Compensation are not centered on preventing poverty, but rather seek to cushion income losses for all households. In terms of the formal goals of these programs, payments to even quite affluent families might be considered desirable. Benefits, it follows, could be weighted according to the pretransfer incomes of the recipients, with the weights declining as income rises, but never falling to zero. Though this possibility has merit, the choice of weights requires subjective judgments, which would be as arbitrary as our approach. The zero weight approach, while perhaps not ideal, has the merits of simplifying the calculations and allowing a strong focus on the poverty population. For examples of alternative approaches, see Marilyn Moon, "The Economic Welfare of the Aged: A Measure of Economic Status and an Analysis of the Federal Programs" (Ph.D. diss., University of Wisconsin-Madison, 1974); Timothy M. Smeeding, "Measuring the Economic Welfare of Low Income Households, and the Anti-Poverty Effectiveness of Cash and Non-Cash Transfer Programs" (Ph.D. diss., University of Wisconsin-Madison, 1975); and Harold W. Watts and J.K. Peck, "On the Comparison of Income Distribution Plans," in *The Personal Distribution of Income and Wealth,* ed. James D. Smith, National Bureau of Economic Research, Studies in Income and Wealth, No. 39 (New York: Columbia University Press, 1975).

[14]The result is obtained as follows: Of the $34.3 billion received by the pretransfer poor in 1972, suppose $27.6 billion (equal to the amount received in 1970) was leaked at the 1970 rate of .31. Then this money would have filled $27.6 X .69 = $19.0 billion of the 1972 income gap. In fact, $21.8 billion of the gap was filled, so we infer that the extra $6.7 billion received only filled $21.8 − $19.0 = $2.8 billion. Hence, leakage from this increase was 1 − (2.8/6.7) = .58.

[15]The degree of underreporting is smaller for Social Security (about 10 percent) and larger for public assistance and the four other transfers considered as a group (about 33 percent in both cases).

[16]For example, consider two families with equally low pretransfer incomes, one of which receives public assistance while the other does not. The latter household would receive a greater food stamp subsidy than the former, which would reduce the disparity between them.

[17]Smeeding, "Measuring the Economic Welfare." He imputes benefits at their cash equivalent value to recipients for food stamps, Medicare, Medicaid, and public housing programs. These programs account for more than 90 percent of all in-kind public transfers. See Note 8 in Chapter 4 for further information on this study.

[18]The contribution of medical benefits to the reduction in need may be overstated in these results. Medicare and Medicaid to some extent allowed the poor to purchase medical care with government payment of the costs and to substitute this aid for care formerly provided free by hospitals and doctors.

[19]For this group, the fraction of the pretransfer poverty gap filled by Social Security also declined over these years. Hence, the situation was not one in which total aid received (relative to the pretransfer gap) was rising, yet a smaller percentage of families received enough to actually cross the line in 1972. Social Security benefits paid to these families are largely survivors' benefits. If a larger fraction of these families in 1972 was created by divorce or illegitimacy than in 1965, which appears to be the case, a smaller fraction would be eligible for survivors' benefits. This, in turn, would mean a smaller fraction of these pretransfer poor families would escape poverty due to Social Security.

[20]These two groups, which include all male heads under 65, receive most of the Unemployment Insurance, Workmen's Compensation, and veterans' benefits.

[21]This result is easily explained for the elderly households. Since we count their Social Security benefits first, many families are taken out of poverty before the payments from the other four programs are added, even if these latter benefits in themselves were enough to prevent poverty. The large increase in Social Security's antipoverty impact during the 1965 to 1972 period could, because of our accounting sequence, lead to a smaller impact of these other transfers. This explanation does not apply to families with female heads and children, since Social Security became less effective against poverty.

[22]If we just look at families who were poor after adding all non-public-assistance transfers to their pretransfer income, and ask what fraction of this group was taken out of poverty by public assistance, the answers are 4 percent in 1965 and 9 percent in 1972. These necessarily exceed the table's numbers, but are not appreciably higher. We can still conclude that welfare has done little to move people over the absolute poverty line.

[23]Examining the reduction in the absolute *poverty gap* produced by transfers, we find that, in 1965, cash transfers filled 77 percent of the poverty gap of aged households. For non-aged male-headed families with children, non-aged female-headed families with children, and households with heads under sixty-five and no children, the percentage filled was 22, 48, and 34 percent, respectively. By 1972, these figures had risen to 85, 41, 56, and 44 percent, respectively, when the absolute gap is measured, and to 79, 34, 48, and 40 percent when the relative gap is studied. The relationship among the four groups and its change over time are similar to the patterns in Tables 6.4 and 6.5, which consider the number of living units escaping poverty.

[24]One might speculate whether these observations lend support to our comment in Chapter 2 that different poverty definitions can give rise to different policies. It can be argued that government transfer policy and payment schedules were at least partially chosen to meet the goal of taking a large number of households out of poverty. Benefits, therefore, were adjusted to bring many households over the accepted poverty lines, which were, of course, the absolute ones. If the official poverty standard had been a relative one, perhaps Social Security and public assistance payments would have been higher.

[25]See, for example, Robert Lampman, "Public and Private Transfers as Social Process" in *Redistribution to the Rich and the Poor: The Grants Economics of Income Distribution,* ed. Kenneth Boulding and Martin Pfaff (Belmont, Calif.: Wadsworth, 1972) and Ben Gillingham, "Cash Transfers: How Much Do They Help the Poor?" Institute for Research on Poverty Special Report, University of Wisconsin-Madison, 1971.

[26]The omission of in-kind income from our poverty measure seems especially troublesome in a discussion of equity. The distributions of food stamps, Medicaid, and Medicare benefits differ greatly from that of cash transfers. Combining cash and in-kind assistance may further exaggerate the inequities of the cash system, or perhaps lessen them. For 1965, when the volume of in-kind transfers was small, only minor distortion is possible. But in later years, when in-kind benefits exceeded $10 billion, bias is very likely, though the direction of this bias is uncertain.

[27]The detailed table from which these numbers are drawn is in Appendix D, Table D1.

[28]This is a slight overstatement. Social Security and Unemployment Insurance benefits can be reduced if labor earnings exceed the statutory limits. Nonetheless, eligibility and the maximum benefit from which reductions are made depend on criteria other than one's current income.

[29]These latter two persons might be eligible for food stamps, however, and, in some cases, AFDC-UP. Agricultural employees are not covered by Unemployment Insurance. The food stamp program helps reduce inequities in the cash transfer system in two ways. It provides aid to families that may be ineligible for any cash transfer. Second, the food stamp subsidy declines as cash income rises. Thus, of two equal-size families, the one with higher cash transfers receives a smaller food stamp bonus than the one with lower cash benefits. Hence,

the difference in the total packages of aid—cash plus food stamps—will be smaller than the differences in cash benefits. However, in this program, the national participation rate of eligible households has been under 50 percent. (Gary Bickel and Maurice MacDonald, "Participation Rates in the Food Stamp Program: Estimated Levels, by State," Institute for Research on Poverty Discussion Paper 253-75 (University of Wisconsin-Madison, 1975).)

[30] If the analysis could be conducted within a life-cycle framework, leapfrogging might be less prevalent. For example, an aged recipient of Social Security may leapfrog over a young earner in the current period even though, over a lifetime, the two may receive equal transfer benefits. A table indicating the extent of leapfrogging in 1965 and 1972 is in Appendix D, Table D2.

[31] The complete statistical results are in Appendix D, Table D3.

[32] This reasoning may also partly explain the male—female difference. All else held constant, men usually earn more than women. However, the connection is not so strong as the racial case, we believe, because for both Social Security and Workmen's Compensation, the widow's benefits are based on her husband's earnings, not her own.

[33] Once again, excluding food stamps and other in-kind benefits may have influenced this conclusion.

[34] We divided households into three groups according to whether their pretransfer welfare ratios were zero or less, between .01 and .50, or between .51 and .99.

7 Progress Against Poverty: Summary and Outlook for the Future

The previous five chapters have given a detailed statistical analysis of changes in the incidence of poverty and the composition of the poverty population between 1965 and 1972. Progress against pretransfer poverty has been charted, and an assessment made of the effect of macroeconomic factors on pretransfer poverty. Changes over the period in posttransfer poverty have been documented, along with the effects of the system of cash transfers. The first section of this final chapter summarizes some of the main findings and themes of previous chapters. The second section looks to the future and points to likely issues for social policy debate during the next decade.

I. PROGRESS AGAINST POVERTY, 1965–1972: SUMMARY

In this study, the position of the poor has been viewed from two major perspectives. Because they measure different things, both are important. Both perspectives have policy objectives associated with them; an appraisal of the success of past policies is dependent on which perspective one adopts.

The first perspective is the official government poverty definition, which specifies a fixed amount of real cash income (determined by family size and residential location) below which a family is considered poor. This is an absolute definition of poverty. The second has been called the "relative definition of poverty" throughout the book, but can equally well be thought of as one indicator of the degree of inequality in the distribution of income (that is, a measure of how incomes of various families or persons compare with one another). This relative definition is related to the official poverty lines. Each family's current income is divided by its official poverty line, yielding an index (welfare ratio) of income relative to need. A family is defined as poor in the relative sense if it has a welfare ratio that is less than a certain fraction of the median welfare ratio of the U.S. population.[1]

Rising average real incomes do not affect the absolute measure of poverty. However, the relative poverty lines increase at about the same rate as average incomes. A society can reduce the problem of poverty in an absolute sense by moving people above a given poverty threshold. The same society may simultaneously become less egalitarian as measured by the distance of its poorest citizens from the typical standard of living. The absolute measure would show progress; the relative measure would not.

Poverty as Officially Defined

Pretransfer Poverty

In any given year, the economy generates a set of earnings, property incomes, and private transfers (for example, alimony payments and gifts) among households. The magnitude and distribution of this income determines the level of poverty that exists before the government redistributes income through public transfers (pretransfer poverty). For the poor, the overwhelming proportion of this pretransfer income is received in the form of earnings.

In 1965, as documented in Chapter 5, $25\frac{1}{2}$ percent ($15\frac{1}{2}$ million) of U.S. households[2] were poor before goverment transfers. In 1968, after three years of strong economic growth and falling unemployment rates, this amount had dropped by three percentage points. After 1968, however, poverty incidence rose. Over the whole period from 1965 to 1972, the incidence of household pretransfer poverty dropped by less than one percentage point.

Beneath these overall averages, poverty incidence fell for all the demographic subgroups (usually by small amounts) except for families headed by prime-age white females and elderly females, for which it rose.[3]

Two major factors influencing pretransfer income status are the aggregate rate of economic growth and the unemployment rate. A rise of 1 percent in the pretransfer income of the average family was associated over this period, other things equal, with a decline of almost 1 percent in the incidence of absolute pretransfer poverty among families. But other things were not equal. Although mean pretransfer income steadily rose between 1965 and 1972, the incidence of absolute poverty did not decline proportionately, because the unemployment rate, another direct influence on the level of pretransfer poverty, increased. A 10 percent change in the unemployment rate was associated with a change in the incidence of family pretransfer poverty of between 2.5 and 3 percent. Between 1965 and 1972, the unemployment rate rose—from 4.5 percent to 5.6 percent—and one-half million more families were made poor in consequence.

Differences among demographic groups are hidden in these broad movements. A 1 percent rise in mean pretransfer family income was associated with a fall in poverty incidence of 2.1 percent for families with prime-age white male heads and 3.0 percent for families with black male heads. A change in the unemployment rate of 10 percent was associated with a 5.8 percent change in poverty incidence for black prime-age male-headed families and 3.4 percent for comparable white families. Families with working-age female heads, the elderly, and unrelated individuals were, in contrast, much less responsive to changes in macroeconomic conditions.

Macroeconomic effects are, obviously, greatest on those who can earn. For those demographic groups that are deficient in labor market skills or that do not participate in the labor market by reason of age, child care responsibilities, or disability, a low unemployment rate and healthy economic growth are not enough to ensure minimally decent living standards. As economic growth takes more people over the poverty threshold, those remaining in poverty will be progressively less sensitive to further growth, because they increasingly will become those who are not affected by labor market conditions. For this reason, we must also be concerned with other instruments of antipoverty policy.

Social Welfare Expenditures Going to the Poor

During this period, economic growth has occurred simultaneously with a growing budget for social welfare expenditures. In Chapter 3, the amount spent by federal, state, and local government on social welfare during the period from 1965 to 1972 was analyzed, and the

proportion that wound up going to the pretransfer poor was estimated. The expenditures examined encompass cash transfer programs, as well as those in-kind public expenditures that provide food,
housing, manpower training, health, and education benefits.[4] It is
relevant to keep in mind here that, except for those programs
designed explicitly for low-income groups (that is, those for which
eligibility is conditioned on having low income), these expenditures
are designed to promote the well-being of the population, in general.
It is not to be expected, therefore, that the proportion going to the
pretransfer poor should ever approach 100 percent. It is of interest,
however, to see how much does go to poor families and to trace how
(or whether) this proportion has changed over time.

In 1965, 75\frac{1}{2}$ billion was spent by all levels of government on
social welfare—39 percent of all public spending. By 1968, this had
climbed to $109 billion. But total public spending had increased
proportionately, so that the fraction going to social welfare expenditures stayed the same, 39 percent. By 1972, social welfare expenditures had risen to $185 billion and, as a fraction of total public
spending, had risen to 46 percent. Between 1965 and 1968, the
composition of those expenditures changed markedly, mainly because of the introduction of Medicare and Medicaid and, to a lesser
extent, because of the growth of OEO and related antipoverty
programs. Between 1968 and 1972, the composition changed again,
although less noticeably, mainly in the direction of larger proportions going for in-kind programs. Over the 1965–1968 period, cash-
transfer programs grew more slowly than the aggregate; between
1968 and 1972, they regained only part of that relative loss.

How much of these social welfare expenditures went to the pretransfer poor? In 1965, nearly 42 percent—$31 billion—went to the
15$\frac{1}{2}$ million pretransfer poor households. Between 1965 and 1968,
the dollar expenditures that went to the poor increased to $44
billion, but the fraction going to the poor decreased to 40 percent,
largely because of a decrease in pretransfer poverty from nearly 26
percent to just over 23 percent of total households. By 1972, the
amount going to the poor had nearly doubled ($79 billion), and the
fraction of the total had become slightly higher than the 1965 figure.
In constant dollars adjusted for inflation, the social welfare expenditures that went to the poor increased by 69 percent, and those that
went to the nonpoor increased by 55 percent.

Why didn't these substantial and rapidly growing social welfare
expenditures result in the disappearance of posttransfer poverty? The
answer has several parts. First, the official definition of poverty only

includes cash income, so any expenditures for goods or services provided to the poor do not reduce measured poverty. Second, about 20 percent of the social welfare expenditures on the poor over this period took the form of education, manpower, and community programs, whose effects on poverty status are long run in nature. In the short run, indeed, such programs—by diverting people from the labor force—might increase measured poverty. Third, macroeconomic policy also affects the status of the poor (in particular, through the unemployment rate, the rate of growth, and the rate of inflation), and may have counteracted the antipoverty effectiveness of direct social welfare expenditures.

Cash Transfers and the Poor

Because cash transfers contribute directly to a reduction in income poverty, their effect on the poor was examined in Chapter 6.

In 1965, 33 percent of all pretransfer poor households were taken out of poverty by cash transfers. By 1972, 44 percent of households that were pretransfer poor received enough income from public transfers to escape poverty. Further, cash transfers decreased the pretransfer poverty-income gap by 53 percent in 1965 and 64 percent seven years later. The poverty-reducing effect of those transfers did, however, vary across demographic groups, with the elderly being heavily favored over other groups throughout the period, largely because of Social Security. In 1965, cash transfers moved over the threshold 51 percent of households with an aged head, and in 1972, this percentage had increased to 63. In 1965, cash transfers lifted 11 percent of non-aged male-headed households over the line, and by 1972, this had doubled to become 23 percent. Non-aged female-headed households made minimal progress over the period, the percentage made nonpoor by cash transfers only increasing by one percentage point, from 22 to 23 percent. Finally, the percentage taken out of poverty of households with no children and headed by a non-aged person increased from 19 to 26 percent.

In every year, the total amount paid out in cash transfers would have been more than enough to fill the poverty-income gap had it been distributed in a way that exactly matched the amount each family needed to reach the poverty line. In 1972, indeed, even the amount paid to the pretransfer poor was sufficient to close the gap. That posttransfer poverty remained is due to the functioning of the system of transfers, whereby some nonpoor families receive transfers, some poor families receive nothing (31 percent in 1965, 22 percent in 1972), and others receive more than enough to make them nonpoor.

Posttransfer Poverty

Macroeconomic fluctuations and the improvement in the ability of the cash transfer system to prevent poverty led to changes in the incidence of posttransfer poverty between 1965 and 1972. In 1965, 15.6 percent of the population (29.9 million persons) lived in post-transfer poor households. By 1968, a prosperous year with low levels of unemployment, 12.8 percent (25.1 million) of all Americans were poor. Macroeconomic conditions deteriorated between 1968 and 1972, but their adverse impact on poverty was more than offset by the growth of cash transfers. As a result, the incidence of posttransfer poverty dropped to 11.9 percent in 1972.

As this overall progress took place, the composition of posttransfer poverty changed. Compared to 1965, the 1972 posttransfer poor more often lived in female-headed households and in households with young heads. Heads of poor households in 1972 were more likely to have a high school or college education and less likely to have any labor market activity during the year than their 1965 counterparts.

Correcting for In-Kind Transfers, the Tax System, and Underreporting[5]

The discussions in the previous subsections have concentrated on the poverty-decreasing effects, as poverty is officially measured, of cash transfers. There are several reasons why this may be considered an inadequate measure of the poverty-reducing effect of government policy. First, during the last decade, as we have seen, the relative importance of in-kind transfers has increased substantially. Second, it has been estimated that about 20 percent of all cash transfer income was not reported in the data used to derive the above estimates.[6] Third, no account is taken in the above statistics of the positive taxes paid by the poor. Here we discuss how the picture changes if these three considerations are taken into account.

In 1968, 52 percent of pretransfer poor households were taken out of poverty, when underreporting and in-kind transfers are accounted for, as compared with the official figure of 35 percent—that is, about one-quarter of the households remaining poor after cash transfers were lifted over the line. By 1972, 72 percent of pretransfer poor households were taken out of poverty as compared with 44 percent by the official figures—one-half of those remaining poor after cash transfers were lifted over the line. The revised figures thus show more progress against poverty for both years and also show a more rapid rate of decline of posttransfer poverty over the 1965–1972 period.

Analogous calculations for the poverty-income gap show, again, that when these corrections are made, measured progress against poverty was consistently greater throughout the period, and the rate at which posttransfer poverty declined over the period was also faster.

Relative Poverty—A Measure of Inequality in the Income Distribution

We have said nothing so far about those whose incomes fall so far below the median (that is, the typical) pretransfer income level that they are poor by our relative definition.

Pretransfer Relative Poverty

In overall terms, relative poverty[7] dipped between 1965 and 1968; after 1968, however, it rose. In 1972, a higher fraction of the population than in 1965 lived in families with private income opportunities below the relative poverty line. Within this overall picture, only two demographic groups reduced their level of relative poverty: families headed by nonwhite prime-age males and families headed by white males over sixty-five. For all other demographic groups, the extent of relative poverty increased.

As with absolute poverty, a rise in average incomes was associated during this period with a decrease in relative poverty, although a somewhat smaller one—a 1 percent increase in mean family pretransfer income being associated with only a one-third-of-1-percent fall in the incidence of pretransfer relative poverty. The effect on the various demographic subgroups was basically similar to those for absolute poverty (though smaller). For changes in unemployment, the situation was almost identical for relative as for absolute pretransfer poverty.

Posttransfer Relative Poverty and the Effect of Cash Transfers

On a relative basis, cash assistance made no overall progress during this period in getting people out of poverty. On our relative measure, 33 percent of the pretransfer poor were taken out of poverty by transfers in 1965. This percentage dropped to 31 percent in 1968 and 1970, then returned to 33 percent in 1972. The fraction of the poverty-income gap filled by transfers did get progressively larger, however, as increasing cash benefits brought people closer to the median but not near enough to cross the relative benchmark. Disaggregating the overall figures, we find that the relative position of the elderly poor improved a little, 51 percent being moved over the relative line in 1965 and 52 percent in 1972. Childless households with non-aged heads also improved their position, but minimally. For families with children and prime-age male heads, the situation did improve substantially, with the fraction of relative poor lifted over the threshold by cash transfers increasing from 11 to 17 percent. The position with respect to prime-age female heads with children, in contrast, deteriorated. In 1965, cash transfers took 22 percent of them over the relative line, but in 1972, this figure dropped to 15 percent—in spite of the increases in AFDC payments over the period. Because transfers did not become more effective against poverty, the incidence of posttransfer relative poverty did not decline during this period. In 1965, 15.6 percent of the nation fell below the relative poverty line; the incidence fell to 14.6 percent in 1968, but rose again to reach 15.7 percent in 1972. However, changes in the composition of the relative posttransfer poor were similar to those for the absolute poor.

While no estimates are available of how correction for underreporting and in-kind transfers would affect these estimates, it is safe to say that they would show somewhat more progress but would not change the basic picture as much as when the absolute poverty measure is used.

What Happened between 1972 and 1975?[8]

Pretransfer Poverty

In contrast to the 1965–1972 period, average real pretransfer incomes have been steadily falling since 1972. In the most recent period, as in the earlier period, the unemployment rate increased, but much more sharply than before (from 5.6 percent in 1972 to somewhere between $8\frac{1}{2}$ percent and 9 percent for 1975). Both these effects increase pretransfer poverty.

Macroeconomic effects are, as we saw in Chapter 5, stronger for prime-age male-headed families than for any other demographic groups. Since 1972, therefore, while pretransfer poverty has probably increased for all demographic groups, poverty incidence will have risen relatively more for prime-age male-headed families, shifting the composition of the poor since 1972 in the direction of containing more of the "working" poor.

In the 1972–1975 period, the rate of inflation has increased. Between 1965 and 1972, inflation affected the poor's purchasing power about the same way as that of the general population. In this recent period, however, the prices affecting the poor the most (necessities such as food and housing) have risen significantly faster than the general price level, and inflation has thus had a more than proportionate effect on the spending power of the poor. Inflation (and this has been true for the whole 1965–1975 period) also affects the net worth of the poor adversely, unlike most of the middle-income and upper-middle-income groups whose net worth increases during inflation.

Both these effects of inflation in the most recent period will have led to progressive deterioration in the economic welfare of the pretransfer poor in comparison to the rest of society—over and above what shows in the poverty statistics themselves. These price-level effects are, however, minor compared with the effect of the current recession on those poor families that are labor market oriented.

Social Welfare Expenditures Going to the Poor[9]

Social welfare spending increased by $50 billion between 1972 and 1974. The 1973–1974 increase, in current dollars, was the largest absolute increase ever, with the 1972–1973 increase not far behind it; in percentage terms, the annual increases were slightly smaller. In real terms, the annual percentage increases were much less than those from 1965 to 1972. Between 1972 and 1973, the real rate of increase was 7 percent; in the 1965–1972 period, it was 9 percent; between 1973 and 1974, the real increase had shrunk to 3 percent, the smallest since 1960.

As a percentage of the Gross National Product, social welfare spending continued to rise, to 18 percent in 1974. As a proportion of total government spending, it also rose, to 56 percent in 1974. A number of compositional changes during the 1972–1974 period make it probable that an increased proportion of social welfare spending went to the poor during that time.

First, federal social welfare spending as a proportion of the total grew between 1972 and 1974 from 56 percent to 58 percent. As we saw in Chapter 3, 52 percent of such federal spending has gone to the poor compared with only 30 percent of state and local social welfare expenditures.

TABLE 7.1.   SOCIAL WELFARE SPENDING 1972-1974. TOTALS AND
SELECTED CATEGORIES

	Percentage Increases in Spending		Percentage Going to the Poor[a]
	1972-1973	*1973-1974*	
Total	11.3	13.2	42.6
Federal	15.3	13.9	52
State and local	6.5	12.2	30
Selected programs:			
Food stamps	19.0	27.0	85
SSI[b] + cash public assistance	2.8	13.5	87
Medicare	7.3	19.4	48
Medicaid	19.0	22.0	75
Housing	63.8	18.4	55
Social Security + railroad benefits	22.0	13.5	58
Education	7.7	11.5	19

*Source: Alfred M. Skolnik and Sophie R. Dales, "Social Welfare Expenditures, Fiscal
Year 1974,"* Social Security Bulletin *38 (January 1975); and Chapter 3,   Table 3.4.*

[a]*These are 1972 proportions; we are assuming they stayed roughly the same over the next
two years.*

[b]*SSI was not introduced until 1974.*

Second, expenditures on the major programs that go predominantly to the poor increased faster than the overall total. Table 7.1
shows (for fiscal 1972–1973 and 1973–1974) percentage increases in
total social welfare spending, the progress made in the major programs predominantly directed to the poor, and the actual percentage
of each expenditure category that has been estimated to reach the
poor.

As can be seen from the table, food stamps, Medicaid, housing,
Social Security, and Railroad Retirement all grew at more than the
average rate over the two-year period. In all these programs, more
than 50 percent of the benefits go to the poor. Cash public assistance
grew little in 1972–1973, but in 1973–1974, with the introduction
of the Supplemental Security Income (SSI) program, it grew as much
as the overall average. Expenditures on education, which are not

highly targeted on the poor, grew less than the average in both years, but the growth they did show came mainly in 1973–1974, and was largely in elementary and secondary education at the state and local government level—which is why the overall proportion spent by state and local government rises during the 1973–1974 period.

The Antipoverty Effectiveness of the Cash and In-Kind Transfer System

These trends indicate that the system is moving continuingly toward spending a smaller proportion on cash assistance to the needy and a larger proportion on in-kind transfers. The introduction of SSI is a partial offset to that for the elderly, blind, and disabled, but benefits from the other major income-conditioned cash program, AFDC, are not being raised proportionately with the other cash transfer programs. In-kind programs are, however, increasing rapidly, particularly the food stamp program. Moreover, since 1972, Social Security, SSI, and food stamps have had automatic cost-of-living increases built in. Except for AFDC recipients, therefore, those poor who are predominantly outside the labor market are automatically compensated for inflation.

Has this progress been enough to reduce the percentage of post-tax-and-transfer poor below the 1972 level? From the evidence just discussed, it seems that the elderly and the disabled are almost certainly less posttransfer-poor than in 1972. Posttransfer poverty incidence among female-headed families may be slightly higher, if increased food stamp and AFDC participation have not entirely offset the effects of unemployment. Able-bodied male-headed poor families have been eligible for food stamps in all states since mid-1974, but this will not have been enough to offset the effects of the fall in real income and the rise in the unemployment rate.[10] Posttransfer poverty incidence for this group is, therefore, certainly higher than in 1972. Our overall judgment is that about 12.7 percent of the entire population will be poor (as defined by the government) in 1975, compared to 11.9 percent in 1972.

II. THE SOCIAL POLICY AGENDA FOR THE DECADE TO COME

Certain major observations stand out from the preceding summary. First, pretransfer poverty as measured by the official absolute poverty definition hardly decreased at all between 1965 and 1972, and has certainly increased since 1972. This means that a larger percentage of people than ten years ago live in families where earnings and other nontransfer income are unable to lift them over the poverty line. Second, the American transfer system has grown enormously in the last decade, and because of it, official posttransfer poverty has been reduced. Third, cash transfers are constituting a steadily decreasing proportion of the benefits going to the poor from the American system of transfers. Fourth, in-kind benefit programs have grown substantially, both proportionately and in absolute terms. This renders the official poverty definition, which counts only cash income, an increasingly inappropriate measure for assessing posttransfer poverty status. Expanding the definition of income to include in-kind transfers reduced posttransfer poverty incidence in 1972 by about four percentage points, and the appropriate correction factor has probably increased since then.[11] Fifth, although poor families headed by an able-bodied male benefited significantly from the overall system of cash transfers during the 1965 to 1972 period, there are few benefits for those who do not qualify for Unemployment Insurance or the other social insurance programs. Further, the poor have been adversely affected most by the dramatic deterioration in macroeconomic conditions since 1972. Finally, the distribution of pretransfer income has become more unequal. The fraction of people with incomes less than 44 percent of the median has grown. The growth of transfers over the period served to compensate for this increase in inequality, but did not reverse the trend. Our relative poverty measure shows the proportion of posttransfer poor to have been static between 1965 and 1972, and there are no indications that it has decreased since then.

These observations lead to several issues that will be on the nation's future policy agenda. The rest of this final section will address them.

Should the Current System of Transfers Be Modified by a New Comprehensive Welfare Reform?

Between 1965 and 1972, the percentage of pretransfer poor families receiving nothing from the cash transfer system shrank from 31 percent to 22 percent. When in-kind transfers are included (and since the universalization of food stamps), that number must be still smaller. With respect to adequacy of benefits, when underreporting and in-kind transfers are corrected for, private earnings combined with the social insurance and income-support systems left only 7 percent of U.S. households below the poverty line in 1972. The problem of absolute posttransfer poverty in the United States, therefore, has changed substantially during the decade since the war on poverty was declared.

This is not to say that an ideal system of public assistance is in place nor that the current one has evolved in any sense as policy planners and social policy experts might have wished. An ideal system, it would be generally agreed, should have nationally uniform eligibility standards, benefit levels, definitions of the family unit, and definition of income. It should also be a system that covers those in need (by some suitable definition) without discouraging their will or incentive to work. Such a system should provide horizontal equity (that is, people with the same characteristics in the same circumstances should be treated the same) and vertical equity (that is, those in greater need should receive greater assistance and those who earn more should end up with a larger total amount). It should be operated with a minimum loss of dignity and self-respect on the part of those receiving the benefits, and such a system should be straightforward and economical to administer, so that a minimum amount of the budget goes into administration rather than benefits.[12]

Welfare satisfied none of these criteria well in the sixties. So with the establishment of OEO and the focusing of attention on the poor, criticism of welfare began to mount. These criticisms led to support for proposals to replace existing welfare programs with a universal income-support plan—culminating in the Republican Administration's efforts between 1969 and 1972 to introduce the Family Assistance Plan, a broadly based negative-income-tax proposal for families with children. These efforts failed, and a similar effort in 1974 never reached the stage of a legislative proposal.

The reasons for their failure must be viewed as largely political. First, there seems to be a continuing fear on the part of Americans that if able-bodied persons are presented with a transfer payment option they will stop working. The history of social programs attests to the fact that the American voter is more generous when a potential recipient can be characterized as in some way hindered in his efforts to participate in the labor market. People with no disability other than insufficient income, in general, are assumed to be able to find work if they want and, further, are assumed to be unlikely to want it if they can get "something for nothing." To test this second assumption, OEO (and later HEW) funded a series of field experiments in which some families were paid negative-income-tax payments and some were not. Data from the first of these (the New Jersey Experiment) have now been analyzed and indicate that able-bodied male heads-of-household show very little disincentive to work associated with a negative-income-tax plan at moderate tax rates and guarantee levels.[13] Some of these data were used as evidence in the Family Assistance Plan debates, but other issues proved to be overriding.

Belief in the value of work and the need to make sure that those who *can* work do goes very deep, as is shown by the fact that no income-conditioned cash assistance program has been passed without a work or training requirement. If one takes the position that the only causes for concern are the economic costs associated with a widespread reduction of work effort, factual evidence of no such reduction may be persuasive. It seems, however, that the concern is with guarding against violation of the work ethic per se. In the most recent years, this concern that persons should work has extended progressively to female heads of families with dependent children, as manifested in recent debates over AFDC. When survivor's insurance and Aid to Dependent Children were started, one objective for these programs was stated as enabling mothers to stay at home while their children were young. As the brief history in Chapter 1 shows, by the mid-sixties this had changed: AFDC was being made progressively more stringent in terms of work or training requirements.

A second reason for failure of welfare reform is public unwillingness to give untied money to the able-bodied poor. This is based on the apprehension that they do not know how to spend money "wisely," and will waste it on nonessentials. Here, again, there is factual evidence; the poor are much like everyone else in their spending habits. But whether such evidence is persuasive depends on values.

There is a third reason, though, which differs sharply from the first two. Beneficiaries of existing programs (and, therefore, potential beneficiaries of the new proposals) were vocally and vehemently opposed to the idea of averaging out and universalizing benefits—which to them meant the possibility of averaging down. This points up a major problem with large-scale welfare reform. Certain areas of the country have high benefit levels. And certain groups receive higher benefits than other groups. Proposals typically contain "grandfather" clauses to guard against any current recipient's becoming worse off by any change, but it is not lost on the recipients that program replacement is designed, in part, to save taxpayers' money by reducing, not only administrative costs, but also certain of the high benefit levels.

Developments since 1965 (and even more since 1972) *have,* however, increased the universality of coverage and decreased the extent of benefit variability.[14] AFDC was liberalized by the 1967 amendments, which specified that the benefit-reduction rate on earnings could not exceed 67 percent. (In fact, the benefit-reduction rate is rarely even as high as that because of the deductibility of work expenses, exemption of initial earnings, rent allowances, and, in some instances, caseworker discretion.) AFDC has also been liberalized by court rulings outlawing (1) the cutting of benefit levels during any year to match a fixed-sum appropriation, (2) state residence requirements, (3) state rules requiring support from "a man in the house," and (4) counting expected contributions from relatives. All these changes have contributed to an extremely high participation rate by those eligible. AFDC guarantee levels still vary widely by geographic area. However, food stamps have reduced this variation because of the inverse relationship between food stamp bonus values and AFDC payments. When food stamp bonuses are combined with AFDC, the guarantee level for a family of four becomes $5046 in Hawaii (a high-benefit state) and $2316 in Mississippi (a low-benefit state). This ratio is only two to one, rather than the six-to-one ratio one gets from comparing AFDC guarantees alone. The advent on 1 January 1974 of Supplemental Security Income as a nationwide negative income tax for the aged, blind, and disabled—with guarantees almost at the poverty line in all states, uniform eligibility and benefit provisions, and a 50 percent benefit-reduction rate on earnings—and in 1 July 1974 of food stamps as a national, universal, and uniform guaranteed minimum income for food have already been noted.

All these developments add up to a significantly more generous, comprehensive, and uniform system than existed in 1965. This piecemeal but real progress, when combined with the political fate of proposals for a major overhaul of the transfer system, suggests that remaining inadequacies are likely to be tackled in an incremental way.

Major inadequacies that will be on the policy agenda for resolution in the coming years are discussed briefly below. They include continuing inadequate coverage of the working poor, horizontal inequities within the AFDC program, cumulative benefit-reduction rates creating a work-disincentive effect, and irrational financing structures underlying the transfer system.

Improving Coverage of the "Working Poor"

As we have seen, the incidence of absolute poverty among the working poor (that is, prime-age male-headed families) decreased on both a pretransfer and a posttransfer basis between 1965 and 1972. However, for those who cannot earn enough to raise themselves above the poverty level and who are not eligible for social insurance programs,[15] the transfer options open to them are still inadequate. They can apply for food stamps, and increasing numbers of them are doing so, but there is no other significant program available to them. This leads to significant horizontal inequity between them and female-headed families, the aged, and the disabled. Liberalizing the eligibility requirements of AFDC-UP might be a partial answer, but it would also have to be mandated to operate in every state for it to be an effective option.

Another option, which is gaining progressively more support, is an earnings subsidy. This would be a program whereby earnings below a certain level would be supplemented at an appropriate rate. The 1975 Tax Reduction Act has instituted such a subsidy on a temporary basis. People without a job would not qualify, but when it is remembered that in 1972 one-quarter of all poor families were headed by persons who worked at least fifty weeks and more than one-half by persons who worked at least one week, an earnings subsidy can be seen as reaching many of the poor that the current system passes over. Obviously, it requires a relatively buoyant economy with low unemployment rates for earnings subsidies to provide effective income support.

In addition, the working poor form the remaining poor group that, in general, is not eligible for any health benefits. Nationalizing Medicaid would fill this major hole, and it would also promote much greater horizontal equity by narrowing the benefit gap significantly between intact poor families and the other poor groups.

Reforming AFDC

Even though the advent of food stamps has narrowed the effective benefit differentials in the AFDC program, combined benefit levels in some states are still well below the poverty line and less than one-half the levels in the high-benefit states. The key objective of reform could be to raise the benefit levels in the low-benefit states without further increasing either the existing differentials among various state supplements within the AFDC program or the disparity between benefit options available to female-headed families and those available to male-headed families. This joint objective could be achieved with regulations analogous to those stipulated by Congress with respect to SSI. Those regulations required the federal government to pick up the extra costs of extending any *existing* state supplements to all eligibles under the new SSI program. Any future increases in generosity of any state supplements, however, were to be financed entirely by the state budgets. The federal government would, therefore, only contribute to the financing of uniform federal across-the-board benefit increases. The prediction is that, as federal benefit levels rise, the relative importance of state supplements will progressively diminish.

Another needed reform is overdue. AFDC lacks an automatic correction factor for inflation. Enacting such a cost-of-living adjustment would protect female-headed poor families from falling real incomes in periods of inflation. It would also decrease the horizontal inequity between them and the aged, blind, and disabled who now have a semi-annual cost-of-living adjustment in SSI.

Lowering High Cumulative Benefit-Reduction Rates[16]

Another important defect of the current income-support system is that combined benefit-reduction rates from the various programs can get high enough to create powerful work disincentives. For example, for families receiving food stamps and AFDC, an increase of $100 in earnings may lead to a $77 reduction in benefits. Low-income persons not on AFDC or SSI lose $30 of their food stamp bonus for every $100 rise in earnings, face additional benefit-reduction rates on child care benefits, and must pay Social Security taxes, and, in many cases, positive personal income taxes. So it would appear that many family heads may face implicit benefit-reduction rates on earnings well above 50 percent in certain income ranges. If new income-tested programs are to be added (as in some health proposals), the rates will rise yet further. This problem is exacerbated when full benefits are received up to a certain income level and then suddenly and completely withdrawn above that level. Such a "notch" creates strong incentives to keep income below the benefit-cutoff level.

High benefit-reduction rates can be lowered by regulations requiring the benefit from one program to be included as countable income in computing the benefits from another program. This would have the effect of lowering the benefits received by those with no earnings, but it would not change the break-even level. The rate of benefit reduction as earnings increase, therefore, would be slowed down. Another way of producing the same effect is by folding one program into the proposed budget of another, producing a new combined guarantee lower than each program alone would dictate. (This was done, in effect, with food stamps when SSI was introduced.)

Rationalizing the Financing Structures of Social Welfare Expenditures

The routes through which social welfare programs are financed have not been treated in this book. A word should be said about them here, however. To decide to live with incremental reforms to the delivery part of the system instead of pursuing major change in the direction of universal noncategorical cash assistance does not necessarily mean that the financing structures underlying these programs should also remain unchanged.

Public assistance and Medicaid have been financed by federal grants-in-aid to states, which must match a designated fraction of the grants with their own funds. This system may require major redesign. The use of matching federal funds grew through efforts to get benefits to special populations that state and local programs have tended to ignore. Starting in 1968 and proceeding rapidly since then, statutes and court orders have been accruing on the basis of civil rights legislation that can be used to enforce coverage. Hence, the federal government no longer has to bribe states to cover certain categories; it can sue them. Given the changed legal environment, it is important to formulate a coherent framework to guide the allocation of federal revenue sharing and grants-in-aid moneys for public assistance programs.

The financing of the Unemployment Insurance system and Social Security are also in need of restructuring. The recent high unemployment rates have shown how shaky the system of Unemployment Insurance reserves can be. The changing demographic structure of the population is highlighting how regressive the payroll tax can be as a means of financing Social Security. The payroll tax rate on earned income is already over 10 percent (counting the employer's contribution), and it is only levied on incomes up to $14,300. Any earned income above that level, therefore, is exempt from the tax, meaning that the higher the earnings, the lower the average payroll tax rate. If financing changes are not made, this 10 percent rate will have to be increased substantially over the next decade, because the changing demographic structure is increasing the number of elderly persons receiving benefits in proportion to the rest of the population—whose earnings are taxed to pay for those benefits.

. . .

All the points made so far have ignored an important set of issues concerning the degree of inequality in the distribution and redistribution of income. Far from getting closer to resolution during the last decade, these issues have become more conspicuous and very possibly, from the point of view of society, more politically divisive. This chapter will conclude with a discussion of them.

If anyone had predicted in 1964 that the great society and war on poverty programs would leave unchanged the posttransfer distribution of money income and that the pretransfer distribution of earnings would have worsened after ten years, few people would have believed the prediction. But that is what has happened. More people fell below our relative benchmark in terms of their pretransfer income—both in absolute terms and as a proportion of the population—in 1972 than in 1965, and this trend has almost certainly continued since then.[17]

Expenditures on education in the 1960s appear to have made little difference by this measure, despite the substantial increases in high-school-graduation rates and in the ratio of college-educated to non-college—educated workers. This is partly due to the fact that much of the shift in education over the period has been a shifting up of the average level rather than a change in the proportions of people with education significantly above that level. But it has also proved far less easy than anyone thought in 1964 to improve test scores over the long run by spending more on education. And it is difficult to show in any case, that test score improvements increase earnings.[18]

It has also been hard to demonstrate that manpower programs judged cost effective in themselves have placed previously unemployed workers into jobs that would have been otherwise unfilled. Their effect has probably been, at least partly, to put newly trained workers into jobs previously filled by other workers, who were simply displaced. And the real new employment created by public employment programs, as a percentage of the new jobs created on paper, is estimated at 51 percent after one year, 44 percent after two years, and 4 percent "under a permanent program".[19]

To this rise in income inequality must be added the increase in inequity in the redistribution of income. This development has been a direct consequence of improvements in the system of transfers for the poor since 1965. The increase of the "leapfrogging" phenomenon with respect to cash transfers during the period has been documented in Chapter 6. To the extent that this rise reflects the aged on Social

Security overtaking the working near-poor, it might be considered justifiable reward for past effort. It might even be argued that large benefits to the aged improve the economic welfare of the near-poor themselves, since some of these aged would have to be supported by their near-poor children had the state not taken over.

Part of the growth of leapfrogging, however, has taken place because public assistance recipients—by means of cash and in-kind transfers—have obtained incomes close to and sometimes exceeding those of the near-poor who have earned their way just above the income eligibility lines for food stamps, welfare, and Medicaid, and who are paying income and payroll taxes on their earnings. This problem can only have been exacerbated by the economic recession, which has clipped earnings relative to transfer benefits.

In short, the working near-poor have watched the welfare-eligible poor catch up and, in some cases, even surpass them, at the same time as they have watched the median or typical standard of living recede further from their grasp. This cannot help but be a potentially explosive state of affairs.

Perhaps the most important order of policy business over the next period, therefore, will turn out to be questions of income redistribution: How much redistribution does society want, who shall receive the benefits, and who shall pay the taxes? As the elimination of absolute poverty increasingly is achieved and certain minimum standards are established for all, these issues may force themselves to the forefront of the policy debate.

Such debates will, of course, take place in the political arena. Experts know something in a technical sense about the potential effects of various legislative proposals, although they do not have a history of being sensitive to the political contours of social policy debates. The experience of the last ten years, however, has a lesson that is relevant here. The consequences of specific programs for income inequality are much harder to predict and a lessening of such income inequality much harder to accomplish, both politically and technically, than was assumed in 1964.[20]

NOTES

[1]The fraction that was chosen (.44) yields identical poverty-counts for 1965 for the two definitions—thus facilitating comparisons of progress made since then.

[2]Defined as families plus unrelated individuals.

[3]Part of this effect is probably due to increasing numbers of women choosing to receive AFDC benefits rather than to work, live with relatives, or remarry.

[4]Expenditures that are essentially public goods (national defense, for example) or that promote individual well-being only indirectly (such as research) are omitted.

[5]Data limitations necessitate a 1968–1972 comparison in this section rather than the 1965–1972 one used in the rest of the summary. For the statistical analysis underlying this section, see Timothy M. Smeeding, "Measuring the Economic Welfare of Low Income Households, and the Anti-Poverty Effectiveness of Cash and Non-Cash Transfer Programs" (Ph.D. diss., University of Wisconsin-Madison, 1975).

[6]Underreporting is corrected in what follows by sequentially adjusting CPS transfer income and recipient totals keeping the relative size distribution of income unchanged, assuming that the propensity to underreport is proportional to the income reported.

[7]This, again, is a measure of cash income.

[8]This section returns to a discussion of absolute poverty.

[9]The data used in this and the following section have come from Alfred M. Skolnik and Sophie R. Dales, "Social Welfare Expenditures, Fiscal Year 1974," *Social Security Bulletin* 38 (January 1975). Though not strictly analogous to the data used in Chapter 3, they are close enough to produce rough comparability.

[10]Significant increases in the coverage and duration of benefits during the last few years have mitigated the effects of unemployment. See Edward M. Gramlich, "The Distributional Effects of Higher Unemployment," *Brookings Papers on Economic Activity* 2 (1974).

[11]If further adjustment is made for underreporting and for intrahousehold transfers among persons living in the same living unit, the correction factor implies a poverty population less than one-half as large as the official estimates.

[12]See Michael C. Barth, George J. Carcagno, and John L. Palmer, *Toward an Effective Income Support System: Problems, Prospects, and Choices,* with an Overview Paper by Irwin Garfinkel (Madison, Wis.: Institute for Research on Poverty, 1974).

[13]*The New Jersey Income-Maintenance Experiment,* vol. 2, *Labor-Supply Responses,* ed. Harold W. Watts and Albert Rees (New York: Academic Press, forthcoming).

[14]The following points are made in Robert J. Lampman, "Scaling Welfare Benefits to Income: An Idea That is Being Overworked," *Policy Analysis* 1 (Winter 1975).

[15]The recent Supreme Court decision (7 June 1975, Paul L. Philbrook vs. Jean Glodgett) that those eligible for Unemployment Insurance may choose whether to apply for that or public assistance (AFDC-UP) is a liberalizing factor here, because public assistance benefits are more generous than Unemployment Insurance in many states. If AFDC-UP programs existed in every state, this would be an extremely important development.

[16]This section also has benefited from Robert J. Lampman, "Scaling Welfare Benefits to Income."

[17]Further discussion of this phenomenon may be found in Sheldon Danziger and Robert Plotnick, "Demographic Change, Government Transfers, and the Distribution of Income," Institute for Research on Poverty Discussion Paper 274-75 (University of Wisconsin-Madison, 1975).

[18]Henry M. Levin, "A Decade of Policy Developments in Improving Education of Low-Income Children," in *A Decade of Federal Antipoverty Policy: Achievements, Failures, and Lessons,* ed. Robert H. Haveman (New York: Academic, forthcoming).

[19]George J. Johnson and James Tomola, "An Impact Evaluation of the Public Employment Program," Technical Analysis Paper no. 17, Office of the Assistant Secretary for Policy Evaluation and Research, Department of Labor, April 1974.

[20]See Alice M. Rivlin, "Income Redistribution—Can Economists Help?" The Richard T. Ely Lecture, *Papers and Proceedings of the American Economic Association* (May 1975), p. 30.

Appendix A

The tables in this appendix contain detailed estimates of government social welfare expenditures benefiting the poor. (These listings we are calling "budgets.") Federal programs, arranged by functional area, appear first, followed by state–local programs. The sources for total expenditure data and the methods used to determine the poor's share are explained in the key to the tables, preceding Table A1.

The estimates in these tables were derived from a combination of computer tabulations; publicly available agency data; unpublished work provided by the Department of Health, Education, and Welfare (derived from data supplied by the Office of Economic Opportunity and other federal agencies); published research; best guesses; and extrapolations. For a handful of major expenditures, estimates came from micro observations from the Survey of Economic Opportunity (SEO) and Current Population Survey (CPS) data tapes and are as accurate as currently available techniques allow. These programs—all cash transfers (except temporary disability), Medicare, Medicaid, public assistance social services, and local schools—accounted for 78, 76, and 75 percent of all social welfare spending in 1965, 1968, and 1972, respectively. For nearly all the remaining programs, our methods are as reliable as possible within the limitations of the data, and we are fairly confident of them. In only four cases was it necessary to resort to informed guesses.

It should be observed that the expenditure figures in these tables are for fiscal years (fiscal 1972 covers July 1971–June 1972, for example), whereas the SEO and CPS data are for the same numbered calendar years. This difference does not, in our judgment, undermine any of our findings. We direct the reader's attention to the following note included at the request of the Department of Health, Education, and Welfare:

> Where noted, estimates of program benefits going to the *post*-transfer poor were supplied by HEW. However, because of severe technical problems involving the data base and the possibility of its transformation to pre-transfer poverty status, HEW must dissociate itself from estimates appearing in these tables of benefits going to the *pre*-transfer poor. (In cases where estimates of benefits to the *pre*-transfer poor were derived solely from SEO or CPS data or from tabulations of tape records of *A Panel Survey of Income Dynamics,* however, no objection is raised.) There are also marked differences of opinion between HEW and the author concerning the concept of presenting estimates of non-cash benefits going to the *pre*-transfer poor, since where there are means tests for non-cash programs, such tests almost always relate to *post*-transfer income, not *pre*-transfer income.

However, we would argue that, for the purpose of this study, estimates of benefits to the pretransfer poor are preferable to estimates of benefits to the posttransfer poor. Our interest in preparing these estimates was to see how the poor fared in obtaining government benefits compared to the rest of the population. Comparing benefits of the posttransfer poor to those received by everyone else overlooks the point that the statistics used to identify the number of posttransfer poor already directly incorporate the effect of cash transfers.

KEY TO TABLES A1–A3

Numbers appearing next to program names refer to the sources used to obtain total expenditure figures. Letters appearing in right-hand column refer to the sources and method used to distribute benefits to pretransfer poor. Rows without numerical entries indicate the program was not functioning in that year.

Sources of Total Expenditure Data

1. Ida Merriam and Alfred Skolnik, Alfred Skolnik and Sophie Dales, "Social Welfare Expenditures," unpublished tables of the Social Security Administration based upon the

expenditure series in *Social Welfare Expenditures Under Public Programs in the United States, 1929–66,* Social Security Administration, Office of Research and Statistics Research Report 25, 1968.

2. For 1965, U.S., Bureau of the Budget, *The Budget of the United States Government for the Fiscal Year Ending June 30, 1967; Appendix* (Washington, D.C.: U.S. Government Printing Office, 1966), (PrEx 2.8:967). For 1968, U.S., Bureau of the Budget, *The Budget of the United States Government, Fiscal Year 1970; Appendix* (Washington, D.C.: U.S. Government Printing Office, 1969), (PrEx 2.8:970). For 1972, U.S., Office of Management and Budget, *The Budget of the United States Government, Fiscal Year 1974; Appendix* (Washington, D.C.: U.S. Government Printing Office, 1973), (PrEx 2.8:974).

3. Estimated as a percentage of total administrative costs.

4. U.S., Office of Management and Budget, *Special Analyses: Budget of the United States Government, Fiscal Year 1974* (Washington, D.C.: U.S. Government Printing Office, 1973), pp. 120, 122, 123, and 133, (PrEx 2.8/5:974).

5. Same as (1), but for 1965 and 1968 the entries include medical vendor payments that did not fall under either Medical Assistance for the Aged or Medicaid.

6. Unpublished data, U.S., Office of Economic Opportunity and Department of Health, Education, and Welfare, supplied by Gordon Fisher (received by him from the federal agencies involved).

7. U.S., Office of Management and Budget, *Special Analyses: Budget of the United States Government, Fiscal Year 1967* (Washington, D.C.: U.S. Government Printing Office, 1966), pp. 97–99, (PrEx2.8/5:967).

8. U.S., Office of Management and Budget, *Special Analyses: Budget of the United States Government, Fiscal Year 1970* (Washington, D.C.: U.S. Government Printing Office, 1969), p. 135, (PrEx2.85:970).

9. U.S., Office of Management and Budget, *Special Analyses: Budget of the United States Government, Fiscal Year 1971* (Washington, D.C.: U.S. Government Printing Office, 1970), p. 131, (PrEx2.8/5:971).

10. U.S., Veterans Administration, *Annual Report 1972,* Administration of Veterans Affairs (U.S. Government Printing Office, 1973), (VA1.1:972).

11. U.S., Department of Health, Education, and Welfare, Education Division, National Center for Education Statistics, *Digest of Educational Statistics* (Washington, D.C.: U.S. Government Printing Office, 1970), (HE5.210:10024-969).

12. U.S., Department of Health, Education, and Welfare, Education Division, National Center for Education Statistics, *Digest of Educational Statistics* (Washington, D.C.: U.S. Government Printing Office, 1972), (HE5.210:10024-71).

13. U.S., Department of Health, Education, and Welfare, Education Division, National Center for Education Statistics, *Digest of Educational Statistics* (Washington, D.C.: U.S. Government Printing Office, 1973), (HE5.98:972).

14. U.S., Department of Health, Education, and Welfare, Education Division, National Center for Education Statistics, *Digest of Educational Statistics* (Washington, D.C.: U.S. Government Printing Office, 1974), (HE5.98:973).

15. Supplementary Medical Insurance premiums paid by recipients are subtracted from total benefits to obtain this figure. For source of premiums and total payments see (2).

Sources and Methods for Allocating Benefits to the Poor

In the following notes, the tabulations cited as sources for estimates are obtained from the 1966 Survey of Economic Opportunity for

1965 material, the March 1969 Current Population Survey for 1968 material, and the March 1973 Current Population Survey for 1972 material.

a. Tabulations of share of income received by pretransfer poor from appropriate transfer program.

b. Tabulations of number of households receiving public assistance. Assumes each household receives the same amount of social services.

c. Tabulations of the number of persons in households receiving public assistance income. Assumes each person gets the same (insurance) benefit from Medicaid. For 1965, only recipients of OAA are considered for MAA benefits.

d. Tabulations of the fraction of school-age children in pretransfer poor families. They are assumed to receive 5 percent less than the average per child expenditure.

e. Begins with unpublished work kindly provided by Gordon Fisher of HEW (formerly of OEO) that provides estimates of program benefits going to posttransfer poor. (These estimates were, in most cases, derived from data supplied to him by the various federal agencies involved.) To convert this to pretransfer poor benefits, we assume that benefits going to the posttransfer *nonpoor* are uniformly distributed. Then, the posttransfer nonpoor who were pretransfer poor are assigned their share of these evenly distributed benefits. This figure is added to the HEW estimate to produce our results. (For HEW's position on the question of preparing estimates of benefits to the *pretransfer* poor, see the note on page 192 of this Appendix.) For programs in which the posttransfer poor receive more than proportional benefits, it is probable that the pretransfer-poor–posttransfer-nonpoor group also receives more than its proportionate share. In these cases, this method is likely to give underestimated benefits to the pretransfer poor. Conversely, if posttransfer poor get less than proportional benefits, this approach may yield overestimates.

For all programs with (*e*), the above procedure is applied to *families* only.

f. Based on data provided by G. Fisher of HEW (derived from data supplied to him by the various federal agencies involved) and on program descriptions.

g. These are unchanged HEW estimates of benefits to the posttransfer poor (derived from data supplied by the various federal agencies involved). They are used when the estimate is 100 percent to the posttransfer poor (and hence 100 percent to the pretransfer poor), or when the method outlined in (5) was inapplicable and other distributional data was not available.

h. See (*e*). Here *all* households, including unrelated individuals, are considered.

i. For 1965 and 1968, based on data giving the posttransfer incomes of rehabilitated clients, projected backwards, from U.S., Department of Health, Education, and Welfare, Social and Rehabilitation Service, Rehabilitation Services Administration, *Characteristics of Clients Rehabilitated in Fiscal Years 1967–1971,* prepared by Division of Monitoring and Program Analysis, Statistical Analysis and Systems Branch, Social and Rehabilitation (SRS) No. 73-25055, (HE17.102:426/967-71). For 1972, based on unpublished data from this agency. For method of converting posttransfer income distribution to pretransfer poverty, see (*o*).

j. For 1965, uses tabulations of public housing tenants. For 1968 and 1972, uses data giving the distributions of beneficiaries by posttransfer income classes in U.S., Department of Housing and Urban Development, *1968 HUD Statistical Yearbook,* (Washington, D.C.: U.S. Government Printing Office, 1970), (HH1.38:968). See also U.S., Department of Housing and Urban Development, *1972 HUD Statistical Yearbook* (Washington, D.C.: U.S. Government Printing Office, 1974), (HH1.38:972). See (*o*) for further explanation.

k. Uses estimate derived as in (*i*).

l. Takes HEW estimates as base and adds to them the average of two other estimates. One of these assumes all posttransfer nonpoor veteran-headed families receive equal health benefits and, as in (*e*), gives the pretransfer poor who are posttransfer nonpoor their share of these benefits. The second estimate assumes that each pretransfer poor veteran-headed family receives the same average benefit as did the posttransfer poor families. Pretransfer family data obtained from tape tabulations.

m. Uses same percentage as (*l*).

n. Weighted average of percentages for federal vocational- and adult-education programs (weights are the federal expenditures).

o. Basic data are tables giving the distribution of days lost from work among posttransfer income classes. Sources are (1) U.S., Department of Health, Education, and Welfare, Public Health Service, National Center for Health Statistics, *Data from the National Health Survey: Disability Days, United States, July 1963–June 1964,* Table 22 (Public Health Service Publication No. 1000; Vital and Health Statistics Series 10, No. 24) (Washington, D.C.: U.S. Government Printing Office, 1965). (2) U.S., Department of Health, Education, and Welfare, Public Health Service, Health Resources Administration, National Center for Health Statistics, *Data from the National Health Survey: Disability Days, United States, 1971,* Table 11 (DHEW Publication No. (HRA) 74-1517; Vital and Health Statistics Series 10, No. 90) (Washington, D.C.: U.S. Government Printing Office, 1974). (3) U.S., Department of Health, Education, and Welfare, Public Health Service, Health Services and Mental Health Administration, National Center for Health Statistics, *Data from the National Health Survey: Time Lost from Work Among the Currently Employed Population, United States, 1968,* Table 3 (DHEW Publication No. (HSM) 72-1053; Vital and Health Statistics Series 10, No. 71) (Washington, D.C.: U.S. Government Printing Office, 1972). We assume the pretransfer poor receive the same fraction of total benefits as the fraction of days lost from work that they accounted for.

Our method of converting a distribution among posttransfer income classes into a distribution between pretransfer poor and nonpoor is best explained by example. Suppose we had a distribution of program beneficiaries as shown in Row 1 below. And suppose a tape tabulation showing the fraction of households in a given posttransfer income class that were pretransfer poor gave Row 2.

	Posttransfer income					
	$0– $1999	$2000– $2999	$3000– $3999	$4000– $4999	$5000– $7999	$8000 and more
Percent of recipients	10	15	20	25	15	15
Fraction pretransfer poor	.99	.88	.66	.46	.22	.01

Then, assuming the incidence of poverty among recipients in each income class was the same as the average (e.g., .66 for $3000–$3999), multiplying entires in Row 1 by the corresponding entry in Row 2 and summing the results will yield the fraction of recipients who are pretransfer poor. In this example we get $(.99 \times 10) + (.88 \times 15) + (.66 \times 20) + (.46 \times 25) + (.22 \times 15) + (.01 \times 15) = 51.25$, which we round to 51 percent.

p. Tabulations of the fraction of families receiving AFDC that were pretransfer poor.

q. Estimated fraction of full-time students attending universities who were from pretransfer poor families. Basic data for 1965 giving distribution of full-time freshmen across posttransfer family income classes are from American Council on Education, Office of Research, *National Norms for Entering College Freshmen—Fall 1966,* by Alexander W. Astin, Robert J. Panos, and John A. Creager. ACE Research Reports, Vol. 2, No. 1 (Washington, D.C.: American Council on Education, 1967). For 1968 and 1972, same publication series is used, but the data are for fall 1968 and fall 1972. These posttransfer income class data are converted to pretransfer poverty statistics using method described in (*o*).

For 1965, an alternative source not available in other years based on a sample of *all* college students gave very similar estimates as the freshman sample. Hence, the restricted sample of freshmen may not give very biased results.

r. Estimated fraction of all higher-education students from pretransfer poor families. See (*q*) for data reference. We took estimates based on the full-time sample and added two percentage points since part-time students are generally poorer.

s. Estimated fraction of full-time higher-education students from pretransfer-poor families. A breakdown of state—local expenditures and students' families' incomes among junior colleges, four-year colleges, and universities was available. For 1965 and 1968, expenditure break-down from Tables D-2(a) and D-3 in E. Becker, "The Financing of Higher Education: A Review of Historical Trends and Projections for 1975–76," in U.S., Department of Health, Education, and Welfare, Office of Education, Bureau of Higher Education, *Trends in Postsecondary Education* (Washington, D.C.: U.S. Government Printing Office, 1970), (HE 5.250:50063). Trends in the share of funds going to each type of institution were projected for 1972.

t. Based on Table 10 in J. Bonnen, "The Absence of Knowledge of Distributional Impact: An Obstacle to Effective Public Program Analysis and Decisions," in U.S., Congress, Joint Economic Committee, *The Analysis and Evaluation of Public Expenditures: The PPB System,* a compendium of papers submitted to the Subcommittee on Economy of the Joint Economic Committee (Washington, D.C.: U.S. Government Printing Office, 1969), (Y4.Ec7:Ex7/5v.1).

u. Of the total expenditures on the extension, part was spent on "Improved Family Living" and "Improved Nutrition." The share of these funds going to the pretransfer poor was estimated using HEW posttransfer poor estimates derived from data supplied by the Agriculture Department. The remainder was divided between poor and nonpoor in proportion to the share of farm income received by each group, as determined by tabulations.

v. Estimated fraction of *full-time* higher-education students from pretransfer poor families. See (*q*) for source.

w. Same as (*v*), but only for four-year public colleges.

x. Same as (*v*), but excludes two-year colleges.

y. Same as (*v*), but only for all four-year colleges.

z. Based on program descriptions, private conversation, and best guesses.

aa. Uses estimated percentage for corresponding federal program.

bb. Same as (*h*), but restricted to elderly families and individuals.

cc. Same as (*h*), but restricted to school-age children (ages 6–18).

dd. Based on tabulations of persons over 65 who are pretransfer poor.

ee. Based on tabulations of tape records of *A Panel Survey of Income Dynamics* estimated for 1965. Result for 1972 based on data for 1971. Key in The Regents of the University of Michigan, Survey Research Center, *A Panel Study of Income Dynamics: Study Design, Procedures, Available Data; 1968–1972 Interviewing Years (Waves I–V), Vol. I* (Ann Arbor, Michigan: Institute for Social Research, The University of Michigan). Conducted under contract to the Office of Economic Opportunity.

ff. Based on posttransfer income distribution of students in "Vocational Education: Characteristics of Teachers and Students, 1969," p. 26, U.S. Office of Education. See (*o*) for further explanation. We estimated the data for 1965 and projected it for 1972.

gg. Same as (8), but restricted to central-city residents of SMSAs.

hh. Uses method described in (*e*), but data are from U.S., Department of Labor, *Manpower Report of the President; A Report on Manpower Requirements, Resources, Utilization, and Training* (Washington, D.C.: U.S. Government Printing Office, 1973), (L1.42/2:973).

ii. Same as (*gg*), but data from U.S., Department of Labor, *Manpower Report of the President; A Report on Manpower Requirements, Resources, Utilization, and Training* (Washington, D.C.: U.S. Government Printing Office, 1974), (L1.42/2:974).

TABLE A1.   ANTIPOVERTY BUDGET, 1965
(in thousands of dollars)

	Expenditures	Benefits to Pretransfer Poor	Percentage Spent on Pretransfer Poor
FEDERAL PROGRAMS	37,773,579	19,951,862	52.8
I. Cash transfers	30,167,751	17,609,900	58.4
A. Social Security[1]	16,488,383	10,161,800	61.6[a]
B. Railroad Retirement[1]	1,117,690	688,500	61.6[a]
C. Railroad Disability[1]	43,984	27,100	61.6[a]
D. Public Employee Retirement[1]	3,215,940	1,656,200	51.5[a]
E. Unemployment Insurance[1]	2,506,320	601,500	24
1. Federal employees and exservicemen	132,235		
2. Railroad	71,260	601,500	24[a]
3. State administered	2,302,825		
F. Workmen's Compensation[1]	73,454	19,800	27
1. Regular	73,454	19,800	27[a]
2. Black lung	—		
G. Public assistance[5]	2,614,032	2,323,000	88.9
1. AFDC	956,470	926,800	96.9[a]
2. OAA, AB, APTD and emergency assistance	1,657,562	1,396,200	84.3[a]
H. Veterans' income maintenance[10]	4,107,948	2,132,000	51.9
1. Compensation and pensions	4,042,144		
2. Burial benefits	56,728		
3. Special allowances	139	2,132,000	51.9[a]
4. Vocational rehabilitation allowances	8,937		
II. Payments to farmers[2]	2,244,567	202,000	9
A. Conservation	248,532		
B. Soil Bank	193,698		
C. Cropland adjustment	—		
D. Sugar Act	92,108		
E. Wool	20,209	202,000	9[t]
F. Price support	333,344		
G. Set aside and diversion	946,645		
H. Milk and beekeeper indemnity	261		
I. Wheat certificates	409,770		

TABLE A1.—(continued)

III. Nutrition[1]	792,522	324,600	41
A. Food stamps	35,561	32,200	95[ee]
B. Child nutrition	500,260	61,400	12.3
1. Donated food, sec. 32, 416	212,949 ⎫		
2. Cash—School Lunch, sec. 4	130,435 ⎬	42,100	10.5[cc]
3. Food bought, sec. 6	59,459 ⎭		
4. Special cash assistance, sec. 11	—		
5. Special food services, sec. 13	—		
6. Supplemental cash, sec. 32	—		
7. Milk program	97,417	19,300	19.8[d]
8. School breakfast	—		
9. Nonfood cash assistance	—		
C. Surplus commodities	256,701	231,000	90
1. Needy families	226,883	204,200	90[f]
2. Institutions	29,818	26,800	90[f]
IV. Housing	226,565	117,300	51.8
A. Public housing[1]	218,995	111,700	51[j]
B. Rent supplements	—		
C. Homeownership and rental housing assistance, sec. 235, 236	—		
D. Rural housing programs[1]	2,318	1,700	75[g]
E. Model Cities	—		
F. College housing debt service grants	—		
G. Neighborhood facilities grants	—		
H. Special disabled veterans' housing benefits[10]	5,252	3,600	69[k]
V. Health	1,990,165	791,036	39.7
A. Medicare	—		
B. Medicaid and MAA[1]	271,288	262,000	96.7[c]
C. Mental health programs	—		
1. Community mental health centers (staffing grants only)	—		
2. Children's services	—		
3. Drug abuse	—		
4. Alcoholism	—		

TABLE A1.—(continued)

	Expenditures	Benefits to Pretransfer Poor	Percentage Spent on Pretransfer Poor
D Maternal and child health[1]	70,281	60,900	87
1. Maternal and child health services	33,038	28,500	86[e]
2. Crippled children services	33,110	28,500	86[e]
3. Child dental health	—		
4. Special projects for comprehensive child health	—		
5. Special projects for maternal and child health	4,133	3,900	94[e]
E. Family planning (HEW)	—		
F. Indian health services[2]	62,208	52,900	85[f]
G. Indian sanitation facilities[2]	9,165	7,800	85[f]
H. Migrant health[2]	2,336	2,336	100[g]
I. Comprehensive health services—formula grants to states[6]	36,200	24,800	69[h]
J. Health services development grants and family health centers[6]	28,000	15,700	56[h]
K. St. Elizabeth's Hospital[2]	9,309	8,400	90[f]
L. Veterans' medical services[10]	1,144,011	228,800	20[l]
M. Health facilities construction (nonveteran)[1]	280,371	112,000	40[z]
N. Veterans' medical facility construction[10]	76,996	15,400	20[m]
VI. Welfare and OEO services	239,349	214,016	89.3
A. Public assistance social services[3]	164,000	154,200	94[b]
B. Child welfare[1]	33,857	23,700	70[g]
C. Indian welfare and guidance[1]	13,028	13,000	100[g]
D. Cuban refugee programs[1]	21,955	16,900	77[h]
E. Aging programs	—		
F. OEO	6,509	6,200	96
1. Community Action Programs[6]	4,000	3,800	95[f]
2. Health and nutrition	—		
3. Legal services	—		
4. Migrant farmworkers aid[1]	1,116	1,116	100[g]
5. Community Economic Development	—		
6. VISTA[1]	1,393	1,300	95[f]

TABLE A1.—(continued)

VII. Employment and manpower	627,435	391,500	62.4
A. *Employment services*	199,554	86,900	44
1. *State employment agencies*[1]	187,554	74,900	40[h]
2. *Computerized job placement*	—		
3. *Indian employment and training*[2]	12,000	12,000	100[g]
B. *Vocational rehabilitation*	101,213	69,600	69
1. *Social Rehabilitation Service*[6]	95,616	65,700	69[i]
2. *Social Security administration*	—		
3. *Veterans' administration*[10]	5,597	3,900	69[k]
C. *Manpower training*	326,669	235,000	72
1. *MDTA—institutional*[7]	230,000	140,300	61[h]
2. *MDTA—OJT, JOBS Optional*[7]			
3. *Neighborhood Youth Corps—in-school and summer*[7]	30,000	30,000	100[f]
4. *Neighborhood Youth Corps—out-of-school*[7]	1,000	1,000	100[f]
5. *Job Corps*[7]	34,000	34,000	100[f]
6. *Public Service Careers*	—		
7. *JOBS*	—		
8. *Concentrated Employment Program*	—		
9. *Operation Mainstream*	—		
10. *Work Experience*[1]	20,668	19,400	94[p]
11. *Work Incentive (WIN)*	—		
12. *Public assistance social service*[6]	11,000	10,300	94[p]
13. *Veterans' OJT*	—		
14. *Employment for disadvantaged youth*	—		
D. *Emergency Employment Assistance (PEP)*	—		
VIII. Education	1,485,225	301,510	20
A. *Student support*	487,646	33,300	7
1. *Fellow/traineeships*[1]	177,563	5,900	5[q]
2. *Training grants*[1]	283,545	14,200	5[q]
3. *Indian scholarships*[1]	1,242	1,100	90[z]
4. *Work-study and cooperative education*[12]	25,296	12,100	48[h]
5. *Educational opportunity grants*	—		

TABLE A1.—(continued)

	Expenditures	Benefits to Pretransfer Poor	Percentage Spent on Pretransfer Poor
6. Insured loans—interest reduction payments	—		
7. Health and nursing professions	—		
B. Preschool, elementary and secondary education	624,479	206,910	33
1. Shared revenue from public lands[1]	51,507	10,200	19.8[d]
2. Indian education[1]	87,541	74,400	85[f]
3. Assistance in special areas[1]	28,808	5,700	19.8[d]
4. School aid to federally affected areas[12]	349,671	69,200	19.8[d]
5. NDEA, III, instructional aid[12]	50,615	10,000	19.8[d]
6. NDEA, V, guidance and testing[12]	17,322	3,400	19.8[d]
7. NSF science education[1]	3,403	670	19.8[d]
8. Head Start and Follow Through[6]	33,900	32,900	97[f]
9. Elementary and Secondary Education Act	1,712	340	19.8
a. Educationally deprived	—		
b. Bilingual education	—		
c. Drop-out prevention	—		
d. Library resources	—		
e. Supplementary education centers	—		
f. Strengthening state departments of education[12]	1,712	340	19.8[d]
10. Teacher Corps	—		
11. Handicapped early childhood aid	—		
12. Handicapped education	—		
13. Emergency school assistance	—		
C. Higher education	152,707	24,900	16
1. Higher Education Act	—		
2. Upward Bound	—		
3. Language development[12]	8,117	700	9[x]
4. NSF grants[1]	48,370	4,400	9[x]
5. Land-grant colleges[12]	14,500	1,800	12[w]
6. Educational exchange (Fulbright-Hays)[1]	37,425	3,400	9[x]

TABLE A1.—(continued)

7. Special institutions (Howard/Gallaudent, Eisenhower, Nat'l Tech. Inst. for the Deaf)[1]	11,564	1,200	10[y]
8. Construction grants	7,161	600	9
a. Higher Education Facilities Act[12]	1,288 ⎫		
b. Health professions teaching facilities	— ⎬	600	9[r]
c. Special institutions	5,873 ⎭		
9. Veterans' education benefits[10]	25,570	12,800	50[a]
1. Vocational-technical training[1, 2, 12]	131,855	21,100	16[ff]
2. Adult basic education[12]	3,146	2,000	63[h]
3. Agricultural extension[1]	85,392	13,300	16[u]
D. Vocational and adult education	220,393	46,600	21
STATE AND LOCAL PROGRAMS[1]	36,707,504	11,098,900	30.2
I. Cash transfers	5,971,771	3,395,700	56.9
A. Public employee retirement	1,861,000	958,400	51.5[a]
B. Temporary disability insurance	253,214	63,000	25[o]
C. Workmen's Compensation	1,689,559	454,500	27[a]
D. Public assistance[5]	2,147,595	1,909,200	88.9[a]
1. AFDC	768,414	744,600	96.9[a]
2. OAA, AB, APTD and general assistance	1,379,181	1,164,600	84.1[a]
E. Veterans' bonuses and compensation	20,403	10,600	51.9[a]
II. Nutrition—child nutrition	113,682	14,000	12.3[aa]
III. Housing	79,957	40,500	50.7[j]
IV. Health	3,665,206	2,314,400	63.1
A. Medicaid, vendor medical	252,406	244,100	96[c]
B. Hospital and medical care	2,377,600	1,585,000	66[z]
C. Maternal and child health	155,921	134,200	86
1. Maternal and child health services	88,246	75,900	86[aa]
2. Crippled children services	66,641	57,300	86[aa]
3. Child dental health	—		
4. Special projects for comprehensive child health	—		

TABLE A1.—(continued)

	Expenditures	Benefits to Pretransfer Poor	Percentage Spent on Pretransfer Poor
5. Special projects for maternal and child health	1,034	1,000	95[aa]
D. School health services	142,200	28,100	19.8[d]
E. Other public health	448,079	150,000	33[z]
F. Medical facilities construction	289,000	173,000	60[z]
V. Welfare services	1,172,821	694,000	59.2
A. Public assistance social services[3]	102,000	95,900	94[b]
B. Child welfare	315,821	221,100	70[aa]
C. Institutional care	755,000	377,000	50[z]
VI. Manpower-vocational rehabilitation	65,987	45,400	69[i]
VII. Education	25,638,080	4,594,900	18
A. Elementary and secondary schools (operating and construction)	21,580,944	4,266,900	19.8[d]
B. Higher education (operating and construction)	3,609,426	252,700	7[s]
C. Vocational and adult education	447,710	76,300	17[n]

TABLE A2.   ANTIPOVERTY BUDGET, 1968
(in thousands of dollars)

	Expenditures	Benefits to Pretransfer Poor	Percentage Spent on Pretransfer Poor
FEDERAL PROGRAMS	58,572,385	29,702,888	50.7
I. Cash Transfers	38,232,301	20,790,100	54.4
A. Social Security[1]	22,653,137	13,094,000	57.8[a]
B. Railroad Retirement[1]	1,403,177	811,000	57.8[a]
C. Railroad Disability[1]	55,747	32,200	57.8[a]
D. Public Employee Retirement[1]	4,160,613	1,760,000	42.3[a]
E. Unemployment insurance[1]	2,204,070	383,500	17.4
1. Federal employees and exservicemen	107,401 ⎫		
2. Railroad	41,698 ⎬	383,500	17.4[a]
3. State administered	2,054,971 ⎭		
F. Workmen's Compensation[1]	98,208	32,400	33
1. Regular	98,208	32,400	33[a]
2. Black lung	—		
G. Public assistance[5]	3,058,236	2,510,800	81.2[a]
1. AFDC	1,404,405	1,321,500	94.1[a]
2. OAA, AB, APTD and emergency assistance	1,653,831	1,189,300	71.9[a]
H. Veterans' income maintenance[10]	4,599,113	2,166,200	47.1
1. Compensation and pensions	4,519,304 ⎫		
2. Burial benefits	63,798 ⎪		
3. Special allowances	388 ⎬	2,166,200	47.1[a]
4. Vocational rehabilitation allowances	15,623 ⎭		
II. Payments to Farmers[2]	3,019,961	211,400	7
A. Conservation	247,046 ⎫		
B. Soil Bank	121,802 ⎪		
C. Cropland adjustment	83,744 ⎪		
D. Sugar Act	83,829 ⎪		
E. Wool	69,423 ⎬	211,400	7[t]
F. Price support	932,859 ⎪		
G. Set aside and diversion	754,558 ⎪		
H. Milk and beekeeper indemnity	264 ⎪		
I. Wheat certificates	726,436 ⎭		

TABLE A2.—(continued)

	Expenditures	Benefits to Pretransfer Poor	Percentage Spent on Pretransfer Poor
III. Nutrition[1]	876,123	384,200	43.9
A. Food stamps	187,159	172,200	92ee
B. Child nutrition	541,701	79,500	14.7
1. Donated food, sec. 32, 416	220,456 ⎫		
2. Cash—School Lunch, sec. 4	154,947 ⎬	56,000	13cc
3. Food bought, sec. 6	55,521 ⎭		
4. Special cash assistance, sec. 11	4,807	3,700	76cc
5. Special food services, sec. 13	—.		
6. Supplemental cash, sec. 32	—		
7. Milk program	101,752	17,700	17.4d
8. School breakfast	3,469	1,900	54cc
9. Nonfood cash assistance	749	200	28cc
C. Surplus commodities	147,263	132,500	90
1. Needy families	124,016	111,600	90f
2. Institutions	23,247	20,900	90f
IV. Housing	309,092	217,800	70.5
A. Public housing[1]	294,737	209,300	71j
B. Rent supplements[1]	2,124	1,500	69e
C. Homeownership and rental housing assistance, sec. 235, 236	—		
D. Rural housing programs[1]	1,128	1,100	98f
E. Model Cities[2]	1,630	600	39h
F. College housing debt service grants	—		
G. Neighborhood facilities grants[1]	4,637	2,100	46h
H. Special disabled veterans housing benefits[10]	4,836	3,200	69k
V. Health	8,222,553	4,072,900	49.5
A. Medicare[15]	4,411,328	2,073,300	47dd
B. Medicaid and MAA[1]	1,644,693	1,256,600	76.5c
C. Mental health programs[2]	59,926	38,700	66
1. Community mental health centers (staffing			

TABLE A2.—(continued)

grants only)	43,359	25,700	59[h]
2. Children's services	—		
3. Drug abuse	16,567	13,000	78[h]
4. Alcoholism	—		.
D. Maternal and child health[1]	155,230	139,000	90
1. Maternal and child health services	46,630	40,100	86[e]
2. Crippled children services	47,712	41,000	86[e]
3. Child dental health	—		
4. Special projects for comprehensive child health	30,896	29,400	95[e]
5. Special projects for maternal and child health	29,992	28,500	95[e]
E. Family planning (HEW)	—		
F. Indian health services[2]	82,290	65,800	80[f]
G. Indian sanitation facilities[2]	12,050	9,600	80[f]
H. Migrant health[2]	7,200	7,200	100[g]
I. Comprehensive health services—formula grants to states[6]	56,075	38,000	68[h]
J. Health services development grants and family health centers[6]	57,699	38,000	66[h]
K. St. Elizabeth's Hospital[2]	10,668	9,600	90[f]
L. Veterans' medical services[10]	1,372,301	274,500	20[l]
M. Health facilities construction (nonveteran)[1]	305,100	113,000	37[z]
N. Veterans' medical facility construction[10]	47,993	9,600	20[l]
VI. Welfare and OEO services	1,033,652	941,400	91.1
A. Public assistance social services[1]	346,654	305,400	88[b]
B. Child welfare[1]	46,571	32,600	70[g]
C. Indian welfare and guidance[1]	20,200	20,200	100[g]
D. Cuban refugee programs[1]	35,713	26,400	74[h]
E. Aging programs	—		
F. OEO	584,514	556,800	95
1. Community Action Program[6]	426,100	404,800	95[f]
2. Health and nutrition[6]	50,100	47,600	95[f]
3. Legal services[6]	35,500	33,700	95[f]
4. Migrant farmworkers aid[1]	32,400	32,400	100[g]
5. Community Economic Development[6]	12,700	12,000	95[f]
6. VISTA[1]	27,714	26,300	95[f]

TABLE A2.—(continued)

	Expenditures	Benefits to Pretransfer Poor	Percentage Spent on Pretransfer Poor
VII. Employment and manpower	1,906,697	1,519,054	79.7
A. Employment services	322,104	144,754	45
1. State employment agencies[1]	300,650	123,300	41[h]
2. Computerized job placement	—		
3. Indian employment and training[2]	21,454	21,454	100[g]
B. Vocational rehabilitation	284,516	196,300	
1. Social Rehabilitation Service[6]	277,384	191,400	69[i]
2. Social Security administration	—		
3. Veterans' administration [10]	7,132	4,900	69[k]
C. Manpower training	1,300,077	1,178,000	89
1. MDTA—institutional[8]	254,000	173,500	68[h]
2. MDTA—OJT, JOBS Optional[8]	67,000	36,000	54[h]
3. Neighborhood Youth Corps—in-school and summer[9]	198,000	198,000	100[g]
4. Neighborhood Youth Corps—out-of-school[9]	143,000	143,000	100[g]
5. Job Corps[9]	318,000	318,000	100[g]
6. Public Service Careers[8]	24,000	24,000	100[g]
7. JOBS[8]	4,000	4,000	100[g]
8. Concentrated Employment Program[9]	68,000	68,600	100[g]
9. Operation Mainstream[8]	31,000	31,000	100[g]
10. Work Experience[1]	98,477	91,000	93[p]
11. Work Incentive (WIN)	—		
12. Public assistance social service[6]	24,300	22,600	93[p]
13. Veterans' OJT[9]	5,000	3,000	60[z]
14. Employment for disadvantaged youth[6]	65,300	65,300	100[g]
D. Emergency Employment Assistance (PEP)[4]	—		
VIII. Education	4,972,006	1,566,034	31.5
A. Student support	936,708	132,134	14
1. Fellow/traineeships[1, 11]	244,863	12,200	5[q]
2. Training grants[1, 11]	428,391	21,400	5[q]
3. Indian scholarships[1]	2,134	2,134	100[f]

TABLE A2.—(continued)

4. *Work-study and co-operative education*[12]	116,839	45,800	39[f]
5. *Educational opportunity grants*[13]	103,104	41,200	40[f]
6. *Insured loans—interest reduction payments*[13]	28,947	5,500	19[f]
7. *Health and nursing professions*[6]	12,430	3,900	31[e]
B. *Preschool, elementary and secondary education*	2,574,458	1,146,400	47.8
1. *Shared revenue from public lands*[12]	52,294	9,100	17.4[d]
2. *Indian education*[1]	112,441	90,000	80[f]
3. *Assistance in special areas*[14]	58,286	10,500	17.4[d]
4. *School aid to federally affected areas*[12]	506,372	88,100	17.4[d]
5. *NDEA, III, instructional aid*[12]	85,916	14,900	17.4[d]
6. *NDEA, V, guidance and testing*[12]	23,093	4,000	17.4[d]
7. *NSF science education*[1]	4,547	800	17.4[d]
8. *Head Start and Follow Through*[6]	379,900	368,500	97[f]
9. *Elementary and Secondary Education Act*[12]	1,343,742	553,100	41
a. *Educationally deprived*	1,049,116	504,600	48[f]
b. *Bilingual education*	—		
c. *Drop-out prevention*	—		
d. *Library resources*	91,054 ⎫		
e. *Supplementary education centers*	161,256 ⎬	48,500	17.4[d]
f. *Strengthening state departments of education*	26,297 ⎭		
10. *Teacher Corps*[12]	16,019	5,600	35[cc]
11. *Handicapped early childhood aid*	—		
12. *Handicapped education*[12]	7,867	1,800	23[cc]
13. *Emergency school assistance*	—		
C. *Higher education*	1,076,371	212,400	20
1. *Higher Education Act*[12]	56,818	5,600	10[r]
2. *Upward Bound*[6]	32,100	30,800	96[e]
3. *Talent Search*[6]	2,497	2,400	96[e]
4. *Language development*[12]	17,550	1,600	9[x]
5. *NSF grants*[1]	25,087	2,300	9[x]
6. *Land-grant colleges*[12]	14,500	1,700	12[w]
7. *Educational exchange (Fulbright-Hays)*[14]	41,670	3,800	9[x]

TABLE A2.—(continued)

	Expenditures	Benefits to Pretransfer Poor	Percentage Spent on Pretransfer Poor
8. Special institutions (Howard/Gallaudent, Eisenhower, Nat'l Tech. Inst. for the Deaf)[1]	18,874	2,000	10.5[y]
9. Construction grants	423,123	42,300	10
a. Higher Education Facilities Act[12]	360,246		
b. Health professions teaching facilities[1]	60,689	42,300	10[r]
c. Special institutions	2,188		
10. Veterans' education benefits[10]	444,152	119,900	27[a]
D. Vocational and adult Education	384,469	75,100	20
1. Vocational-technical training[1, 2, 12]	265,738	45,200	17[ff]
2. Adult basic education[12]	28,701	17,800	62[h]
3. Agricultural extension[14]	90,030	12,300	14[u]
STATE AND LOCAL PROGRAMS	50,652,100	14,210,600	28.1
I. Cash transfers	7,331,185	3,785,306	51.6
A. Public employee retirement	2,334,000	987,300	42.3[a]
B. Temporary disability insurance	296,883	47,500	16[o]
C. Workmen's Compensation	2,188,799	722,300	33[a]
D. Public assistance[5]	2,479,003	2,012,900	81.2[a]
1. AFDC	1,137,294	1,070,000	94.1[a]
2. OAA, AB, APTD and general assistance	1,341,709	942,700	70.3[a]
E. Veterans' bonuses and compensation	32,500	15,300	47.1[a]
II. Nutrition—child nutrition	161,973	23,800	14.7[aa]
III. Housing	102,548	72,800	71[j]
IV. Health	5,841,026	3,631,000	62.2
A. Medicaid, vendor medical	1,684,288	1,288,500	76.5[c]
B. Hospital and medical care	2,741,100	1,645,000	60[z]
C. Maternal and child health	176,166	152,800	87
1. Maternal and child health services	97,830	84,100	86[aa]
2. Crippled children services	63,124	54,300	86[aa]

TABLE A2.—(continued)

3. Child dental health	—		
4. Special projects for comprehensive child health	7,724	7,300	95[aa]
5. Special projects for maternal and child health	7,488	7,100	95[aa]
D. School health services	204,648	35,600	17.4[d]
E. Other public health	573,824	172,000	30[z]
F. Medical facilities construction	461,000	253,000	55[z]
V. Welfare services	1,520,991	927,700	61
A. Public assistance social services	200,597	176,700	88[b]
B. Child welfare	455,394	319,000	70[aa]
C. Institutional care	865,000	432,000	50[z]
VI. Manpower-vocational rehabilitation	105,022	72,500	69[aa]
VII. Education	35,589,365	5,697,500	16
A. Elementary and secondary schools (operating and construction)	29,035,586	5,052,200	17.4[d]
B. Higher education (operating and construction)	5,623,300	449,900	8[s]
C. Vocational and adult education	930,479	195,400	21[n]

TABLE A3.   ANTIPOVERTY BUDGET, 1972
(in thousands of dollars)

	Expenditures	Benefits to Pretransfer Poor	Percentage Spent on Pretransfer Poor
FEDERAL PROGRAMS	105,015,829	54,757,259	52.1
I. Cash Transfers	67,331,412	35,610,800	52.9
A. Social Security[1]	38,265,265	22,117,300	57.8[a]
B. Railroad Retirement[1]	2,121,350	1,226,600	57.8[a]
C. Railroad Disability[1]	39,407	22,800	57.8[a]
D. Public Employee Retirement[1]	7,641,818	2,903,900	38.0[a]
E. Unemployment insurance[1]	6,750,800	1,424,400	21.1
1. Federal employees and exservicemen	444,200 ⎫		
2. Railroad	80,684 ⎬	1,424,400	21.1[a]
3. State administered	6,067,000 ⎭		
F. Workmen's Compensation[1]	586,921	193,100	32.9
1. Regular	189,958 ⎱		
2. Black lung	396,963 ⎰	193,100	32.9[a]
G. Public assistance[1]	5,762,170	5,103,100	87.0[a]
1. AFDC	3,610,972	3,372,700	93.4[a]
2. OAA, AB, APTD and emergency assistance	2,151,198	1,640,400	76.3[a]
H. Veterans' income maintenance[10]	6,163,681	2,619,600	42.5
1. Compensation and pensions	6,045,214 ⎫		
2. Burial benefits	75,753 ⎪		
3. Special allowances	663 ⎬	2,619,600	42.5[a]
4. Vocational rehabilitation allowances	42,051 ⎭		
II. Payments to farmers[2]	3,233,754	161,700	5
A. Conservation	209,640 ⎫		
B. Soil Bank	80 ⎪		
C. Cropland adjustment	66,783 ⎪		
D. Sugar Act	86,133 ⎪		
E. Wool	112,766 ⎬	161,700	5[t]
F. Price support	— ⎪		
G. Set aside and diversion	1,877,301 ⎪		
H. Milk and beekeeper indemnity	2,974 ⎪		
I. Wheat certificates	878,077 ⎭		

TABLE A3.—(continued)

III. Nutrition[1]	3,419,286	2,458,400	72
A. Food stamps	1,865,574	1,585,700	85[ee]
B. Child nutrition	1,216,442	556,100	46
1. Donated food, sec. 32, 416[6]	253,253 ⎫		
2. Cash—School Lunch, sec. 4	225,747 ⎬ 141,200		26[cc]
3. Food bought, sec. 6	64,030 ⎭		
4. Special cash assistance, sec. 11	237,047	165,900	70[cc]
5. Special food services, sec. 13	37,059	33,400	90[z]
6. Supplemental cash, sec. 32	250,732	175,500	70[cc]
7. Milk program	90,286	15,800	17.5[d]
8. School breakfast	24,934	14,000	56[cc]
9. Nonfood cash assistance[6]	33,354	10,300	31[cc]
C. Surplus commodities	337,270	316,600	94
1. Needy families	311,508	296,000	95[f]
2. Institutions	25,762	20,600	80[f]
IV. Housing	1,685,015	915,500	54
A. Public housing[1]	743,924	550,500	74[j]
B. Rent supplements[1]	74,513	55,900	75[j]
C. Homeownership and rental housing assistance, sec. 235, 236[1]	298,590	71,700	24[j]
D. Rural housing program[1,2]	32,505	9,400	29[g]
E. Model Cities[2]	499,515	209,800	42[gg]
F. College housing debt service grants[1]	2,716	300	10[v]
G. Neighborhood facilities grants[1]	23,177	11,100	48[h]
H. Special disabled veterans' housing benefits[10]	10,075	6,800	67[k]
V. Health	14,720,133	7,809,655	53
A. Medicare[15]	7,023,082	3,371,100	48[dd]
B. Medicaid and MAA[1]	4,002,553	3,041,900	76[c]
C. Mental health programs[2]	276,715	180,700	65
1. Community mental health centers (staffing grants only)	135,084	82,400	61[h]
2. Children's services	9,979	6,100	61[h]
3. Drug abuse	62,308	49,200	79[h]
4. Alcoholism	69,344	43,000	62[h]

TABLE A3.—(continued)

	Expenditures	Benefits to Pretransfer Poor	Percentage Spent on Pretransfer Poor
D. Maternal and child health[1]	247,980	223,200	90
1. Maternal and child health services	68,475	58,900	86[e]
2. Crippled children services	67,929	58,400	86[e]
3. Child dental health	1,818	1,700	95[e]
4. Special projects for comprehensive child health	54,550	51,800	95[e]
5. Special projects for maternal and child health	55,208	52,400	95[e]
E. Family planning (HEW)[2]	54,315	39,600	73[e]
F. Indian health services[2]	144,828	108,600	75[f]
G. Indian sanitation facilities[2]	24,771	18,600	75[f]
H. Migrant health[2]	16,155	16,155	100[g]
I. Comprehensive health services—formula grants to states[6]	81,658	56,300	69[h]
J. Health services development grants and family health centers[6]	106,149	82,800	78[h]
K. St. Elizabeth's Hospital[2]	23,905	21,500	90[f]
L. Veterans' medical services[10]	2,269,186	499,200	22[i]
M. Health facilities construction (nonveteran)[1]	341,500	126,400	37[z]
N. Veterans' medical facility construction[10]	107,336	23,600	22[m]
VI. Welfare and OEO services	2,680,068	2,294,190	85.6
A. Public assistance social services[1]	1,598,215	1,294,600	81[b]
B. Child welfare[1]	44,663	26,800	60[g]
C. Indian welfare and guidance[1]	57,482	57,482	100[g]
D. Cuban refugee programs[1]	118,874	99,900	84[h]
E. Aging programs[1]	44,768	32,200	72[g]
F. OEO	816,066	783,208	96
1. Community Action Program[6]	458,000	439,700	96[h]
2. Health and nutrition[6]	180,000	172,800	96[e]
3. Legal services[6]	60,100	57,700	96[e]
4. Migrant farmworkers aid[1]	36,608	36,608	100[g]
5. Community Economic Development[6]	27,400	26,000	95[f]
6. ACTION (VISTA, Foster Grandparents, etc.)[1]	51,958	50,400	97[f]

TABLE A3.—(continued)

VII. Employment and manpower	3,749,812	2,692,200	72
A. Employment services	449,753	227,900	51
1. State employment agencies[1]	378,753	174,200	46[h]
2. Computerized job placement[4]	32,000	14,700	46[h]
3. Indian employment and training[4]	39,000	39,000	100[g]
B. Vocational rehabilitation	621,959	417,100	67
1. Social Rehabilitation Service[6]	569,943	381,900	67[k]
2. Social Security administration[1]	29,079	19,800	68[k]
3. Veterans' administration[10]	22,937	15,400	67[k]
C. Manpower training	2,119,100	1,891,200	86
1. MDTA—institutional[4]	406,000	276,100	68[hh]
2. MDTA—OJT, JOBS Optional[4]	68,000	45,600	67[e]
3. Neighborhood Youth Corps—in-school and summer[4]	376,000	376,000	100[g]
4. Neighborhood Youth Corps—out-of-school[4]	125,000	125,000	100[hh]
5. Job Corps[4]	188,000	188,000	100[g]
6. Public Service Careers[4]	117,000	111,200	95[e]
7. JOBS[4]	127,000	127,000	100[g]
8. Concentrated Employment Program[4]	158,000	158,000	100[g]
9. Operation Mainstream[4]	75,000	74,300	99[hh]
10. Work Experience	—		
11. Work Incentive (WIN)[4]	171,000	159,000	93[p]
12. Public assistance social service[6]	107,000	99,500	93[p]
13. Veterans' OJT[4]	124,000	74,400	60[z]
14. Employment for disadvantaged youth[6]	77,100	77,100	100[g]
D. Emergency Employment Assistance (PEP)[4]	559,000	156,000	28[ii]
VIII. Education	8,196,349	2,814,814	34
A. Student support	1,687,562	347,014	21
1. Fellow/traineeships[1,14]	308,690	18,500	6[q]
2. Training grants[1,14]	677,827	40,700	6[q]
3. Indian scholarships[1]	20,914	20,914	100[f]
4. Work-study and co-operative education[14]	276,253	138,100	50[e]
5. Educational opportunity grants[13]	167,600	90,500	54[e]

TABLE A3.—(continued)

	Expenditures	Benefits to Pretransfer Poor	Percentage Spent on Pretransfer Poor
6. Insured loans—interest reduction payments [14]	201,321	38,300	19[e]
7. Health and nursing professions [6]	34,957	13,300	38[e]
B. Pre-School, elementary and secondary education	3,467,678	1,573,800	45
1. Shared revenue from public lands [14]	73,285	12,800	17.5[d]
2. Indian education [1]	138,052	103,500	75[f]
3. Assistance in special areas [14]	156,757	27,400	17.5[d]
4. School aid to federally affected areas [14]	648,608	113,500	17.5[d]
5. NDEA, III, instructional aid [14]	42,629	7,500	17.5[d]
6. NDEA, V, guidance and testing	—		
7. NSF science education [1]	1,868	300	17.5[d]
8. Head Start and Follow Through [6]	437,785	394,000	90[f]
9. Elementary and Secondary Education act [14]	1,835,564	879,200	48
a. Educationally deprived	1,570,388	816,600	52[cc]
b. Bilingual education	26,010	17,200	66[cc]
c. Drop-out prevention	9,112	5,100	56[cc]
d. Library resources	74,648		
e. Supplementary education centers	122,527	40,300	17.5[d]
f. Strengthening state departments of education	32,879		
10. Teacher Corps [14]	23,887	8,400	35[cc]
11. Handicapped early childhood aid [14]	6,687	1,900	28[cc]
12. Handicapped education [14]	32,657	7,800	24[cc]
13. Emergency school assistance [14]	69,899	17,500	25[z]
C. Higher education	2,407,365	719,300	30
1. Higher Education Act [14]	9,597	1,200	12[r]
2. Upward Bound	24,993	22,500	90[e]
3. Talent Search and higher education remedial services [14]	18,970	17,100	90[e]
4. Language development [14]	8,659	900	10[x]
5. NSF grants	—		
6. Land-grant colleges [14]	12,600	1,800	14[w]
7. Educational exchange (Fulbright-Hays) [14]	37,837	3,800	10[x]

TABLE A3.—(continued)

	Expenditures	Benefits to Pretransfer Poor	Percentage Spent on Pretransfer Poor
D. School health services	295,000	51,600	17.5[d]
E. Other public health	1,304,749	430,600	33[z]
F. Medical facilities construction	800,000	440,000	55[z]
V. Welfare services	2,609,652	1,527,900	59
A. Public assistance social services	562,315	455,500	81[b]
B. Child welfare	487,337	292,400	60[aa]
C. Institutional care	1,560,000	780,000	50[z]
Manpower-vocational rehabilitation	154,178	103,300	67[aa]
Education	54,042,280	8,915,300	16
Elementary and secondary schools operating and construction)	42,147,551	7,375,800	17.5[d]
higher education operating and construction)	9,700,000	970,000	10[s]
vocational and adult education	2,194,729	69,500	26[n]

TABLE A3.—(continued)

8. *Special institutions (Howard/Gallaudent, Eisenhower, Nat'l Tech. Inst. for the Deaf)* [1]	44,568	5,300
9. *Construction grants*	361,075	43,300
a. *Higher Education Facilities Act* [13]	198,204 ⎫	
b. *Health professions teaching facilities* [1]	147,477 ⎬	43,300
c. *Special institutions*	15,394 ⎭	
10. *Veterans' education benefits* [10]	1,889,066	623
D. *Vocational and adult education*	633,744	1
1. *Vocational-technical training* [1,2,14]	407,962	
2. *Adult basic education* [14]	55,971	
3. *Agricultural extension* [14]	169,811	

STATE AND LOCAL PROGRAMS [1]   79,856,199

I. Cash transfers	12,778,40/
A. *Public employee retirement*	4,050,(
B. *Temporary disability insurance*	40
C. *Workmen's Compensation*	3,2
D. *Public assistance*	5
1. *AFDC*	
2. *OAA, AB, APTD and general assistance*	
E. *Veterans' bonuses and compensation*	

II. Nutrition—child nutrition

III. Housing

IV. Health
  A. *Medicaid, vendor m*
  B. *Hospital and medi*
  C. *Maternal and chi*
    1. *Maternal and health servi*
    2. *Crippled (services*
    3. *Child d*
    4. *Specia comp. health*
    5. *Special projects maternal and child health*

Appendix B

This appendix contains supplementary tables of poverty statistics for 1965 and 1972. Tables B1–B6 present the composition and incidence of relative poverty among persons. We do not repeat here the statistics on the composition of the total population because they are the same as in Tables 4.3–4.8. Tables B7–B12 contain data on the incidence and composition of absolute and relative poverty (denoted by A and R, respectively) among *families,* as well as information on the composition of all families. Tables B13–B18 present similar data, but for unrelated individuals. To determine the number of poor families (unrelated individuals) with a given characteristic, multiply the composition percentage by the total number of poor families (unrelated individuals) in Table 4.1. Finally, Table B19 contains data on the poverty gaps for families and unrelated individuals. Statistics for 1965 are derived from Survey of Economic Opportunity data tapes, for 1972 from Current Population Survey data tapes.

TABLE B1.   PERSONS IN RELATIVE POVERTY ACCORDING TO RACE
AND SEX OF HEAD OF HOUSEHOLD
(in percentages)

	White Male	Nonwhite Male	White Female	Nonwhite Female	All
Composition					
1965	48.0	20.1	18.6	13.3	100
1972	43.0	13.5	26.4	17.1	100
Incidence					
1965	9.5	35.8	31.9	66.2	15.6
1972	8.8	25.6	37.6	65.2	15.7

TABLE B2.   PERSONS IN RELATIVE POVERTY ACCORDING TO AGE OF
HEAD OF HOUSEHOLD
(in percentages)

	Years of Age					All
	14-22	23-36	37-50	51-64	65 & Above	
Composition						
1965	5.2	29.3	28.5	17.5	19.6	100
1972	7.4	30.6	26.4	15.7	19.9	100
Incidence						
1965	30.4	15.7	12.0	13.6	27.6	15.6
1972	32.7	15.6	12.3	12.0	27.0	15.7

TABLE B3.   PERSONS IN RELATIVE POVERTY ACCORDING TO
EDUCATION OF HEAD OF HOUSEHOLD
(in percentages)

	Years of Schooling			All
	0-8	9-12	13 or More	
Composition				
1965	59.5	34.0	6.5	100
1972	42.3	47.0	10.7	100
Incidence				
1965	30.8	11.1	4.7	15.6
1972	30.2	14.1	6.1	15.7

TABLE B4.   PERSONS IN RELATIVE POVERTY ACCORDING TO WEEKS
WORKED BY HEAD OF HOUSEHOLD
(in percentages)

| | Weeks Worked | | | | |
	0	1-26	27-49	50-52	All
Composition					
1965	33.1	15.9	19.5	35.1	100
1972	44.6	15.8	12.7	26.9	100
Incidence					
1965	41.4	44.3	19.4	7.9	15.6
1972	44.5	40.2	17.9	6.3	15.7

TABLE B5.   PERSONS IN RELATIVE POVERTY ACCORDING TO REGION
OF RESIDENCE
(in percentages)

	North-east	North-central	South	West	All
Composition					
1965	15.7	22.4	48.0	13.9	100
1972	18.5	21.2	43.1	17.2	100
Incidence					
1965	10.0	12.5	24.5	12.9	15.6
1972	12.3	12.1	21.6	15.3	15.7

TABLE B6.   PERSONS IN RELATIVE POVERTY ACCORDING TO
LOCATION OF RESIDENCE
(in percentages)

	Central City	Suburban	Non-metropolitan	All
Composition				
1965	30.9	15.8	53.3	100
1972	36.5	23.2	40.3	100
Incidence				
1965	15.7	7.2	23.8	15.6
1972	19.0	9.5	20.1	15.7

TABLE B7.   FAMILIES IN ABSOLUTE AND RELATIVE POVERTY
ACCORDING TO RACE AND SEX OF HEAD OF FAMILY
(in percentages)

	White Male	Nonwhite Male	White Female	Nonwhite Female	All
Composition					
1965	55.4	17.0	14.5	13.0	100
1972A	45.5	12.1	22.4	20.1	100
1972R	49.5	12.0	21.2	17.3	100
Incidence					
1965	8.3	28.8	23.8	60.8	12.4
1972A	5.3	16.2	24.3	53.3	9.3
1972R	7.7	20.7	31.0	60.9	12.5
Composition of all families					
1965	82.5	7.3	7.5	2.6	100
1972	80.5	7.3	8.6	3.6	100

Notes: *A* indicates absolute poverty; *R* indicates relative poverty. Absolute and relative poverty populations are identical in 1965.

TABLE B8.   FAMILIES IN ABSOLUTE AND RELATIVE POVERTY
ACCORDING TO AGE OF HEAD OF FAMILY
(in percentages)

	Years of Age					
	14-22	23-36	37-50	51-64	65 & Over	All
Composition						
1965	5.9	27.0	24.8	19.5	22.8	100
1972A	8.6	32.8	23.2	18.2	17.3	100
1972R	8.0	31.5	23.5	17.7	19.6	100
Incidence						
1965	23.7	12.5	9.5	10.1	20.0	12.4
1972A	20.5	10.3	7.5	7.0	11.6	9.3
1972R	25.5	13.4	10.3	9.1	17.7	12.5
Composition of all families						
1965	3.1	26.6	32.3	23.9	14.1	100
1972	3.9	29.5	28.7	24.0	13.9	100

Notes: *A* indicates absolute poverty, *R* indicates relative poverty. Absolute and relative poverty populations are identical in 1965.

TABLE B9.   FAMILIES IN ABSOLUTE AND RELATIVE POVERTY
ACCORDING TO EDUCATION OF HEAD OF FAMILY
(in percentages)

| | Years of Schooling | | | |
	0-8	9-12	13 or More	All
Composition				
1965	59.6	34.6	5.8	100
1972A	41.9	48.7	9.4	100
1972R	42.2	47.9	10.3	100
Incidence				
1965	24.0	8.9	3.4	12.4
1972A	17.5	8.9	3.3	9.3
1972R	23.6	11.8	4.7	12.5
Composition of all families				
1965	30.7	48.1	21.2	100
1972	22.4	50.9	26.7	100

Notes: *A* indicates absolute poverty; *R* indicates relative poverty. Absolute and relative
poverty populations are identical in 1965.

TABLE B10.   FAMILIES IN ABSOLUTE AND RELATIVE POVERTY
ACCORDING TO WEEKS WORKED BY HEAD OF FAMILY
(in percentages)

| | Weeks Worked | | | | |
	0	13-26	27-49	50-52	All
Composition					
1965	36.0	16.7	14.8	32.5	100
1972A	46.2	18.9	11.3	23.5	100
1972R	44.6	17.1	12.2	26.1	100
Incidence					
1965	31.3	35.5	14.7	6.0	12.4
1972A	27.4	27.4	9.6	3.3	9.3
1972R	35.3	33.3	13.8	5.0	12.5
Composition of all families					
1965	14.1	5.8	12.4	67.4	100
1972	15.9	6.5	11.2	66.4	100

Notes: *A* indicates absolute poverty; *R* indicates relative poverty. Absolute and relative
poverty populations are identical in 1965.

TABLE B11.   FAMILIES IN ABSOLUTE AND RELATIVE POVERTY
ACCORDING TO REGION OF RESIDENCE
(in percentages)

	North-east	North-central	South	West	All
Composition					
1965	15.2	21.8	49.5	13.6	100
1972A	16.5	21.4	45.5	16.7	100
1972R	18.1	20.7	44.4	16.8	100
Incidence					
1965	7.6	9.6	19.9	10.0	12.4
1972A	6.6	7.3	13.4	8.8	9.3
1972R	9.7	9.5	17.5	12.0	12.5
Composition of all families					
1965	24.5	28.1	30.7	16.7	100
1972	23.4	27.4	31.7	17.6	100

Notes: *A* indicates absolute poverty; *R* indicates relative poverty. Absolute and relative poverty populations are identical in 1965.

TABLE B12.   FAMILIES IN ABSOLUTE AND RELATIVE POVERTY
ACCORDING TO LOCATION OF RESIDENCE
(in percentages)

	Central City	Suburban	Non-metropolitan	All
Composition				
1965	28.9	15.8	55.3	100
1972A	36.0	22.0	42.0	100
1972R	35.1	23.2	41.8	100
Incidence				
1965	11.7	5.7	19.5	12.4
1972A	11.3	5.4	12.3	9.3
1972R	14.8	7.8	16.4	12.5
Composition of all families				
1965	30.7	34.3	35.1	100
1972	29.8	38.3	32.0	100

Notes: *A* indicates absolute poverty; *R* indicates relative poverty. Absolute and relative poverty populations are identical in 1965.

TABLE B13.   UNRELATED INDIVIDUALS IN ABSOLUTE AND RELATIVE POVERTY ACCORDING TO RACE AND SEX
(in percentages)

	White Male	Nonwhite Male	White Female	Nonwhite Female	All
Composition					
1965	19.7	7.6	60.8	11.8	100
1972A	20.9	7.9	59.8	11.4	100
1972R	21.4	7.3	60.9	10.4	100
Incidence					
1965	23.7	38.3	40.2	65.7	36.7
1972A	18.7	32.6	32.6	49.6	29.2
1972R	23.7	37.5	41.3	56.2	36.3
Composition of all unrelated individuals					
1965	30.6	7.3	55.4	6.6	100
1972	32.7	7.1	53.5	6.7	100

Notes: *A* indicates absolute poverty; *R* indicates relative poverty. Absolute and relative poverty populations are identical in 1965.

TABLE B14.   UNRELATED INDIVIDUALS IN ABSOLUTE AND RELATIVE POVERTY ACCORDING TO AGE
(in percentages)

	Years of Age					All
	14-22	23-36	37-50	51-64	65 & Over	
Composition						
1965	11.6	6.3	8.1	21.4	52.5	100
1972A	15.2	9.7	7.3	20.8	47.1	100
1972R	13.7	9.3	6.9	19.3	50.7	100
Incidence						
1965	57.4	17.0	20.1	30.2	50.5	36.7
1972A	45.2	13.9	18.2	28.1	37.5	29.2
1972R	50.8	16.7	21.4	32.7	50.2	36.3
Composition of all unrelated individuals						
1965	7.4	13.6	14.9	26.0	38.2	100
1972	9.8	20.3	11.7	21.5	36.7	100

Notes: *A* indicates absolute poverty; *R* indicates relative poverty. Absolute and relative poverty populations are identical in 1965.

TABLE B15.   UNRELATED INDIVIDUALS IN ABSOLUTE AND RELATIVE POVERTY ACCORDING TO EDUCATION
(in percentages)

| | Years of Schooling | | | |
	0-8	9-12	13 or More	All
Composition				
1965	56.0	28.7	15.3	100
1972A	48.3	34.7	17.0	100
1972R	47.8	34.9	17.3	100
Incidence				
1965	51.3	28.4	24.6	36.7
1972A	45.9	24.8	17.6	29.2
1972R	56.5	30.8	22.3	36.3
Composition of all unrelated individuals				
1965	40.1	37.1	22.8	100
1972	30.7	41.3	28.2	100

Notes: *A* indicates absolute poverty; *R* indicates relative poverty. Absolute and relative poverty populations are identical in 1965.

TABLE B16.   UNRELATED INDIVIDUALS IN ABSOLUTE AND RELATIVE POVERTY ACCORDING TO WEEKS WORKED
(in percentages)

| | Weeks Worked | | | | |
	0	1-26	27-49	50-52	All
Composition					
1965	65.7	16.0	7.1	11.3	100
1972A	68.0	15.1	7.4	9.5	100
1972R	68.1	14.4	7.6	9.8	100
Incidence					
1965	61.6	55.8	18.0	11.5	36.7
1972A	48.9	44.5	19.0	7.2	29.2
1972R	60.9	52.7	24.4	9.4	36.3
Composition of all unrelated individuals					
1965	39.2	10.5	14.4	35.9	100
1972	40.6	9.9	11.4	38.1	100

Notes: *A* indicates absolute poverty; *R* indicates relative poverty. Absolute and relative poverty populations are identical in 1965.

TABLE B17.   UNRELATED INDIVIDUALS IN ABSOLUTE AND RELATIVE
POVERTY ACCORDING TO REGION OF RESIDENCE
(in percentages)

	North-east	North-central	South	West	All
Composition					
1965	22.8	29.6	29.8	17.9	100
1972A	22.7	26.0	33.4	17.9	100
1972R	23.5	25.7	31.5	19.3	100
Incidence					
1965	30.6	37.4	45.6	33.2	36.7
1972A	26.6	29.1	35.4	24.5	29.2
1972R	34.1	35.8	41.5	32.9	36.3
Composition of all unrelated individuals					
1965	27.3	29.0	24.0	19.7	100
1972	25.0	26.1	27.6	21.3	100

Notes: *A* indicates absolute poverty; *R* indicates relative poverty. Absolute and relative
poverty populations are identical in 1965.

TABLE B18.   UNRELATED INDIVIDUALS IN ABSOLUTE AND RELATIVE
POVERTY ACCORDING TO LOCATION OF RESIDENCE
(in percentages)

	Central City	Suburban	Non-metropolitan	All
Composition				
1965	40.9	19.4	39.7	100
1972A	40.5	23.9	35.7	100
1972R	40.9	24.6	34.4	100
Incidence				
1965	33.0	31.0	46.2	36.7
1972A	27.2	23.9	38.0	29.2
1972R	34.2	30.7	45.6	36.3
Composition of all unrelated individuals				
1965	45.5	23.0	31.5	100
1972	43.5	29.1	27.4	100

Notes: *A* indicates absolute poverty; *R* indicates relative poverty. Absolute and relative
poverty populations are identical in 1965.

TABLE B19.   POVERTY GAP OF POOR FAMILIES AND UNRELATED INDIVIDUALS
(in millions of 1972 dollars)

	Families	Unrelated Individuals
1965	9,523	4,271
1968A	8,086	4,155
1970A	7,942	4,433
1972A	7,950	4,534
1968R	9,880	4,971
1970R	10,787	5,811
1972R	12,530	6,735

Notes: *A* indicates absolute poverty; *R* indicates relative poverty. Absolute and relative poverty populations are identical in 1965.

Appendix C

This appendix describes the method used to obtain our multivariate estimates of the relationship between the odds of a household being poor and its demographic characteristics. These results were discussed in Chapter 4. Also, this section contains the 1965 coefficients for the absolute poverty analysis and the statistical results based on the relative poverty measure.

The estimates were derived using a technique developed by Leo Goodman for the analysis of probability models and other models where the dependent variable takes only discrete values (see his article "A Model for the Analysis of Surveys," *American Journal of Sociology* 77 (May 1972): 1035–1085 and references cited therein). In our case, the dependent variable is poverty status. Each household is assigned a value of one if it is below the line and zero if above the line. Predicting the probability of poverty using a linear regression model may lead to serious statistical distortions (see any standard econometrics text), so we adopted Goodman's logit approach. To implement it, we group the households into cells, each cell containing the number of poor (or nonpoor) households with a specific combination of demographic characteristics. For example, a cell might indicate the number of poor households that had *all* of the following traits: male head, black, head had 9–12 years of school, head's age between 14 and 29, household was a family, lived outside of South, and lived in an SMSA. Another cell would indicate the number of nonpoor households with the identical traits. The full array of cells becomes the input and the technique estimates the effects of each specified variable on the odds of being poor. It also computes interaction effects if we specify them. In particular, we test for differences in the coefficients between 1965 and 1972 by pooling the input for both years and checking for the presence of any statistically significant interactions between time, which can be viewed as simply another independent variable, and the other independent variables. Only one appeared for the absolute analysis and none was found when data based in the relative measure were used. Hence, we conclude that for each variable except age, the association between it and absolute poverty remained constant over time, while in the relative case, all relationships did not change.

The Goodman technique is not a least squares estimation method and does not generate the usual R^2 statistic. The goodness of fit is instead measured by considering the χ^2 statistic. In a model that fits the data perfectly, the value of χ^2, which measures the degree to which the distribution of the actual data and the distribution of the model's predictions differ, is zero. The χ^2 will be much larger for a model that assumes the chances of poverty are totally unrelated to socioeconomic characteristics (an independent logit model), because such a model provides a very bad fit to the data. The χ^2 for the model we present—a conditional logit model—falls somewhere between these two extremes. Dividing the χ^2 for our final model by the χ^2 for the independent logit model and subtracting the result from one provides a measure of the explanatory power of our model. For example, a value of .9 means the χ^2 for the final model is 90 percent smaller than the χ^2 of the independent logit model, so that in some sense (see Goodman's work), the model accounts for 90 percent of the variance.

TABLE C1.   THE EFFECT OF DEMOGRAPHIC CHARACTERISTICS ON THE ODDS OF BEING POOR, 1965 AND 1972
(absolute poverty definition)

	(1)	(2)	(3)	(4)	(5)	(6)	(7)	(8)
	Non-South				South			
	Families		Unrelated Individuals		Families		Unrelated Individuals	
	Male	Female	Male	Female	Male	Female	Male	Female
1965:								
Constant	.1525	.6531	.4946	1.0182	.1946	.8336	.6313	1.5281
White and other	.5513	.5513	.7001	.7001	.5513	.5513	.7001	.7001
Black	1.8138	1.8138	1.4285	1.4285	1.8138	1.8138	1.4285	1.4285
Age 14-29	1.2003	3.4508	1.6274	1.4550	1.2003	3.4508	1.6274	1.4550
Age 30-64	.6559	.7298	.5720	.5415	.6559	.7298	.5720	.5415
Age 65 or above	1.2705	.3973	1.0740	1.2695	1.2705	.3973	1.0740	1.2695
0-8 years school	2.1391	2.1702	1.8485	1.8753	3.0356	3.0796	2.6232	2.6613
9-12 years school	.8552	1.1279	.6784	.8948	.9012	1.1886	.7149	.9429
13+ years school	.5465	.4086	.7972	.5961	.3655	.2732	.5331	.3986
Lives in SMSA	.7320	.7320	.7320	.7320	.7320	.7320	.7320	.7320
Lives outside SMSA	1.3662	1.3662	1.3662	1.3662	1.3662	1.3662	1.3662	1.3662
1972:								
Constant	.1048	.4490	.3400	.6999	.1338	.5730	.4340	1.0504
Age 14-29	1.2256	3.5233	1.6616	1.4856	1.2256	3.5233	1.6616	1.4856
Age 30-64	.7893	.8557	.6884	.6516	.7893	.8557	.6884	.6516
Age 65 or above	1.0304	.3234	.8741	1.0331	1.0341	.3234	.8741	1.0331

All other coefficients identical to those for 1965.

Goodness of fit: reduction of χ^2 is 92.1 percent.

231

TABLE C2. THE EFFECT OF DEMOGRAPHIC CHARACTERISTICS ON THE ODDS OF BEING POOR, 1965 AND 1972
(relative poverty definition)

	(1)	(2)	(3)	(4)	(5)	(6)	(7)	(8)
	Non-South				South			
	Families		Unrelated Individuals		Families		Unrelated Individuals	
	Male	Female	Male	Female	Male	Female	Male	Female
Constant:								
1965	.1524	.6347	.4574	.9457	.1968	.8192	.5904	1.2207
1972	.1624	.6761	.4872	1.0074	.2096	.8727	.6289	1.3003
White and other	.5559	.5559	.7143	.7143	.5559	.5559	.7143	.7143
Black	1.7989	1.7989	1.3999	1.3999	1.7989	1.7989	1.3999	1.3999
Age 14-29	1.2182	3.1855	1.4850	1.3442	1.2182	3.1855	1.4850	1.3442
Age 30-64	.6803	.8145	.5910	.5793	.6803	.8145	.5910	.5793
Age 65 or above	1.2066	.3856	1.1391	1.2843	1.2066	.3856	1.1391	1.2843
0-8 years school	2.1494	2.2087	1.8716	1.9232	2.9506	3.0319	2.5692	2.6401
9-12 years school	.8742	1.1325	.6872	.8901	.8690	1.1257	.6830	.8848
13+ years school	.5323	.3999	.7774	.5840	.3901	.2931	.5697	.4280
Lives in SMSA	.7408	.7408	.7408	.7408	.7408	.7408	.7408	.7408
Lives outside SMSA	1.3499	1.3499	1.3499	1.3499	1.3499	1.3499	1.3499	1.3499

Goodness of fit: reduction of χ^2 is 92.1 percent.

Appendix D

Tables in this appendix were the sources of some of the material in Chapter 6. For further discussion of how to interpret the estimates in Tables D3 and D4, consult Chapter 4 and Appendix C.

TABLE D1.   HORIZONTAL AND VERTICAL INEQUITY AMONG
POOR RECIPIENTS OF PUBLIC TRANSFERS, 1965 AND 1972

Posttransfer Welfare Ratio	Pretransfer Welfare Ratio					
	<0	0	.01-.25	.26-.50	.51-.75	.76-1.0
1965						
<0	33	—	—	—	—	—
0	0	0	—	—	—	—
.01-.25	10	2	4	—	—	—
.26-.5	17	17	14	5	—	—
.51-.75	16	32	23	17	11	—
.76-1	15	25	21	22	17	14
1-1.25	0	10	15	23	21	25
1.26-1.5	0	7	9	14	20	20
1.51-2	0	5	9	14	23	31
2+	4	2	5	6	8	11
N =	82	3,186	2,756	1,932	1,573	1,298
1972						
<0	29	—	—	—	—	—
0	0	0	—	—	—	—
.01-.25	11	2	2	—	—	—
.26-.5	12	12	11	4	—	—
.51-.75	14	23	18	11	6	—
.76-1	8	25	21	19	14	6
1-1.25	11	17	18	18	16	15
1.26-1.5	6	10	13	16	17	16
1.51-2	4	6	9	20	29	32
2+	4	3	8	11	19	31
N =	114	5,197	3,184	1,875	1,794	1,613

TABLE D2. LEAPFROGGING IN THE TRANSFER SYSTEM, 1965 AND 1972

Posttransfer Welfare Ratio	Pretransfer Welfare Ratio								
	<0	0	.01-.50	.51-.75	.76-1.0	1-1.25	1.26-1.5	1.51-2.0	2+
1965									
<0	71	—	—	—	—	—	—	—	—
0	0	14	—	—	—	—	—	—	—
.01-.5	13	16	34	—	—	—	—	—	—
.51-.75	7	27	15	48	—	—	—	—	—
.76-1	7	22	16	10	59	—	—	—	—
1-1.25	2	9	14	12	10	66	—	—	—
1.26-1.5	0	6	8	12	10	12	75	—	—
1.51-2	0	4	8	13	15	12	15	84	—
2+	2	1	4	5	5	10	10	16	100
N =	184	3,722	6,254	2,709	2,740	2,799	3,415	7,156	31,658

TABLE D2.—(continued)

1972

	<0	0	.01-.5	.51-.75	.76-1	1-1.25	1.26-1.5	1.51-2	2+
<0	64	—	—	—	—	—	—	—	—
0	0	10	—	—	—	—	—	—	—
.01-.5	12	13	27	—	—	—	—	—	—
.51-.75	7	21	13	35	—	—	—	—	—
.76-1	4	23	16	10	44	—	—	—	—
1-1.25	6	15	15	11	9	56	—	—	—
1.26-1.5	3	9	11	12	10	8	63	—	—
1.51-2	2	6	11	20	19	16	15	74	—
2+	2	3	7	13	18	20	22	26	100
N =	224	5,797	6,295	2,603	2,714	2,633	2,833	6,194	41,784

Entries in each column give the percentage distribution of posttransfer welfare ratios for all households with pretransfer ratios within the specified range. The row of numbers in the N = row tells us the number of households (times 1000) in each pretransfer welfare ratio class.

TABLE D3.   THE EFFECT ON THE ODDS OF ESCAPING ABSOLUTE
PRETRANSFER POVERTY VIA CASH TRANSFERS OF DEMOGRAPHIC
CHARACTERISTICS

	Under 65		Over 65	
	South	Elsewhere	South	Elsewhere
Constant:				
1965	.1025	.1604	.7354	1.1505
1972	.1849	.2893	1.3266	2.0755
Male	.9873	.9873	1.5608	1.5608
Female	1.0129	1.0129	.6407	.6407
White and other	1.6382	1.3279	1.6382	1.3279
Black	.6104	.7531	.6104	.7531
0-8 years school	.7963	1.1386	.4993	.7139
9-12 years school	.9843	1.0736	1.0290	1.1223
13+ years school	1.2756	.8179	1.9468	1.2471
Family	1.3780	1.3780	1.3780	1.3780
Unrelated				
individual	.7257	.7257	.7257	.7257

Goodness of fit: reduction of χ^2 is 93.4 percent.

TABLE D4. THE EFFECT ON THE ODDS OF ESCAPING RELATIVE PRETRANSFER POVERTY VIA CASH TRANSFERS OF DEMOGRAPHIC CHARACTERISTICS

| | Under 65 | | | | Over 65 | | | |
| | South | | Elsewhere | | South | | Elsewhere | |
	White	Black	White	Black	White	Black	White	Black
Constant:								
1965	.1765	.0728	.2295	.1399	1.1475	.4735	1.4918	.9096
1972	.1944	.0802	.2528	.1541	1.2642	.5216	1.6435	1.0020
Male	.9859	.9859	.9859	.9859	1.5920	1.5920	1.5920	1.5920
Female	1.0143	1.0143	1.0143	1.0143	.6821	.6821	.6821	.6821
0-8 years school	.7743	.7211	1.0574	.9847	.4924	.4586	.6723	.6261
9-12 years school	1.0342	.9143	.9960	.8806	1.0500	.9283	1.0113	.8940
13+ years school	1.2486	1.5165	.9493	1.1530	1.9348	2.3500	1.4711	1.7868
Family	1.3874	1.3874	1.3874	1.3874	1.3874	1.3874	1.3874	1.3874
Unrelated individual	.7208	.7208	.7208	.7208	.7208	.7208	.7208	.7208

Goodness of fit: reduction of x^2 is 92.7 percent.

Index